Macintosh Hard Disk Management

Macintosh Hard Disk Management

Charles Rubin and Bencion Calica

fff

HAYDEN BOOKS

A Division of Howard W. Sams & Company
4300 West 62nd Street
Indianapolis, Indiana 46268 USA

FIRST EDITION
FIRST PRINTING—1988

International Standard Book Number: 0-672-48403-X
Library of Congress Catalog Card Number: 88-60993

Acquisitions Editor: Greg Michael
Development Editor: Jennifer Ackley
Technical Reviewer: Keith Thompson
Coordinating Editor: Katherine S. Ewing
Manuscript Editor, Compositor, and Indexer: Brown Editorial Service
Cover Art: Celeste Design

Printed in the United States of America

For Doris and Daniel.

—Charles

To Gillian, who brings out the best in me.

—Ben

Contents

Acknowledgments

Many individuals and developers contributed their time, advice, and products to the preparation of this book. In particular, we would like to thank Seth Lipkin at General Computer Corporation, Rob Hafer, who always pushes the edge of hard disk technology, Jack Hodgson, who was always a good sounding board, and everybody at Alsoft, Inc., Apple Computer Developer Services, CE Software, Fifth Generation Systems, Software Research Technologies, and SuperMac Software.

We would also like to thank these individuals: Brad Roth, Keith Thompson, all the hard-working editors and artists at Howard W. Sams & Company, Virginia Worthington, and Lynn Brown.

Trademarks

All terms mentioned in this book that are known to be trademarks or service marks are listed below. In addition, terms suspected of being trademarks or service marks have been appropriately capitalized. Howard W. Sams & Co. cannot attest to the accuracy of this information. Use of a term in this book should not be regarded as affecting the validity of any trademark or service mark.

Apple is a registered trademark of Apple Computer. AppleShare, Disk First Aid, Font/DA Mover, HyperCard, the Macintosh Logo, ImageWriter, ImageWriter II, LaserWriter, LaserWriter IINT, LaserWriter IINTX, LaserWriter IISC, and MultiFinder are trademarks of Apple Computer.

Art Grabber and Cheap Paint are trademarks of MacroMind.

Bernoulli Box is a trademark of Iomega Corp.

Copy II Mac and MacTools are trademarks of Central Point Software.

DataFrame Hard Disks is a trademark of SuperMac Technologies.

DiskExpress and Font/DA Juggler are trademarks of Alsoft, Inc.

DiskFit, Super Laser Spool, and SuperSpool are trademarks of SuperMac Software.

DiskTop 3.0 and QuicKeys are trademarks of CE Software.

Fastback is a trademark of Fifth Generation Systems, Inc.

Findswell is a trademark of Working Software.

1st Aid Kit is a trademark of 1st Aid Software.

HDBackup is a trademark of PBI Software.

HFS Backup is a trademark of Personal Computer Peripherals Corporation.

HFS Navigator and LaserSpeed are trademarks of Think Technologies.

MacTree is a trademark of Software Research Technologies.

MacBottom Hard Disks is a trademark of Personal Computer Peripherals Corporation.

MegaDrive is a trademark of Jasmine Technologies.

Microsoft and Excel are registered trademarks of Microsoft Corporation.

PhoneNet Plus is a trademark of Farallon Computing, Inc.

PowerStation is a trademark of Software Supply.

SideKick is a trademark of Borland International.

Suitcase is a trademark of Software Supply.

SuperGlue is a trademark of Solutions International.

Tempo is a trademark of Affinity Microsystems.

Thunder is a trademark of Electronic Arts.

TOPS is a trademark of TOPS, a Sun Microsystems Company.

Introduction

If you're reading this book because you already own or are seriously contemplating purchasing a hard disk for your Mac, congratulations. Dollar for dollar, day in and day out, a hard disk will add more performance and convenience to your system than any other peripheral you could buy. When you first get a Mac, the 800K floppy disk drive may look like an adequate storage device, but you quickly realize that it isn't. Many application programs occupy at least half that much space, and when you include sample files, Help files, and the System files you need to run your Mac, an 800K floppy disk begins to look cramped. The more you use your Mac the worse it gets, because soon you're using two, three, or more application programs, each with its own disk, and you've begun to build a collection of data disks as well.

Even if you just run one program all the time, having 25 floppy disks' worth of storage space or more on a hard disk makes things much more convenient. There's no more hunting for the right data or program disk: You can just turn on your hard disk in the morning and work all day without ever touching a floppy to load a program or data.

How This Book Can Help You

Hard disks are a simple way around the floppy-swapping blues, and they're simple to set up and use. But having a hard disk presents an organizational challenge many people aren't prepared for. Many of us aren't very good at organizing things, but without an organizing scheme, your Mac's hard disk can become like your attic, basement, or that junk drawer in the kitchen where you throw things in one at a time: It's simple enough to store things, but you're often at a loss to find any one of them later.

And unfortunately, while you may only have to root through the attic or basement once in awhile, you will probably have to use your hard disk every day. The purpose of this book is to help you organize your hard disk and make use of some inexpensive programs and techniques so you can find the file you want when you want it with a minimum of delay.

How This Book Is Organized

This book is divided into four parts: "Hard Disk Basics," "Hard Disk Strategies," "Supercharging a Hard Disk," and "Troubleshooting and Maintenance." Part One presents the fundamental information you need to understand the tips and techniques described in the rest of the book:

- Chapter 1 explains the hardware technology: where hard disks came from and how they work.
- Chapter 2 covers the basic operation of the System Folder and its files, and how these affect a hard disk.
- Chapter 3 details the operation of the Finder, and how it can help or hinder your attempts at organizing hard disk files.
- Chapter 4 describes fonts, desk accessories, and the Font/DA Mover program, and shows how these operate on a hard disk system.

After the basics, we'll move on to specific strategies for making the most of a hard disk in Part Two:

- Chapter 5 explains how to organize hard disk files so you can locate and manage them more easily.
- Chapter 6 describes the basics of using a hard disk on a local area network.
- Chapter 7 covers the use of file and disk copying programs.

- Chapter 8 discusses print spoolers that use a hard disk to speed printing from your Mac.
- In Chapter 9, we'll explore the vital procedure of backing up hard disk data and look at the various hardware, software, and techniques for maintaining duplicate files.

Part Three covers enhancement programs and techniques for moving beyond basic hard disk management to even greater performance and convenience:

- In Chapter 10 we look at hard disk optimizing utilities such as file-finding aids, disk performance optimizers, and file cataloging programs.
- One of the big advantages to having a hard disk is the ability to store lots of extra fonts, desk accessories, and other System files, so in Chapter 11, we'll explore font and desk accessory management programs that let you work with hundreds of fonts or desk accessories at a time.
- Chapter 12 explains FKeys, Init programs, and Chooser resources, which are other System files that can make the Mac easier to use.
- In Chapter 13, we'll test drive some Finder alternatives (including MultiFinder and Switcher) to see how they can make locating or managing files or programs easier.

The last part covers preventive measures and troubleshooting techniques that can help you prevent hard disk problems, or overcome them when they occur.

- Chapter 14 offers practical advice about how to prevent or minimize problems with your hard disk.
- Chapter 15 presents a series of techniques for isolating and recovering from hard disk errors.

Finally, there's a Glossary in Appendix A, and Appendix B lists all the products mentioned in the book with their prices and their manufacturers' addresses and telephone numbers. For quick reference to the concepts covered in the book, refer to the Index.

How to Use This Book

If you've just purchased your Macintosh, start at the beginning of Part One and read Chapters 1 through 4 first. Then, you can browse among the remaining chapters to locate a specific subject of interest.

If you're a more experienced Mac user, Parts Two, Three, and Four will be more likely places to start reading. If you want to learn about a specific product, check the book's index to zero in on the exact page or pages where that product is covered.

In either case, we strongly urge you to read Chapters 14 and 15, so you'll be better prepared to avoid (and if necessary deal with) hard disk problems. If something goes wrong with your hard disk, you'll be under enough stress without having to read a vital chapter, so it's best to read up on troubleshooting in advance.

Making Your Hard Disk Work Harder

A hard disk can enhance your productivity more than any other peripheral you can buy for your Macintosh. In capable hands, a hard disk can be an effective extension of your own memory where you can store or retrieve hundreds of pages of information easily and quickly. In the wrong hands, a hard disk can lull you into a false sense of security and then fail you when you need it most. In writing this book, we've done our best to provide you with the technical information, product descriptions, and user tips you need to make your hard disk realize its true potential.

PART ONE

Hard Disk Basics

CHAPTER

1

The Hardware

This chapter provides a history and background of the evolution of hard disks in general, and for the Macintosh in particular. The first few sections explain how hard disks work and how the Mac's design influenced trade-offs in hard disk design. The balance of the chapter discusses the current Small Computer Systems Interface (SCSI) hard disk technology.

How Hard Disks Took Over the World

As large computers became commonplace in corporate America during the late 1950s and early 1960s, data processing professionals began to long for a more efficient way to store the volumes of data they were accumulating. Their main choice at the time was magnetic tape, which could hold lots of information, but couldn't let people retrieve it very quickly. Tape was fine for storing archival data, but it stored and accessed data linearly. Much as you have to advance or rewind an audio tape to play a particular track, data tapes often had to be wound a hundred feet or more in one direction or another to locate the exact piece of data required.

The first improvement over tape was the high-speed hard disk pack, which was a stack of aluminum disks, each coated with a magnetic surface, all enclosed in a cylindrical plastic housing. The housing was inserted into the top of a disk drive, where it was connected to a spindle that turned the disks, and where a set of read/write heads from the disk drive could access the data on the disks. In operation, the disk drive spun the disks at about 3500 rpm, creating a cushion of air on which to "float" the read/write heads very close to the surfaces of the disks.

Thanks to the speed of the disk and the closeness of the read/write heads to the disk surface, data could be recorded fairly densely on these disk packs, allowing for capacities of 100 megabytes or more. And, because all the data was laid out on the surface of the disk, the head could go straight to the data being retrieved, instead of having to advance or rewind a tape to get there. Like tapes, disk packs are removable; thus they provide you with unlimited storage potential on a disk drive. The problem with disk packs is that, because the disks are removed and replaced, the delicate read/write heads are exposed to air, dirt, and other contaminants, and they require a lot of maintenance.

In the early 1970s, IBM researchers came up with the Winchester hard disk drive, which contained the disks and read/write heads in one sealed unit. The disks were not removable (so the amount of data a drive could store was finite), but because the heads were sealed inside the unit, they almost never required maintenance. But Winchester technology was plagued by one of the same potential problems as disk packs—if the air flow created by the disk is interrupted by particles of dirt or dust, the read/write heads can come crashing down upon the surface of the disk itself, wiping out a lot of data in what is agonizingly referred to as a *head crash*. To prevent head crashes, today's hard disks use dense air filters to keep unwanted dirt from the inside of the drive, and the system seems to work. Most hard disks are quite reliable, with mean times between failure (MTBFs) of 10,000 hours or more. Since 1985, the Winchester hard disk has supplanted disk packs as the storage device of choice in most mainframe and minicomputer installations.

The storage options for personal computers followed somewhat the same genesis. In 1975, the earliest personal computers used magnetic cassette tapes to store data. Floppy disk drives followed within two years, and hard disk drives first became available in the early 1980s. Since then, advances in hard disk technology and manufacturing methods have made for dramatic increases in hard disk price/performance ratios. Early personal computer hard disks stored 5 megabytes of data and cost $1500 to $2000. Today's personal computer hard disks store from 20 to over 100 megabytes of data and cost as little as $400.

How Macintosh Hard Disks Evolved

The Macintosh presented a special problem for would-be suppliers of hard disk drives. Most other personal computers contain internal slots that can accept a circuit board, called a *controller,* that allows the computer to communicate properly with a hard disk drive. The 128K and 512K Macs had no internal slots and no external connector that was designed specifically for a hard disk. As for the disk itself, Mac developers used the same 3.5-inch hard disk drives used by developers for other systems, but they had to do some fancy footwork with the hard disk controller.

Would-be suppliers of hard disks for 128K and 512K Macs had to connect them via one of the Mac's serial ports, and they had to design special hard disk systems with built-in controllers to make that connection work. Hard disk controllers on other computers, called DMA controllers (for direct memory access), were designed to send data over a very fast interface (usually over 100K per second) directly between the computer's data bus and the hard disk. But because Mac hard disks had to be connected to a slower serial port (running at 68.5K per second), the special, built-in controllers on Mac hard disks had to convert the high-speed data going to and from the hard disk into lower-speed data that could be sent via the Mac's serial port. The extra engineering and the built-in controller kept prices of Mac hard disks high—early models stored 10 megabytes and sold for $1200–$1500.

The other problem with serial-port hard disks is that you can't start up your Mac from one of them. The 128K and 512K Macs were designed to look only on a floppy disk drive—either the internal drive or an external drive connected to the floppy disk port—for the System file they need to start up. The only way to make a Mac recognize a serial port hard disk is via a floppy disk. Serial port hard disks come with a floppy disk that starts up the Mac, then tells it to access a hard disk through the serial port and switch system control from the floppy disk to the hard disk. (Normally, the disk you first use to start up a Mac is the one that controls the system.) This arrangement has some interesting implications with programs that modify the System file or must be located in the System Folder, as you'll see in Chapters 2 and 11.

Apple Tries Plan B

Apple's first solution to the problem of serial port hard disks was to bring out its own hard disk, the HD20, which connected to the Mac via the external floppy disk drive port. This hard disk still needed its own built-in controller to handle interaction between the Mac and the drive, but because it was connected to the floppy disk port, you could start up your Mac from this hard disk. While this method also offered faster data transfers through the floppy drive port, the transfers still weren't as fast as with a typical DMA controller.

The Internal Option

Another alternative to slow hard disks was pioneered by General Computer in late 1984, when the HyperDrive appeared. This was the first internal hard disk drive for the Mac. Requiring installation by a dealer, the HyperDrive mounted inside a Mac's case and connected directly to the Mac's data bus via a clip around the 68000 processor. This allowed for faster data transfer than either the serial or floppy disk port, the ability to boot from the hard disk itself, plus the added convenience of having a hard disk without hindering the Mac's small size and portability. Other manufacturers such as Rodime and Lapine offer internal hard disks for the Mac SE and Mac II today, and of course Apple itself has endorsed the concept by offering its own internal hard disks for the Mac SE and Mac II.

But the feature that makes an internal hard drive convenient to use also makes it rather inconvenient if it breaks. You can simply unplug a faulty external hard disk and send it off for repairs while you continue using your Mac, but when an internal hard disk goes down, so does your computer—unless you are technically skilled enough to open up the Mac and disconnect the faulty hard disk so you can still run software from a floppy.

Two other problems with early internal hard disks such as the Hyper-Drive were heat and power consumption. Although the internal HyperDrives came with a fan to dissipate heat, the fan wasn't always adequate, and the drive failed after awhile. Also, the Mac 512K, 512KE, and Mac Plus used smaller power supplies that were strained with the addition of an internal hard disk. General Computer has now discontinued production of its original internal HyperDrives, but today's Mac SE and Mac II have larger power supplies and larger built-in fans to correct these problems.

Alternate Mass Storage Technologies

Two other storage options have been marketed for the Mac: Bernoulli boxes and high-density floppy disks. Both technologies feature removable storage media, which means you have an unlimited amount of storage space.

Bernoulli boxes use flexible mylar disks encased in cartridges. Unlike Winchester technology, which floats the read/write heads above the disk, Bernoulli boxes create a cushion of air that raises the storage media itself up close to where the heads are located. These drives are said to be head crash-proof, because if the cushion of air is disturbed by dirt or dust, the media drops safely away from the heads. The drawbacks to Bernoulli boxes are that the flexible storage disks only last a year or two (as opposed to 10 years or more for a hard disk), and these units are the noisiest mass storage devices available for the Mac.

High-density floppy disk drives are floppy disk drives using flexible, removable Mylar disks. The difference between the high-density and regular Mac floppy disk drive is that instead of storing only 400K or 800K of data, high-density disks store 5 or 10 megabytes. One example of such a device is Jasmine's MegaDrive, which uses 10-megabyte floppy disks.

SCSI: The Final Solution

When Apple introduced the Macintosh Plus in early 1986, the new machine included an SCSI (Small Computer Systems Interface, also called "scuzzy") port on the rear of the machine. This port permitted the high-speed data transfer rates (up to 5 megabits per second) that would allow the Mac to make full use of a hard disk's data transfer speed. SCSI was just emerging as a standard hard disk interface in 1986—it has since been adopted by most hard disk manufacturers—but it was quickly adopted by all Apple third-party hard disk developers as the wave of the future. Today, all the older serial port hard disks have been discontinued, and the Mac Plus, Mac SE, and Mac II all use SCSI interfaces. Users of 512K Macs who buy a hard disk today are given an SCSI adapter that attaches through the battery compartment on the rear of the Mac.

Not only is the SCSI interface fast, but the Mac Plus and later machines were designed to read their startup instructions directly from devices connected to the SCSI port, so you could start your Macintosh directly from an SCSI hard disk. The SCSI interface has heightened competition in the Mac hard disk market and made hard disks less expensive to buy. Today, the smallest Mac hard disk can store 20 megabytes and sells for as little as $600.

Note: The explanations throughout the balance of this book assume you are using either an SCSI or internal hard disk. Where the procedures differ for serial or floppy disk port hard disks, we will call special attention to them.

About SCSI Hard Disks

The SCSI interface was designed to allow up to seven hard disks (or other SCSI peripherals, for that matter) to be interconnected. You connect the first device via an SCSI port to the second device, then connect it via a second SCSI port to the third device, and so on. This is known as a *daisy chain*.

In a Macintosh system, the computer itself is an SCSI device, as are hard disks, tape backup devices, and some scanners. You could connect six SCSI hard disk drives and have them all working for you through the single SCSI port on your Mac. The only requirement for doing this is that each device must have a specific SCSI identification, or address, so your Mac knows which device you want to use.

Every SCSI device can have its SCSI address set to a number from 0 through 7. The Mac itself is always identified as SCSI device number 7. When you turn it on, the Mac searches for its startup instructions on the first disk storage device at or below SCSI address number 7. Because the Mac itself is device number 7, the machine looks for startup files first on either its internal or external floppy disk drive. If there is no disk available in a floppy disk drive, it looks for a hard disk numbered from 6 down to 0 for the startup files. On the Mac SE and Mac II, the internal hard disks have their SCSI address set to 0.

You can set the SCSI address for any external hard disk drives. (Apple doesn't supply any tools for changing the addresses of its internal hard disks.) You can change a disk's SCSI address either via a switch somewhere on the case (or underneath a removable panel); by moving a wire jumper—a u-shaped goodie that connects two pins on a circuit board—from one place to another on a board you can expose by removing a small access panel; or by using special software.

If you add a second external hard disk, you will have to change one external drive's address. Because your Mac will always boot from the drive with the highest SCSI address number, you must make sure the drive from which you want to boot your system has the highest SCSI address. If you want to continue booting from the first of two external hard disks, for example, you will have to change its address from 0 to a higher number. If you are using an external drive with a Mac equipped with an internal SCSI hard disk (the SE or the Mac II), your Mac will always boot from the external hard disk, because the internal drive has the lowest address number.

Keep in mind as you set up your system for SCSI identification that you can't use two hard disks with the same address. If you have two hard disks with the same SCSI address, your Mac will probably destroy the directory on one or both drives, making it impossible to use either of them. The only remedy will be to reformat both disks and change one drive's address. One great advantage of drives for which you can set the address via switches or jumpers on the outside of the unit (rather than through software) is that you can see the drive address at any given time, and you can always change the address with the drive shut down if there's a problem. One caution: Never change a drive's address while it and your Mac are running, because this confuses the System file and could result in damage to the hard disk's directory or files.

One final hardware requirement of SCSI drives in a daisy chain is a terminator—a resistor that defines the end of the SCSI daisy chain. Most SCSI drives for the Mac have built-in terminators, but with some drives (such as Apple's HD20SC) you'll have to attach a terminator block in line with the SCSI cable between the last and second-to-last drives. The first device (physically) in the chain requires a terminator, and the last requires one. None of the others should have one. If you want to connect an SCSI drive between two others in a daisy chain, you must use a drive that doesn't have a terminator. You can't easily remove the built-in terminator from a drive that has one, so it's hard to connect such a drive between two SCSI devices in a daisy chain. On the other hand, most people don't connect more than two SCSI devices to a Mac in a daisy chain anyway.

Locating a Hard Disk

Many external Mac hard disks are designed to fit under the base of the Mac itself. This design works because the hard disk's own thickness helps raise the Mac's screen to eye level for most users, and it makes it easy to reach the on–off switch on the back of the disk drive. Another great feature of this design is that you can usually fit the hard disk inside a Mac Plus or Mac SE carrying case right along with your computer.

Some disks, like the DataFrame series, are free-standing, vertically oriented units. The short cables supplied with these drives will encourage you to place such disks close beside your Mac. When you do so, however, make sure there are a couple of inches of air space between the hard disk and the side of your Mac, so air can circulate through the vents in the bottom of the Mac and disk drive cases. Air flow is particularly important with drives that don't have built-in fans, like the DataFrame.

For some people, the noise of a hard disk in operation is incredibly annoying, especially because a Mac 128, 512, Plus, or hard disk-less SE is totally silent. You can buy SCSI extension cables long enough so you can keep your drive across the office or even in the next room. SCSI drives can work with cables up to seven meters long, but these cables can be expensive—$50 or more.

If you decide to exile your hard disk to a remote location, remember that you still have to turn it on every day and warm it up a bit before turning on your Mac. Don't move the disk so far away that turning the power on becomes a chore, or if you have to, try plugging the disk into a power strip located near your computer, and then use the power strip's switch to turn it on and off each day. Also, make sure you haven't placed the disk in front of a leaky window, underneath a shedding cat, or in another place where dirt, smoke, or moisture is likely to assault it.

So these are the basics of hard disk hardware. Now, let's look at the software that really makes a hard disk run.

2

The System Folder Files

The System Folder contains the basic software that makes the Macintosh capable of loading and running programs, storing and retrieving files, and displaying and printing text in various fonts and type styles. The System Folder must be present on any disk you use to start your Macintosh, whether it's a floppy disk or a hard disk. While the Mac's built-in read-only memory (ROM) lights up the screen and tells the computer to look for a disk drive to read, it is the System Folder that tells your Mac where to go from there. This chapter focuses on the System Folder and the different types of files it contains, with special attention to the System file. Because the Finder is a subject in itself, it is covered separately in Chapter 3.

The System Folder

The System Folder, shown in Figure 2–1, contains several different files, called *System files*. At a minimum, the System Folder used to start a Macintosh must contain two files: the System and the Finder. If you want to print a file, the System Folder must also contain a printer driver for the printer you want to use—for an ImageWriter, a LaserWriter, or another printer.

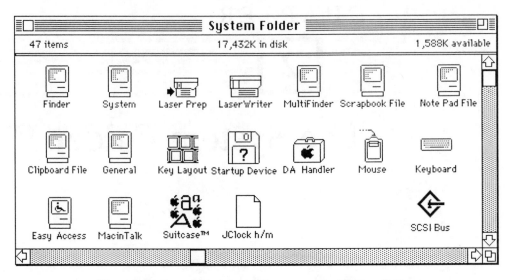

Figure 2–1. Every Mac startup disk must contain a System Folder.

When you turn your Mac on, the ROM instructions tell it to look for a System Folder on the startup disk. The System Folder must be there, or the Mac will eject the disk and wait for you to insert a disk containing the System Folder. If you have placed your System and Finder files in another folder, or they are not on your disk at all, or if you've hidden the System Folder, the Mac can't locate the startup files it needs.

System-type files inside the System Folder are identified by various icons. The System and Finder file icons look like a small Macintosh. Printer driver icons usually look like miniature printers. Files in the System Folder fall into four basic categories

- System files (the System or the Finder)
- Storage files for data created by desk accessories or application programs (such as the Notepad and Scrapbook files)
- Other system resources (called Chooser Resources and cdevs) used by the Chooser or the Control Panel
- Inits, which are programs that are run by the System file upon startup, and which add extra capabilities to your System file or specific application programs.

The System file interacts with the other files in the System Folder in various ways. If you have an ImageWriter printer driver inside the folder, for example, the System is automatically aware of those printing capabilities and presents the ImageWriter as an option when you use the Chooser desk accessory, or when you select Print from the Finder or any application program. Some Init programs tell the System where to store desk accessory data.

We won't describe the System Folder in detail here—it's enough to know that your System files must be contained inside it and that the System Folder must be contained on your hard disk if you want to start your Mac with it. Now, let's look at the different kinds of system-type files.

The System File

The System file itself is a vital, if somewhat invisible, resource for your Macintosh. Invisible though it may be, however, the System file is one of the things that makes a Mac so easy to use. On other computers, there are few standards governing how files are presented to the user. Each developer of an application program has to come up with a method by which the program's user loads or saves files, for example, and users must constantly relearn how to do these basic computer operations.

On the Macintosh, the System file is required for and used by all application programs. It defines standard methods of displaying and manipulating files, and most programs adhere to those methods. Thanks to the System file and the Finder, just about every Macintosh program looks and works the same in terms of file management.

When you use the Open... command inside any application program, you are presented with a list of files like the one in Figure 2–2.

The Mac System file provides a standard Open... box, called the SFGet box, and a standard Save... box, called the SFPut box. Some program developers use the SFGet and SFPut boxes as they are, while other developers vary their functions slightly. Nevertheless, the boxes you see whenever you save or load files are very much the same in every program.

The System file also stores a format for presenting printer commands inside application programs, and these commands are very much the same, if not identical, in every program you use. Another way the system maintains consistency is with *desk accessories (DAs)*. As long as you use the same

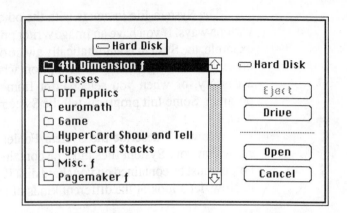

Figure 2–2. The System file stores a standard format for the file boxes you see when you use the Open..., Save, or Save As... commands from inside an application.

System file, the DAs available under the Apple menu are the same in every program. (See Chapter 10 for exceptions.) All this uniformity is due to the System file.

Although you can see the System file's icon inside the System Folder, the system is not an application program—there are no menus and buttons for interacting with it. Instead, the System file contains sets of resources that are used by every other program that runs on your Mac:

- It tells your Mac how to store and organize files, and provides the default SFGet and SFPut boxes that appear when you choose an Open..., Save, or Save As... command from any application program.

- It is the storage facility for the DAs whose names appear on the Apple menu, for the different fonts and type styles that appear on the Font and Style menus, for some other programs, and for Fkeys. (Fkeys are explained later in the chapter.)

- It knows which printer drivers you have in the System Folder and tells your application programs via the Chooser to display different sets of printing options when you issue the Print... command, depending on which printer files you have installed and which printer is currently selected with the Chooser. See Figure 2–3 for an example.

- It searches for and loads Inits that have been placed in the System Folder.

HOWARD W. SAMS & COMPANY

fff

Bookmark

DEAR VALUED CUSTOMER:

Howard W. Sams & Company is dedicated to bringing you timely and authoritative books for your personal and professional library. Our goal is to provide you with excellent technical books written by the most qualified authors. You can assist us in this endeavor by checking the box next to your particular areas of interest.

We appreciate your comments and will use the information to provide you with a more comprehensive selection of titles.

Thank you,

Vice President, Book Publishing
Howard W. Sams & Company

COMPUTER TITLES:

Hardware
- ☐ Apple 140   ☐ Macintosh 101
- ☐ Commodore 110
- ☐ IBM & Compatibles 114

Business Applications
- ☐ Word Processing J01
- ☐ Data Base J04
- ☐ Spreadsheets J02

Operating Systems
- ☐ MS-DOS K05   ☐ OS/2 K10
- ☐ CP/M K01   ☐ UNIX K03

Programming Languages
- ☐ C L03   ☐ Pascal L05
- ☐ Prolog L12   ☐ Assembly L01
- ☐ BASIC L02   ☐ HyperTalk L14

Troubleshooting & Repair
- ☐ Computers S05
- ☐ Peripherals S10

Other
- ☐ Communications/Networking M03
- ☐ AI/Expert Systems T18

ELECTRONICS TITLES:

- ☐ Amateur Radio T01
- ☐ Audio T03
- ☐ Basic Electronics T20
- ☐ Basic Electricity T21
- ☐ Electronics Design T12
- ☐ Electronics Projects T04
- ☐ Satellites T09

- ☐ Instrumentation T05
- ☐ Digital Electronics T11

Troubleshooting & Repair
- ☐ Audio S11   ☐ Television S04
- ☐ VCR S01   ☐ Compact Disc S02
- ☐ Automotive S06
- ☐ Microwave Oven S03

Other interests or comments: _____

_____

_____

Name_____
Title _____
Company _____
Address _____
City _____
State/Zip _____
Daytime Telephone No. _____

A Division of Macmillan, Inc.
4300 West 62nd Street
Indianapolis, Indiana 46268

48403

Bookmark

HOWARD W. SAMS
& COMPANY

HAYDEN *Macintosh Library* BOOKS

Macintosh™ Revealed

Volume One:
Unlocking the Toolbox
Second Edition
Stephen Chernicoff
ISBN: 0-672-48400-5, $26.95

Volume Two:
Programming with the
Toolbox
Second Edition
Stephen Chernicoff
ISBN: 0-672-48401-3, $26.95

Volume Three:
Mastering the Toolbox
(forthcoming)
Stephen Chernicoff
ISBN: 0-672-48402-1, $26.95

Volume Four:
Programming the
Machintosh™ II (forthcoming)
Stephen Chernicoff and Geri Younggren
ISBN: 0-672-48413-7, $26.95

Advanced Macintosh™ Pascal
Paul Goodman
ISBN: 0-672-46570-1, $19.95

How to Write Macintosh™
Software
Second Edition
Scott Knaster
ISBN: 0-672-48429-3, $27.95

MacAccess: Information in
Motion
Dean Gengle and Steven Smith
ISBN: 0-672-46567-1, $21.95

Macintosh™ Multiplan®
Joan Lasselle and Carol Ramsay
ISBN: 0-8104-6555-8, $16.95

MPW and Assembly
Language Programming
Scott Kronick
ISBN: 0-672-48409-9, $24.95

(more titles on the back)

To order, return the card below, or call 1-800-428-SAMS. In Indiana call (317) 298-5699.

Please send me the books listed below.

Title	Quantity	ISBN #	Price

☐ Please add my name to your mailing list to receive more
information on related titles.

Name (please print) ―――――――――――――――

Company ―――――――――――――――――

City ――――――――――――――――――

State/Zip ――――――――――――――――

Signature ――――――――――――――――
(required for credit card purchase)

Telephone # ―――――――――――――――

Subtotal ―――――

Standard Postage and Handling $2.50 ―――

All States Add Appropriate Sales Tax ―――――

TOTAL ―――――

Enclosed is My Check or Money Order for $―――――

Charge my Credit Card: ☐ VISA   ☐ MC   ☐ AE

Account No.   Expiration Date ―――――

☐☐☐☐ ☐☐☐☐ ☐☐☐☐ ☐☐☐☐

48403

**The Macintosh™ Advisor
(Updated for Multifinder)**
Cynthia Harriman and Bencion Calica
ISBN: 0-8104-6569-8, $19.95

**Object-Oriented
Programming for the
Macintosh™**
Kurt J. Schmucker
ISBN: 0-8104-6565-5, $34.95

**dBASE® Mac Programmer's
Reference Guide**
Edward C. Jones
ISBN: 0-672-48416-1, $19.95

HyperTalk™ Programming
Dan Shafer
ISBN: 0-672-48426-9, $24.95

**HyperTalk™ Tips and
Techniques**
Dan Shafer
ISBN: 0-672-48427-7, $21.95

**IBM® PC and Macintosh™
Networking: Featuring TOPS
and AppleShare™**
Steve Michel
ISBN: 0-672-48405-6, $21.95

Nonlibrary Titles

**The Waite Group's
HyperTalk™ Bible**
The Waite Group
ISBN: 0-672-48430-7, $24.95

**Understanding HyperTalk™
(forthcoming)**
Dan Shafer
ISBN: 0-672-27283-0, $17.95

Place
Postage
Here

HOWARD W. SAMS & COMPANY

Dept. DM
4300 West 62nd Street
Indianapolis, IN 46268–2520

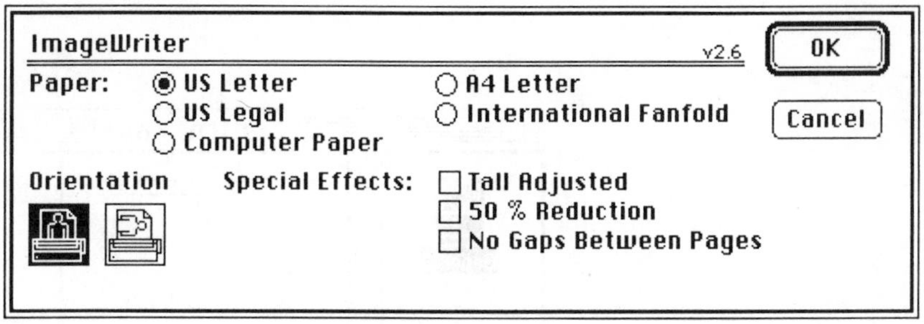

Figure 2–3. Printer options are displayed inside application programs, depending on which printer drivers are installed in the System Folder and which printer you have selected with the Chooser.

Storage Files

Desk accessories are stored in the System file. Files that store the data generated by DAs must reside in the System Folder so the System knows where to find the data. A basic Mac System Folder contains storage files called Scrapbook and Notepad, which hold images you store using the Scrapbook DA, or notes you create with the Notepad DA.

Some other DAs that store information also require you to place a storage file in the System Folder. SideKick, for example, needs a storage file called Phonebook in the System Folder to store telephone numbers. Finally, there are application programs that either use or actually create storage files in the System Folder. Microsoft Word 3.01 creates a file called Word Settings in the System Folder. The Word Settings file stores the user preference information you set in Word.

If you use a lot of data-storing DAs or other programs that have storage files in the System Folder, you may be tempted to place all these files in their own folder inside the System Folder to tidy things up. Resist this temptation! Storage files usually must be only in the System Folder, not in folders of their own, to work properly.

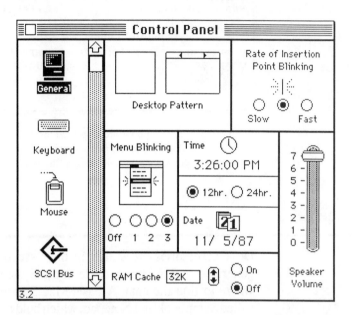

Figure 2–4. cdevs appear as icons on the left side of the Control Panel.

Other System Resources: Chooser Resources and cdevs

Two DAs that relate closely to the System file are the Chooser and the Control Panel. As mentioned earlier, you use the Chooser to select different printers, depending on which printer drivers are in the System Folder. Chooser Resources are like printer drivers, only they are "drivers" for other devices, such as AppleShare volumes, network modems, or alternate "printers" that you use to print files or images to disk.

   cdevs (or control devices) are resources available via the Control Panel desk accessory. Versions of the System beginning with 4.1 have a Control Panel whose user-adjustable settings are divided into groups. The basic Control Panel for the Mac Plus has groups of settings called General (for the cursor blink rate, the desktop pattern, speaker volume, and other functions), Keyboard (for key-repeat rates and other related features), and Mouse (for mouse sensitivity and other features). The particular group of settings shown on the Control Panel at a given time is selected via an icon in a scroll box to the left of the panel adjustments, as shown in Figure 2–4. Each icon representing a group of user settings is called a cdev, and the list of cdevs can vary. On the Mac II, for example, the list of cdevs includes groups of settings for the monitor and for sound.

In order for a cdev to appear in the Control Panel, it must reside in the System Folder. If you have a Mac Plus with System file 4.1 or later, you'll see cdev files in the System Folder for General, Keyboard, and Mouse. Initially, Apple's cdevs were the only ones to be found in the System Folder, but cdevs are a fertile area for programmers. They offer a way to install a utility program on the Apple menu without taking up a desk accessory slot and still make the program easily available. Already, there are public domain cdevs that you can use to install a screen saver program to black out your screen when it isn't in use and one to control the default colors shown on the Mac II screen.

Along with placing cdevs in the System Folder, you can actually control the order in which they appear on the Control Panel. Typically, cdevs are shown in alphabetical order, but if there's a cdev you use frequently that usually appears way down the list, you can rename it to appear higher on the list. In the Mac's alphabetizing scheme, any name with a period in front of it comes before letters of the alphabet. You can rename a cdev with a period in front of the name to move it up the cdev list on the Control Panel, just below the General icon. (Despite the alphabetizing scheme, the cdevs always appear under the General icon.)

You can't simply select a cdev's icon in the System Folder and rename it—the System won't allow this—but you can rename a duplicate of the cdev. So, to rename a cdev, duplicate it first, rename the duplicate with a period in front of it, then throw away the original cdev. Here's the procedure:

1. Quit to the Finder if you're not already there.
2. Open the System Folder.
3. Select the cdev you want to rename.
4. Choose the Duplicate command from the File menu. A second cdev, called Duplicate of *cdev* (where *cdev* is the name of the resource), will appear in the System Folder.
5. Select the duplicate cdev you have just made, if it isn't already selected.
6. Retype the cdev name with a period in front of it and press the Return key.
7. Select the original cdev and drag it to the Trash Can. Click on the Yes button when the Mac asks you if you really want to throw that file away.

cdevs and Chooser Resources automatically appear on the Control Panel and Chooser menu as soon as you drag them into the System Folder. You don't need to restart your Mac first.

Inits

An Init is nothing more than a program of the file type Init. Once a program has the Init file type and is placed in the System Folder, the System will find that program and load it automatically into memory whenever you start up your Mac in the future. The System file always looks for and loads any Inits inside the System Folder before it starts the Finder or any other startup application you have set.

There are many Inits available. One called Startup Sound finds a sound file and plays that sound as your Mac starts up. Apple's Node ID Init automatically enters a user ID you specify into the Chooser's User ID box. Another Init called Findswell adds a new button to the SFGet box in your application programs, so you can find hard disk files more easily. There isn't any absolute limit to the number of Inits you can place inside your System Folder (as long as you have enough disk space), but having too many Inits can cause some problems with your Mac's operation, as we'll see in Chapter 14. We'll look at various types of Inits more closely in Chapter 11.

Which System Should You Use?

The System file has been updated over half a dozen times since the Macintosh was first introduced. Each new version has a number, and each subsequent version has brought new capabilities to the Mac. But the watershed version number for the System was 3.2, which was introduced in 1986 and which gave the Mac a hierarchical filing system that made hard disks much more useful. Some early versions of Mac application programs aren't compatible with the later versions of the System, and many newer versions of application programs aren't compatible with System versions prior to version 3.2.

This book assumes you are using System version 3.2 or later. If you have an earlier version, get an update from your Apple dealer or download it from the Micronetworked Apple User's Group (MAUG) on CompuServe. The latest version of the system at this writing is 4.2, which supports the new MultiFinder. This version of the System is being sold as an update by Apple dealers, complete with a manual, for $49, but you can probably get the software alone for free. The MultiFinder and System version 4.2 present problems and opportunities of their own, however. You'll find more information about the MultiFinder in Chapter 12.

The version of the System that you use must also be compatible with the Finder version you're using. Like the System, the Finder has been updated a number of times since the Mac was new, and very old versions of the Finder won't work with newer versions of the System. If you are updating your System file through a dealer, you will be given a new, compatible version of the Finder to go along with it.

Apple places each new revision of the system on the MAUG bulletin board on CompuServe. While you want to have a newer version of the System, you don't necessarily want to have the very latest. System 3.1, for example, was actually the first version with the new hierarchical filing system, but it was somewhat bug-ridden, so nobody uses that version anymore. If you're not sure which later version to use, ask your local user group or your Apple dealer. Apple doesn't release System upgrades to its dealers until they have been proven to be essentially trouble-free.

Whatever System file you choose, don't choose more than one. In our floppy disk days, many of us got in the habit of placing a System Folder on each of our application program disks, so we could start up from any program disk. In many cases, we gave each System Folder and System file its own collection of fonts, DAs, and even printer files to make the best use of space on each floppy, and to customize the System for each application. Multiple System Folders makes a lot of sense when you're using multiple floppies, but it's totally unnecessary, if not disastrous, on a hard disk.

In most cases, the System Folder you use to start your Mac remains in control of your Mac until you shut it off. If you had two System Folders in the main directory of your hard disk instead of one, your Mac would almost certainly get very confused about which System was in charge, and you could look forward to system crashes, lost files, and other unpleasant problems. Remember, the great thing about a hard disk is that you have plenty of space to include all the fonts, DAs, Inits, printer drivers, and other goodies you like in just *one* System Folder.

If you own a Mac Plus, Mac SE, or Mac II, you received a program called the Installer with your computer that automatically updates your System and Finder files. (If you own an earlier model of the Mac, you can get the Installer along with the System and Finder file updates from a dealer.) The main advantage to using the Installer is that it updates your System file without disturbing the existing fonts and DAs you have installed. If you've spent a lot of time customizing your System file with extra fonts and DAs, you'll want to preserve them when you update. If you simply replace your old System file by copying the new System file in the Finder, all your existing fonts and DAs will be lost.

The Installer updates the whole System file, including the Chooser and Control panel. For the various Macintosh models, different system resources are added. In the Mac II, for example, the Installer adds the Monitor, Color, and Sound cdevs to the Control Panel.

The Installer can't be used to update the disk from which it is running, nor can it update the current startup disk (it's rather like trying to soup up a car while you're driving it). For step-by-step instructions on using the Installer, refer to Chapter 2 of your Macintosh user's manual.

Compatible Systems on Serial Port Hard Disks

Serial port hard disk users must use a startup floppy disk that contains its own System Folder. These startup floppies may also contain an Init program that passes control over the Mac from the floppy disks' System Folder to the System Folder on the hard disk. Other programs on the startup floppy will include hard disk utilities, such as a backup program or a floppy-copying program. The System files on both the floppy and hard disk must be the same version, but they don't otherwise have to be compatible. If you load up your hard disk's System file with lots of space-eating fonts and DAs, you don't have to make the same additions to the System on your startup floppy.

Filing Systems: MFS Versus HFS

Before System version 3.2 came out, the System file used the Macintosh Filing System (MFS) as a means of organizing files on a disk. MFS was an extremely basic filing system that placed every file on a disk on one organizational level, as if all the pieces of paper in a file drawer were spread out side by side across the floor. From the Finder, you could create folders and place groups of files inside them so you didn't have to look at every file on the disk each time you opened a disk window. But the folders were only masks, not actual disk organizing tools. As soon as you loaded an application program and used the Open... command, all the folders disappeared. In the

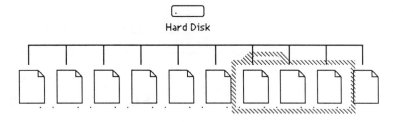

Figure 2–5. Files stored under the MFS are all placed on the same directory level.

displayed list of files, you saw all the files on the disk again. So the "road map" of an MFS disk would look like the one in Figure 2–5.

Here's what MFS looks like in action. Suppose you have three files on a disk and you make a folder in the Finder to store two of them, as in Figure 2–6.

This all looks nicely organized in the Finder, but as soon as you load an application and use the Open... command, the file window shows all three files, as in Figure 2–7. Furthermore, if you open one of the files that had been inside the folder and then save it back to disk later, the file will end up outside the folder when you return to the Finder.

This situation was annoying enough when the two or three dozen files that could be stored on the original Mac's 400K floppy disks were involved, but it became ridiculous with 800K floppies and hard disks. Because folders were only masks and not true disk organizing devices, anyone with several dozen or hundreds of files on a hard disk had to look through a long list of files to find a specific one.

Hard disk manufacturers at the time tackled this problem with software that partitioned the disks into a series of volumes, or file drawers. On the Mac, a *volume* is a discrete storage area, such as a floppy disk. Just as it can only read one disk at a time, MFS would only show the files on one volume at a time. With partitioning software, you could divide a hard disk into several volumes, so groups of files could be viewed and accessed separately. (You can still partition a hard disk into volumes under the HFS filing system today, but most users do not find it necessary because HFS has such good disk organizing tools of its own.)

With System 3.2, Apple introduced a new file organization system, the Hierarchical Filing System (HFS). HFS is a multilevel filing system that organizes files using folders that actually place files on different hierarchical levels, dividing up the disk space, similar to the hierarchical "tree structure"

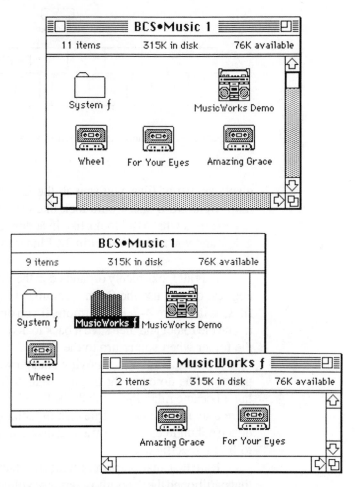

Figure 2–6. Under MFS, folders created in the Finder were merely cosmetic; they didn't move files to a lower level of the file hierarchy.

system of directories and subordinate subdirectories used by the MS-DOS and UNIX operating systems. When you place a file inside a folder under HFS, it stays there. When you use the Open... command in an application program, you can navigate to the folder you want and see only the names of files you've placed in that folder. The "road map" of an HFS disk might look like the one in Figure 2–8.

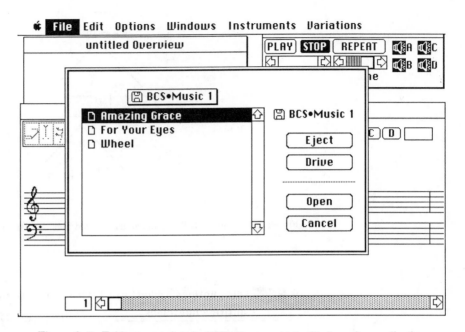

Figure 2–7. Folders created under MFS disappear in the file box of an application.

Let's look at the HFS difference in action. Using our previous example, say you have three files on a disk, and you have placed two of them in a folder, as in Figure 2–6. When you use the Open... command inside a program to produce the file box, you see the folder (which contains the two files), and a third file by itself, as in Figure 2–9. To see only the files inside the folder you created, you can open the folder, as in Figure 2–10.

Notice that when the folder is open, the disk icon at the top of the file listing changes to the name of the folder, so you know you've moved down one level in the file hierarchy, into a folder.

With the ability to place files inside real folders, you can organize your hard disk files into useful groups and greatly limit the amount of hunting to find a particular file.

The danger of HFS is that you can create many levels and sublevels in the file hierarchy, making folders inside folders inside folders. It's actually possible to be *too* organized. You could end up with one or two files each in dozens of different folders, or folders inside folders. You would be back to the MFS mess, only instead of hunting through long lists of files, you would

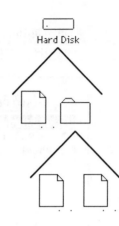

Figure 2–8. Under HFS, folders actually place files in different hierarchical levels.

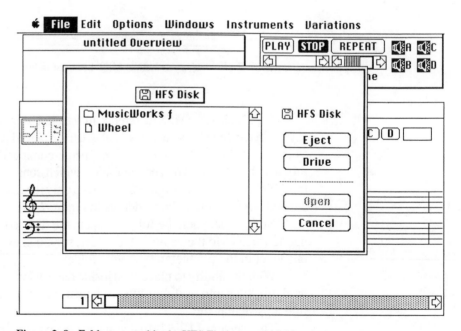

Figure 2–9. Folders created in the HFS Finder remain folders inside application programs.

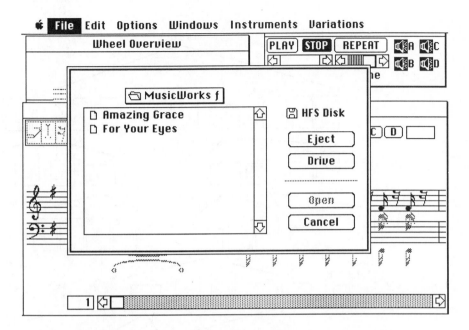

Figure 2–10.   You can navigate into and out of folders under HFS.

navigate endlessly through a maze of folders to find the file you want. An over-organized HFS disk road map might look like the one in Figure 2–11.

Fortunately, there's a way to strike a balance between organizing your files logically in folders and being able to find any one file quickly. Chapter 5 offers a number of file-organizing strategies.

System File Partners: Special DAs

Every Macintosh System file stores two DAs that you use to control some system-type information: the Chooser and the Control Panel. Some hard disks have their own "control panel" DA as well, which you install in your System file using the Font/DA Mover and which you use to control some of the operations of your hard disk.

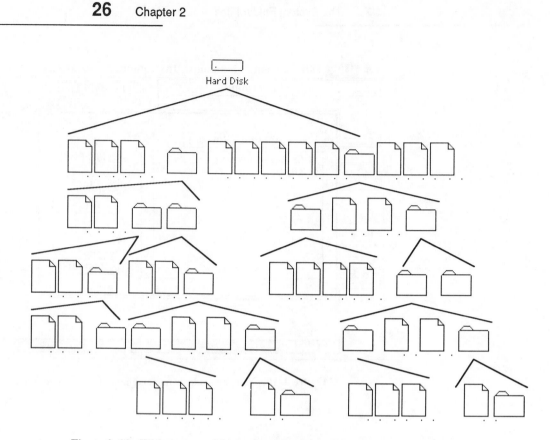

Figure 2–11.   With too many folders on a disk, you trade a file-hunting problem for a folder-hunting problem.

One feature of the System file is its ability to store up to 15 DAs. We'll discuss DAs in detail in Chapter 4. For now, it's enough to say that the System file supplied with every new Macintosh comes with a selection of useful DAs, such as a Notepad and a Calculator, and you can use them, remove them, or add other accessories that are more to your liking. As soon as you add a DA to the System file with the Font/DA Mover, it appears automatically on the Apple menu. Two DAs that come with every Mac System file and that should never be removed are the Chooser and the Control Panel.

The Chooser tells the System file which set of printer options to present to your application programs. When the System Folder contains one or more printer drivers, it lets the Chooser know that those printers are available for use. When you select the Chooser DA from the Apple menu, you see a

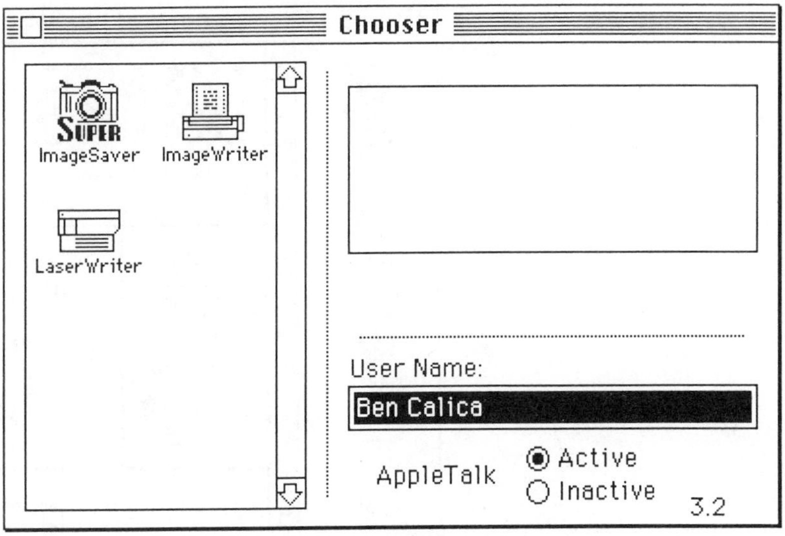

Figure 2–12. With the Chooser, you select icons to choose an output or network device.

collection of icons, one for each printer whose file is contained in the System Folder. If you have stored other Chooser Resources in the System Folder, you'll see icons for them as well, as in Figure 2–12.

To select a printer for use, just click on its icon. If you are using AppleTalk, you select the AppleTalk Active option at the bottom of the Chooser box. If you have chosen a LaserWriter (which must be connected via AppleTalk), your Mac's System file checks across the network to see if a LaserWriter is connected, turned on, and initialized. If there is a LaserWriter ready, the LaserWriter name appears in the list box on the right side of the Chooser box. If the LaserWriter isn't ready for some reason, it won't appear in the list box. Even if the LaserWriter is connected and initialized, you'll get a warning message if you try to print when the LaserWriter is out of paper.

If you're using an ImageWriter, the System file has no way of knowing whether an ImageWriter printer is actually connected to the Mac, turned on, or loaded with paper. If you try to print to an ImageWriter that isn't turned on, though, you'll get a warning message.

You use the Control Panel to adjust some parameters of the System file so your Mac works more the way you want it to. An example of Control Panel settings appears in Figure 2–13. You can set the speed at which the cursor

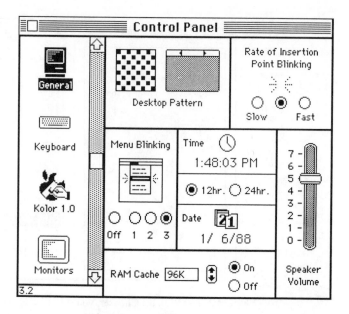

Figure 2–13. A typical Control Panel.

blinks, the sensitivity of the mouse, the time lag needed between double-clicks on the mouse button, the background pattern of the desktop, and other variables.

As a hard disk user, you may have a third DA specific to the operation of your hard disk. Some hard disks come with print spooler programs that are controlled through a desk accessory (see Chapter 7). Other hard disks, particularly older serial port or floppy port models that were designed to operate under MFS, have their own "control panel" DAs. With these DAs you mount or unmount different hard disk volumes or file drawers (to access different groups of files). Some serial port hard disks also featured built-in print spoolers, and their control panels often contained options for controlling the print spooler as well.

While the System does most of its work in the background, the Finder takes the spotlight for every Mac user. In Chapter 4, we'll look at the Mac's most visible program.

3

The Finder

The Finder is the first program you ever encounter on a Macintosh, and it is the program you use the most. Using information from the System file, the Finder lets you work with files, folders, and disks in various ways. The Finder is like a personal secretary that remembers what you called files, when you last worked on them, and where you put them. Like a human secretary, though, the Finder can get bogged down when you ask it to remember too many things. If your files are carefully organized on your disk, the Finder can show you any file quickly and easily, but if your desktop is a jumble of open windows, it will take the Finder longer to find and display the file you want. Your Macintosh user's manual covers the operations of the Finder in some detail, but this chapter expands on those explanations, and we'll explore some additional Finder issues Apple didn't tell you about.

Why the Finder?

The Finder is an application that gives you an easy way to manipulate files and disks on your Macintosh. It is the program that displays the familiar desktop when you start your Mac. When you start a Mac with a disk containing the System Folder, the Mac locates and loads needed parts of the System file, then looks for a Startup Application to run. The Finder is typically the Startup Application, so the desktop is displayed.

With the Finder you load, copy, and otherwise manipulate files and disks, and, like other application programs, it gives you access to your System file's desk accessories (DAs) via the Apple menu. But the Finder is not essential to running a Macintosh. There are other programs, which we call Finder alternatives, that perform many of the Finder's functions in different ways. Some of these alternatives include stacks created with Apple's HyperCard program, the new Apple MultiFinder, and other programs sold by third parties. These alternatives are covered in detail in Chapter 12.

You can even work without a Finder or Finder alternative at all. If you use the Finder to set a different Startup Application, you can then eject the disk, restart your Mac with a different system disk, and delete the Finder from the original startup disk. The next time you boot from that disk, the System file will load the Startup Application and you will never see the desktop. The System file is set up to look for and load the Finder whenever you quit any other application; however, if there's no Finder in the System Folder, your Mac will unceremoniously crash when you quit the application you are running.

The Finder was designed to be very easy to use, and its simplicity is one of the things that make the Mac so appealing. Much of that ease of use, however, comes from presenting files, folders, and disks graphically, and drawing those graphics takes time. After you quit a program, it takes a few seconds for the Mac to re-draw the Finder's desktop so you can perform other tasks. When you start your Mac, it takes several seconds for the desktop to appear. The more windows you have open on the desktop, and the more objects or text displayed in each of those windows, the longer it takes your Mac to draw the desktop each time you run the Finder. That's why it's a good idea to limit the number of windows you have open, and the information displayed in each. (More on this in Chapter 5.)

Which Finder?

As with the System file, there have been many versions of the Finder since the Mac first appeared. But, like System version 3.2, the Finder versions can be divided into two groups: before version 5.3 and after. Finder 5.3 was released with System version 3.2, and it is the first of the Finders that was compatible with the new hierarchical filing system. Version 5.3 offers several new functions over previous versions, such as the Restart command that reboots a hard disk as opposed to shutting it down completely. At this writing, the current version of the Finder is 6.0. This includes the new

MultiFinder that allows you to open and operate several application programs at once. To use the MultiFinder effectively, you need a megabyte or more of memory in your Mac.

Different versions of the Finder are compatible with different versions of the System file. For our purposes, we'll assume you are using Finder 5.3 or later. If you aren't, visit your Apple dealer to get an update, ask among your Mac-using friends for a newer version, or get the latest reliable version from a user group. Finder and System upgrades are usually offered together—you get the latest System and the latest Finder that is compatible with it. As explained in Chapter 2, Apple places each new version of the System and Finder on the Micronetworked Apple User's Group (MAUG) on CompuServe as well as MacNet. It rarely pays to be on the cutting edge, though, because there are frequently problems with new releases. Finder 5.2 was released on CompuServe, for example, but it is never used now because of incompatibilities with existing application software.

To install a Finder update, use the Installer program that came with your Macintosh Plus, SE, or II, or get it from your Apple dealer. The Installer automatically updates your old Finder with the new version. If you need help using the Installer, look in Chapter 2 of your Macintosh user's manual. Now, let's take a look at various features of the Finder and how they relate to hard disk users.

The Desktop

The first thing you notice after you load the Finder is the desktop, that light gray surface with a menu bar at the top, a Trash Can icon in the lower right corner, and an icon for your hard disk (and/or the floppy disk you used to start your Mac) in the upper right corner. The desktop, its icons, and its windows are the main tools you use to organize and present hard disk files so you can find them easily.

Windows always have the same basic appearance, and they always behave in the same way. Knowing the basic rules of how windows look and act is a key to arranging them so you can view and select the files on your hard disk easily.

First of all, windows are always square or rectangular graphic areas that display the contents of a disk or folder. Each window has a title bar at the top, a close box at the left side of the title bar, and scroll bars at the bottom and right side of the window. Finally, there's a size box at the lower right corner, which allows you to adjust the window's size. In Finder versions 5.3 and

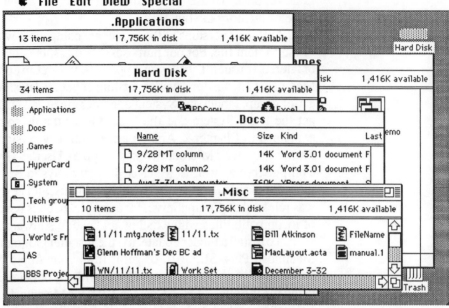

Figure 3–1. With too many windows open on the desktop, it can be difficult to see the files you need.

later, there's also a Zoom box at the right edge of the title bar, which you can click to quickly change the window's size from its maximum size (about 3/4 of the screen) to a smaller size you have preset. Inside an open window, you'll find names or icons representing the files or folders stored on the disk or folder you have opened.

Windows can have different sizes and positions on the desktop, and they can overlap one another. You can have up to 12 windows open at once on the desktop, but you will want to limit the number of open windows yourself so you can see what you're doing. Because windows can hide behind other windows, it's amazingly easy to lose track of the window you want to look into. If you open too many windows, your desktop can quickly look like the one in Figure 3–1.

Another rule is that the position of a window is always exactly where you last left it. If you create a certain window arrangement, that arrangement will be preserved between sessions with the Finder. The next time you return to the Finder, the windows will be in the same place where you left them, so you can create a default window arrangement and be sure that it will be there each time you start up your Mac. We'll look at some effective window arrangements in Chapter 5.

Viewing Files in Windows

When you first open a disk or folder window, each file is represented by an icon. This process is called viewing the window contents by Icon. Using the Finder's View menu you select one of six different ways to view the files in a window. The view you choose applies only to the currently active window. The desktop itself is always viewed by Icon, as long as you're using the Finder. Different window views can be handy for different purposes, and there are some tricks to using the Icon views to their best advantage.

By Icon

Icon view is the standard way to view files in windows. Each application and file is represented as a different icon, with the name of the file beneath it. Along with icons depicting files, this view shows you some other valuable information. At the top of the window, you see the number of items (icons) in the window, the amount of disk space that is in use, and the amount of disk space available. The Icon and Small Icon views are the only two views that display this information.

Icons can be moved around the window, and they can overlap one another. Many applications have their own unique icons that make them easy to identify, as you can see in Figure 3–2.

Icon view is great when you have only a few files in a window, because it's easy to pick out the file or application you want. Icons take up a lot of space in a window, though, and with more than a few files you'll have one of two problems:

1. The icons will be spread out over a wide area, so you'll have to use the window's scroll bars to locate the file you want at any given time, or

2. The icons will overlap one another and it will be difficult to read individual icon names or pick out the one you want.

There are some strategies for minimizing these problems. The Clean Up command rearranges the icons in a window along an invisible grid. It only works on windows displayed with either Icon or Small Icon views. In Icon view, Clean Up tries to place icons in straight horizontal rows and columns.

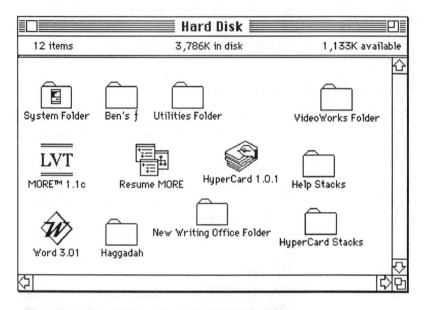

Figure 3–2. Unique icons help you locate specific application programs easily in the Finder.

Clean Up places icons in the closest grid position. In each row, the names of icons will overlap one another, as in Figure 3–3.

When icon names overlap in a window like those in Figure 3–3, you can stagger icons vertically so the names are offset. To do this,

1. Select every other icon in a row by shift-clicking with the mouse.

2. When every other icon is selected, drag the group straight down (or up, if there's room) until the names are below those of the other icons from that row that weren't selected, as in Figure 3–4.

Another tip for making the most of Icon view in a window is to keep icon names as short as possible. Icons themselves are fairly compact, and it is usually the names that end up overlapping one another. With shorter names, you'll be able to squeeze more icons into the visible part of a window.

Finally, you can use the zoom box at the upper right side of the menu bar to fully expand the window and display as many icons as possible. In a zoomed-out window, you can display dozens of icons at once. Of course, the

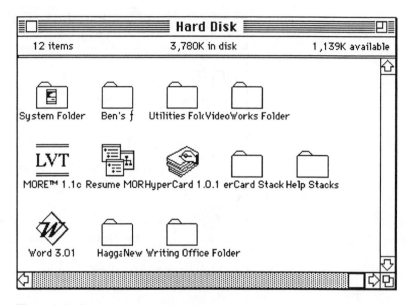

Figure 3–3.   Icon names can overlap when they're arranged side by side with the
Clean Up command.

zoomed-out window will probably obscure other windows underneath it, but
at least you'll be able to locate the icon you want without a lot of scrolling
around.

By Small Icon

Small Icon is a view just like Icon, except (you guessed it) the icons are
smaller. Rather than appearing on top of the filename, as in Icon view, small
icons appear to the left of the filename, as in Figure 3–5.

There are several advantages to using the Small Icon view. First, you
can cram more icons into a smaller area in a window, reducing some of the
space problems possible with Icon view. Like Icon view, it shows you the
amount of space used and space remaining on the disk. Finally, you can use
the Clean Up command to arrange small icons so they don't overlap one
another.

The disadvantage to small icons is that they are squashed versions of
regular icons. It's harder to identify an icon quickly by glancing at it, and
when you do, you'll realize that regular icons are more pleasing to the eye.

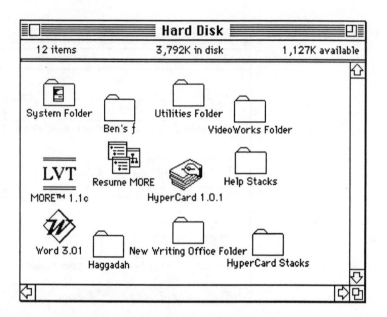

Figure 3–4. You can untangle overlapping icon names by selecting alternate icons in a row and dragging them beneath their neighbors.

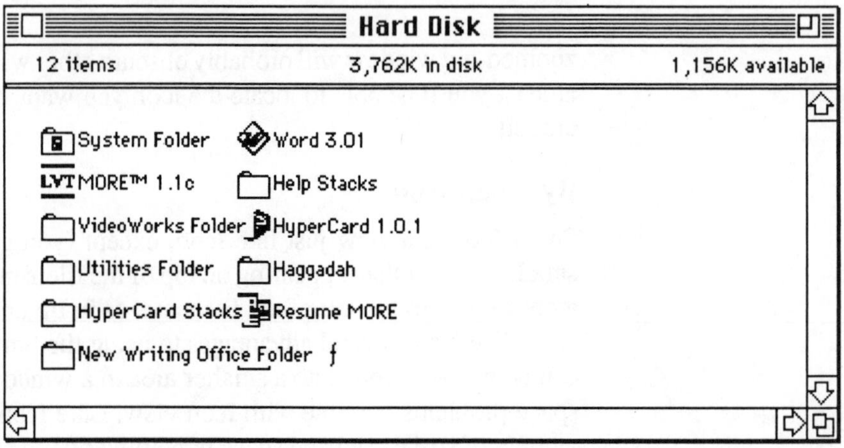

Figure 3–5. Small Icon view places the icon name to the right of the icon, rather than below it.

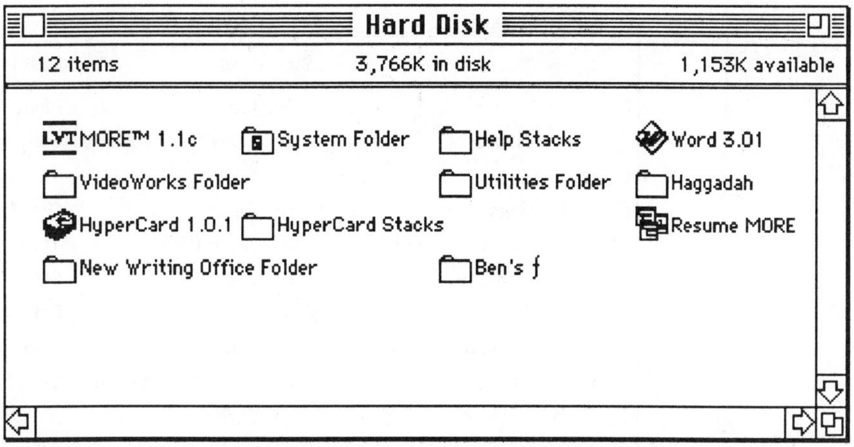

```
┌─────────────────────────────────────────────────────────────────┐
│ ▣ │▭│═══════════════════ Hard Disk ═══════════════════│ ⬚ │▭│    │
├─────────────────────────────────────────────────────────────────┤
│ 12 items              3,766K in disk            1,153K available  │
├───────────────────────────────────────────────────────────────┬─┤
│                                                               │⇧│
│  LVT MORE™ 1.1c    ▣ System Folder    ▢ Help Stacks   ◈ Word 3.01│ │
│                                                                 │ │
│  ▢ VideoWorks Folder      ▢ Utilities Folder    ▢ Haggadah      │ │
│                                                                 │ │
│  ◉ HyperCard 1.0.1  ▢ HyperCard Stacks      ▣ Resume MORE       │ │
│                                                                 │ │
│  ▢ New Writing Office Folder      ▢ Ben's ƒ                     │ │
│                                                                 │ │
│                                                               │⇩│
├───────────────────────────────────────────────────────────────┴─┤
│ ⬅ │                                                    │ ⇨ │⬚│    │
└─────────────────────────────────────────────────────────────────┘
```

Figure 3–6. By pressing the Option key while you select the Clean Up command for the Small Icon view, the Macintosh arranges icons so their names don't overlap.

Even with small icons, your window may become crowded if there are a lot of documents in it. As with Icon view, small icons can overlap one another, and the names can become impossible to read. Again, the Clean Up command comes to the rescue. Using the Clean Up command, the Finder arranges the small icons along an invisible grid, from one edge of the window to the other. Icon names will overlap one another, just as they do when you use Icon view. But with Small Icon view, you can hold down the Option key while you choose Clean Up, and the icons will be arranged farther apart on a grid so no filenames overlap, as in Figure 3–6.

There are some additional features of the Clean Up command you should know. The techniques just described only work if none of the items in the window are selected. The window itself must be selected, though. To select a window without selecting anything in it, click in its title bar. If you choose Clean Up while an icon in a window is selected, that icon itself will be cleaned up—it will be moved to the nearest invisible grid point. If you don't have any windows open on the desktop when you choose the Clean Up command, the Finder will tidy up the disk and Trash Can icons on the desktop itself.

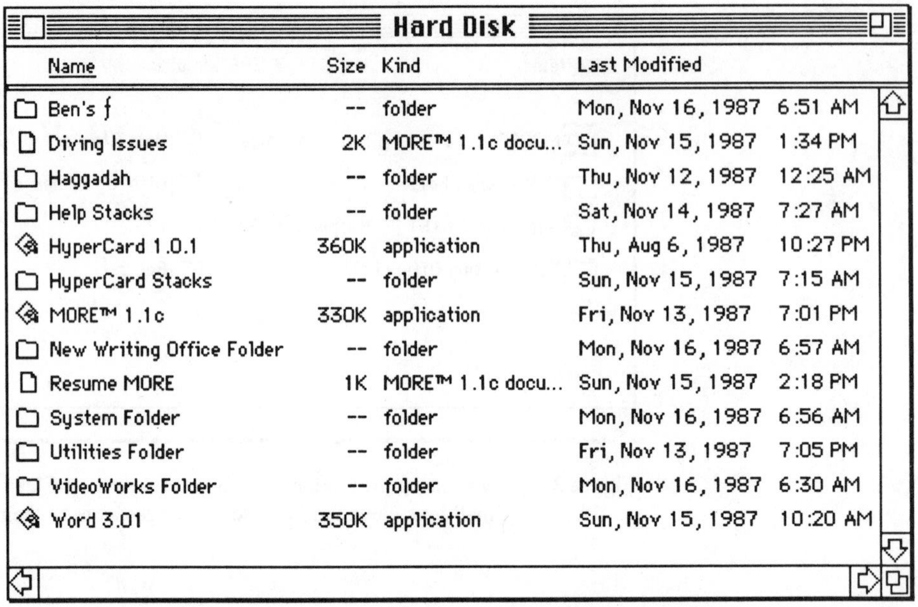

Hard Disk			
Name	Size	Kind	Last Modified
📁 Ben's ʃ	--	folder	Mon, Nov 16, 1987 6:51 AM
📄 Diving Issues	2K	MORE™ 1.1c docu...	Sun, Nov 15, 1987 1:34 PM
📁 Haggadah	--	folder	Thu, Nov 12, 1987 12:25 AM
📁 Help Stacks	--	folder	Sat, Nov 14, 1987 7:27 AM
📁 HyperCard 1.0.1	360K	application	Thu, Aug 6, 1987 10:27 PM
📁 HyperCard Stacks	--	folder	Sun, Nov 15, 1987 7:15 AM
📁 MORE™ 1.1c	330K	application	Fri, Nov 13, 1987 7:01 PM
📁 New Writing Office Folder	--	folder	Mon, Nov 16, 1987 6:57 AM
📄 Resume MORE	1K	MORE™ 1.1c docu...	Sun, Nov 15, 1987 2:18 PM
📁 System Folder	--	folder	Mon, Nov 16, 1987 6:56 AM
📁 Utilities Folder	--	folder	Fri, Nov 13, 1987 7:05 PM
📁 VideoWorks Folder	--	folder	Mon, Nov 16, 1987 6:30 AM
📁 Word 3.01	350K	application	Sun, Nov 15, 1987 10:20 AM

Figure 3–7. Text window views always show file information in four columns, or fields.

The Text Views

The last four options on the View menu display files by name, in text format. The only non-text element in the window is a tiny icon, either a document page, an application, or a folder, next to each filename, which tells you which type of file each name represents.

Text names are always arranged neatly in rows, with one file per row, and the names cannot overlap one another or become disorganized in any way. File information in the text views is displayed in four columns. You see the filename, the file size, the type of file, and the date the file was last modified, as in Figure 3–7. The different text views simply let you sort the files on each of these four columns, or fields of information.

With the Name view, files are arranged alphabetically by filename. Name view is the best option for folders or disks that contain mostly documents, rather than applications. (Many documents in a window are often created by the same application, so the distinguishing feature of each document in the list is its name, rather than its icon. Applications, on the other hand, are more easily distinguished by their unique icons in an Icon view.)

With the Date view, files are listed chronologically by the modification date. (Folder modification dates indicate when you last added a file to them, removed a file from them, or when you created them, if the folder is empty.) This view is useful if you want to select a file or files created on, before, or after certain dates.

The Size view arranges files in descending order by size. If you couldn't remember a file name but you knew it was a 32K file, arranging the files by size would help you find it. (Folder sizes are not shown, and Folders are placed last on the list of filenames, below other files.)

In the Kind view, files are organized in alphabetical order by type. Files are designated either as applications, folders, or X files, where X is the name of the application used to create them. You could use this view if you couldn't remember a filename but you knew it was a MacWrite file, for example.

Deleting and Erasing Files from a Disk

Along with viewing and loading files, the Finder offers a quick file-deleting utility: Trash Can. For a long time, the Trash Can icon on the desktop was the only way to erase a file from a disk. Now, many application programs have their own commands that delete disk files. The advantages to using the Trash Can to delete files are that you can delete groups of files quickly, and you can retrieve deleted files if you change your mind.

You can select multiple files by shift-clicking on them, then dragging them all to the Trash Can at once to delete them as a group. The Trash Can is not bottomless, however. Early Finder versions crash when you attempt to toss out more than a dozen or so files at a time, and even with a recent Finder version, you shouldn't try to get rid of more than 30 files at once.

Note that when you delete a file by dragging it to the Trash Can, then emptying the trash (or use an application's file deleting command), you haven't necessarily done away with the file forever. The file isn't physically erased yet from the disk. Deleting a file in this way tells the disk's directory system—the listing that keeps track of how much disk space is available, where files are, how big they are, and where the available space is—that the space used by that file is now available. Once the directory knows the file space is up for grabs again, it will overwrite the old file with new information as you save it. Unless your disk is full, however (in which case the file you've deleted represents the only available space), the directory will choose other locations in which to store new files for awhile. That means your "deleted" file will actually remain on the disk for some time.

If you delete a file on a floppy disk and decide you made a mistake, the first thing to do is put the disk aside. Don't save any more files on it, because one of the new files may overwrite your old file, and it really will be gone forever. If the file is on your hard disk, stop file modification. Then, use a disk utility program to recover the deleted file. Disk utility programs you can use to recover a deleted file are covered in Chapter 10.

There are also some disk utilities (also covered in Chapter 10) that permanently erase individual files from a disk, rather than "deleting" them in the usual way. Otherwise, the best way to be sure a disk's files are really deleted is to reinitialize the disk using the Erase Disk command from the Special menu in the Finder. This method requires you to erase the entire disk, though, so be sure there aren't any files on it that you want to keep.

Automating Operations in the Finder

Users of non-Mac operating systems such as UNIX and MS-DOS are familiar with the concept of batch operations, which is a feature of the operating system that allows it to automatically execute several tasks without user intervention. In the MS-DOS world, batch operations are performed by batch or command files, which are small programs that tell MS-DOS to load files and do other jobs when the computer starts up.

The Finder has two built-in facilities that you can use to specify one or more activities in advance and then have them performed automatically. In addition, you can use third-party programs to automate many Finder activities.

Loading Applications Automatically

Using the Set Startup command on the Special menu, you choose an application to be loaded automatically when you start your Mac each day. As shipped, your System file has the Startup Application set to the Finder, which is why the desktop appears first after you start your Mac. With the Set Startup command, you can bypass the Finder and directly load an application.

To use Set Startup, select the icon for the application you want, and then choose the Set Startup command. After you've used Set Startup to change the Startup Application, you must restart your Mac to see it work. Set Startup works on either applications or documents. If you choose a document as the Startup Application, your Mac will load the document and the application that was used to create it at the same time.

In System versions prior to 4.2, the Set Startup command could only be used to load one application. In System version 4.2 and later, though, the new MultiFinder helps you manage a series of startups. You can use its Set Startup command to specify several different applications, documents, or even desk accessories to load upon startup.

Sometimes, you may find yourself wishing for the ability to automate several different operations when your Mac starts each day. If you're on a network, for example, and you always check your electronic mail before starting work, you might want your Mac to make the check automatically before loading your favorite application. If you use a print spooler that must be the Startup Application, you might want a way to run the spooler and then load another application. Or, maybe you just want your Mac to load Microsoft Word and then open two or three Word files you need.

The Finder doesn't have the capability to automate more than one activity at once (unless you count the System Folder's Init programs, discussed in Chapter 2), but you can gain more automation with a macro program. Two popular macro programs are Tempo from Affinity Microsystems ($99), and QuicKeys, from CE Software (also $99). Both of these programs help you create small programs, called *macros,* that perform a series of Mac operations automatically. Macros can execute keystrokes, make menu selections, and recreate mouse movements, so they can do just about anything you can do with a Mac yourself.

To automate Finder operations with a macro program, you create a startup macro, which is a macro set to run by itself as soon as you start your Mac. Macros can contain hundreds of keystrokes or mouse movements, so you can design macros that perform some highly complex, sequential operations upon startup. As an example, a startup macro could start a terminal program, log onto a remote database, download some information into a file, quit the terminal program, load a database program, and then load the file of downloaded information, all without user intervention. In addition to automating startup activities, macro programs can also make using applications much easier by automating complex, repetitive operations that you perform regularly within the applications. A good macro program is well worth the money if you're interested in boosting your productivity and saving keystrokes.

Batch Printing

With the Finder's Print command, you can print a series of selected documents in order. To batch print several files, simply shift-click to select all the files you want to print, and then choose the Print command from the File menu.

Generally, all the documents you select for printing in this way must have been created with the same application. If you select several icons for printing, they are printed in order from left to right, then from the top of the window to the bottom. If you are using a text view of a window, selected files are printed in order from top to bottom. To print successfully, the application you used to create the documents you select must be available in a currently installed disk.

When you print files from the Finder, the Finder uses the application used to create those documents for instructions on how to print them. The options you last chose with the Print and Page Setup commands in that application will be the ones used when you print from the Finder.

Batch printing is very useful if you have several lengthy files to print and you don't want to wait around for them. You could print a series of long reports over lunch or overnight and have them ready on your return. If you're using a print spooler, you can use the spooler's batch printing feature to quickly select a series of files to be printed, rather than selecting them one at a time.

Other Disk-Handling Commands in the Finder

Your hard disk holds many megabytes of programs and data, but it's still just a storage device as far as your Mac is concerned. That means you can use the Finder's other disk-handling commands just as easily with your hard disk as you can with a floppy. Let's look at these commands and see how they affect a hard disk.

The Eject command ejects the selected disk from its disk drive. You cannot "eject" your hard disk unless it is one of the large floppies such as Bernoulli or Jasmine's MegaDrive. You can never remove the startup disk's icon from the desktop, whether it's a floppy or hard disk. You can eject the disk itself, but the image of the startup disk remains on the desktop.

You can also eject disks and remove their icons from the desktop by dragging their icons to the Trash Can. This goes for your hard disk as well.

The Restart command clears your Mac's memory, records all the changes to the desktop (window locations and so on), records Control Panel and Chooser changes, ejects any disks from the disk drives, and returns you to the opening Mac screen where an icon prompts you to insert a startup disk. While your hard disk is "ejected," however, it is still connected to your Mac and it is still running (unless you've turned it off). If you choose Restart while you have an operating hard disk connected to your Mac's SCSI or external floppy port, the Mac will automatically reboot from the hard disk.

The Shut Down command does the same thing as the Restart command, only it doesn't automatically display the opening Mac screen. Instead, you'll see a black screen with a button in the center labeled Restart. This black screen gives you an opportunity to either shut off your Mac and hard disk or restart the Mac.

In previous versions of the Finder, the Shut Down command performed the function of the Restart command. Hard disk users had to hurry to turn off the Mac after choosing the old Shut Down command, or else their Macs would restart from the hard disk immediately. The newer Shut Down command means hard disk users don't have to race to hit their Mac power switches.

The Erase Disk command is used to reformat floppy disks when you want to completely erase them. You can also use Erase Disk to reformat a hard disk, however. The ease with which users of MS-DOS and CP/M computers could reformat large disks accidentally has been a subject of jokes for years, but Erase Disk makes this catastrophe possible on a Mac. If the icon for your hard disk is selected and you choose Erase Disk, you'll get a warning message first. One other safety feature is that you can't erase the startup disk, whether it's a floppy or a hard disk. If you have selected a hard disk that isn't the startup disk, and you click the Initialize button in the warning box, that hard disk will be erased.

Now, About All That Storage

In the past two chapters, we've explored the System and Finder files and how their special features apply to hard disk users. One of the big advantages to having a hard disk is the ability to store lots of fonts and DAs inside the System file. We'll look closely at fonts and DAs in Chapter 4.

CHAPTER

4

Fonts, DAs, and the Font/DA Mover

From the beginning, the Mac was designed to give us a lot of control over the fonts and desk accessories (DAs) we use. Being able to select from a wide assortment of different fonts for documents is one of the things that attracted us to the Mac in the first place. And because DAs work along with most application programs, their handy utilities and miniapplications are always available. Some fonts and many DAs are in the public domain, and others are sold commercially, but in any case, there are hundreds of them to choose from. Throughout this book, we mention several DAs that make using a hard disk easier, and Appendix B lists them.

On a floppy disk system, the number of fonts and DAs you can add to the System file on a startup disk is often limited by the amount of available disk space. This problem disappears with a hard disk. But installing fonts and DAs in a hard disk's System file forces us to face other limits of the Macintosh. Relieved of the disk space constraint, we discover that the Mac itself places a limit on the number of DAs we can install on the Apple menu (15), and we realize that although we could have dozens of different fonts available at once, we probably don't need them.

This chapter explores fonts and DAs from a hard disk user's point of view. We'll look at some guidelines for deciding which fonts to install. We'll consider downloadable fonts for the LaserWriter. And we'll check out the

Figure 4–1. Font and DA files are usually represented by suitcase icons, with font files (left) identified by the letter A on the suitcase and DA files (right) identified by a grid on the suitcase.

DA limit and look at some ways to get around it. But first of all, we'll look at fonts and DAs in general, and we'll take a thorough tour of the program that makes adding different fonts and DAs possible.

Fonts and DAs: Individual Files or Part of the System?

Fonts and DAs have two different identities on a Macintosh. Originally, each font and DA begins as a file, called a *suitcase file,* which can be copied, moved, and deleted like any other file on a Mac. Font and DA files are always represented by an icon that looks like a suitcase, as in Figure 4–1.

Each new font and DA you buy or receive usually comes in a suitcase file, but suitcase files can't be opened like regular icons. To use a font or DA, you must install it in your System file using the Font/DA Mover. (In fact, if you open a suitcase file by double-clicking or selecting it and using the Open command, the Font/DA Mover loads.) Using the Font/DA Mover, you can locate a suitcase file, open it, and copy it to the System file. Once a font or DA is copied into the System file, it will always appear on the Font or Apple menu, ready for use. After you copy the suitcase file, however, the suitcase file itself remains on the disk where it was.

Once fonts or DAs have been installed in your System file, you may want to remove them to make way for other fonts or DAs, or simply to gain more space on your disk. At other times, you might want to take a font or DA from your System file and store it as a suitcase file to give to someone else. The Font/DA Mover has options that let you remove fonts and DAs from your System file, or create new suitcase files, along with installing new fonts and DAs.

F /DA Mover 3.5

Figure 4–2. The Font/DA Mover icon looks like a delivery truck.

Using the Font/DA Mover

When the Mac was first introduced, Apple supplied a program called the Font Mover that added or removed only fonts in a System file. In the beginning, the main purpose of the Font Mover was to remove fonts from a System file, so users could gain more storage space on the Mac's original 400K floppy disks. In 1985, the program was renamed the Font/DA Mover and was updated to allow users to add or remove desk accessories as well as fonts.

The Font/DA Mover comes as part of the package with a lot of commercial desk accessory programs. Its basic operations are described in the Macintosh user's manual, and in the manuals for many DAs, but many users find it a source of confusion anyway. Let's clear things up with a close look at how the Font/DA Mover works.

First of all, make sure you are using version 3.2 or later of the Font/DA Mover. Earlier versions are unreliable with System version 3.2 or later. You can check the version number by looking in the upper left-hand corner of the screen after you launch the program. If you find you don't have at least version 3.2, get an update from your local Apple dealer or local user group. The update is free, and sometimes dealers will throw in several public domain fonts or DAs along with the Font/DA mover itself.

The Font/DA Mover icon looks like a delivery truck, as in Figure 4–2. You can launch the Font/DA mover in two ways, by double-clicking on or opening the Font/DA Mover icon in the Finder or by double-clicking on or opening a suitcase file. If you double-click on a suitcase file, the Font/DA Mover opens automatically, and the suitcase file will be opened when the Font/DA Mover screen appears.

Most of the action in the Font/DA Mover occurs in a screen like the one in Figure 4–3. Let's look at the different features of this screen.

At the upper left-hand corner of the screen is the Font/DA Mover version number. Inside the box, above the two list boxes, are two radio buttons, indicating whether fonts or desk accessories are being worked with. The Font button is automatically selected when you launch the Font/DA

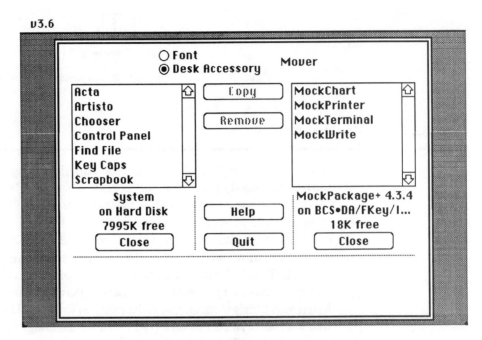

Figure 4–3. Most Font/DA Mover operations are carried out from this screen.

Mover (or if you double-click on a font suitcase file). If you want the Desk Accessory button to be selected automatically, press the Option key when you launch the Font/DA Mover and hold it down until the Font/DA Mover screen appears. The Desk Accessory button will be selected automatically if you've opened the program by double-clicking on a DA suitcase file. The button selected determines which type of file will be displayed in the list boxes.

The two list boxes are the focus of attention on this screen, because using the Font/DA Mover is usually a matter of opening two files and copying a font or DA from one to the other. When you launch the Font/DA Mover, the program automatically opens the System file on the disk from which you launched the program, and the left-hand list box displays all the fonts contained in that System file. Beneath this box, the name of the file whose contents are shown (System), the name of the disk where it is located, and the amount of space available on that disk are shown. Below this information is a Close button. The button changes to read Open... if there is no file currently open.

U3.5

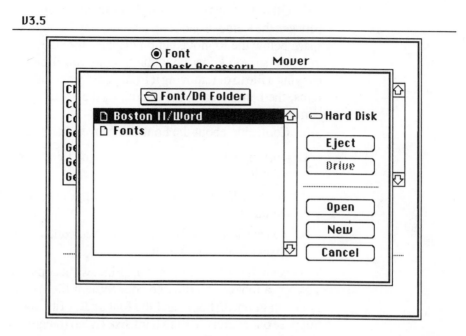

Figure 4–4. When you click the Open... button under one of the list boxes in the Font/DA mover, you'll see a version of the SFGet box that helps you locate different files to open on the current disk or other disks.

The right-hand list box is empty when you load the Font/DA Mover, because there is no file open there. There is no file information underneath the box, and the button below the file information space says Open.... When you click the Open... button, the standard file get (SFGet) box appears, as in Figure 4–4.

The SFGet box locates and opens System or suitcase files on either the current or a different disk. Also on the screen are four buttons between the two list boxes, and a space that displays the size of a selected file. The top two buttons, Copy and Remove, remain inactive until you have selected a file in one of the list boxes. The Copy button only becomes active when files are open in both list boxes and you have selected a file in one of them. The Help button displays two screens of condensed information about using the Font/ DA Mover. The Quit button stops the Font/DA Mover program and returns you to the Finder.

Other features of the Font/DA Mover's main screen are the blank area between the Remove and Help buttons, and the blank area at the bottom. The space below the Remove button displays the size of a selected suitcase file in bytes, so you know how much room you'll be using up or gaining by copying a file to or removing it from your System file. If you're working with fonts, the blank area at the bottom of the screen displays a sample of the currently selected font.

Confusion about the Font/DA Mover arises for several reasons:

1. Opening a file doesn't mean the same thing as it does when you open a file in the Finder.

2. You usually work with two files, copying a font or DA from one file to the other.

3. You can have two files open (and their contents displayed in the two list boxes) from the same disk.

Two examples will clear things up. First, we'll copy a font to the System file. To copy a font or DA file into your System file, you must have the System file open in one list box, and the font or DA file open in the other list box. Suppose our startup disk is a hard disk called (creatively enough) Hard Disk, which contains the Font/DA Mover, and we get a new font called Symbol in a suitcase file. We copy the suitcase file to the hard disk by dragging it in the Finder. To install it in the System file:

1. Double-click on the suitcase file's icon in the Finder. The Font/DA Mover will load, and the contents of the Hard Disk's System File will be displayed in the left-hand list box, as in Figure 4–3.

2. Click the Open... button under the right-hand list box, then navigate through the SFGet box until the Symbol file is displayed in the get box. The list and SFGet boxes show only suitcase files and folders, not documents and applications. Notice that we are navigating to this file on the same disk, but we could just as easily look on a different disk by inserting a floppy or clicking the Drive button.

3. Double-click on the Symbol file, or click on it once and then click the Open button. The Symbol file will be displayed in the right-hand list box on the Font/DA Mover screen.

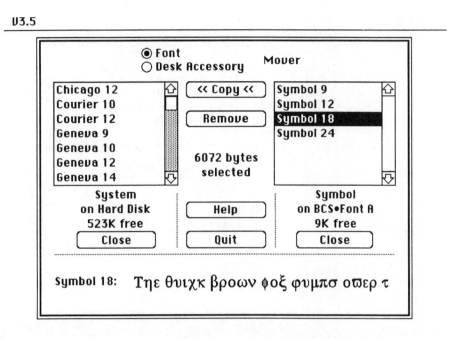

V3.5

Figure 4–5. When you have selected a font file to copy to the System file, the Copy button becomes active, and a sample of the font appears at the bottom of the screen.

4. Click on the Symbol file in the right-hand list box to select it. The Copy button between the two list boxes becomes active, with arrows pointing from the right-hand list box (where the Symbol file is) to the left-hand list box (the System file). The size of the Symbol file is shown below the Remove button, and a sample of the font appears at the bottom of the screen, as in Figure 4–5.

5. Click the Copy button, and the font will be copied to the System file. After this, the font will appear in the Font menu of your application programs.

In the second example, assume we already have the Symbol font in our System file and that we don't have a suitcase file for it. We've just created a document using the font, and we want to send the document to a friend.

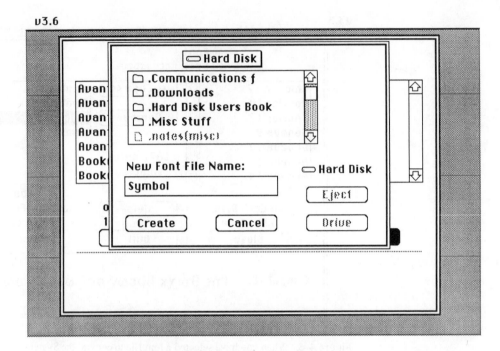

Figure 4–6. When you create a new suitcase file with the Font/DA Mover, you are first prompted to name the new file.

We're not sure our friend has the Symbol font in her system, and we want to send a suitcase file containing the font along with the document, so we'll be sure the friend can print out the document with the same font we used.

1. Double-click on the Font/DA Mover in the Finder to load it. The System file on our disk will be opened, and its fonts displayed in the right-hand list box.

2. Click the Open... button underneath the left-hand list box. The SFGet box will appear.

3. Click the New button. A version of the SFPut box will appear, and we will be prompted to enter a name for the new font file, as shown in Figure 4–6. We're storing the Symbol font, so we'll call the file Symbol.

4. Click the Create button at the bottom of the SFPut box. The standard Font/DA Mover screen will appear, and the new file, Symbol, will be open in the right-hand list box. The list won't contain any files at this point, because the file is a new one.

5. Click on the Symbol font in the left-hand list box to select that font from the System file. The Copy button will be activated, the arrows in the button will point to the right-hand list box, the size of the font will be shown below the Remove button, and a sample of the font will be shown at the bottom of the box.

6. Click the Copy button. The font will be copied to the new Symbol file. If you wanted to at this point, you could copy several other fonts to the Symbol file. If you wanted to copy DAs to a suitcase file, you would have to create a new DA suitcase file using the procedure outlined above.

After the file is copied, you can quit the Font/DA Mover and return to the Finder. If your disk's window is displayed in the Icon view, you'll see the new Symbol suitcase file there.

A time-saving tip: We've discussed selecting files for copying or removal one at a time. You can select more than one file at a time by holding down the Shift key as you click on the various files you want. When you select several files at once, the area below the Remove button shows the total size of all the selected items. This technique is very handy when you want to select an entire font family—all the different sizes of a particular font—for copying or removal.

Now that we've covered the basics of font and DA files and using the Font/DA Mover, let's look at using these types of files more closely and what they all mean to a hard disk user.

All About Fonts

Fonts are different typefaces. In the typographic world, fonts are distinguished by name, size, and style. A font's name is like a family name—there can be many relatives in the family with different styles and sizes, but they all have the same essential look. As you can see in Figure 4–7, three members of the Geneva font family have the same basic look, even though their styles and sizes may be different. Because these are all from the same family, they will always have a different look from fonts in the Helvetica or Times Roman families. No two font families look exactly the same.

This is Geneva Plain 12 point
This is Geneva Bold 14 point
This is Geneva Italic 18 point

Figure 4–7. All fonts in a family have the same basic look, even though different members have different sizes or styles.

In a printer's shop, each family member is distinct: Geneva 12 is a different font from Geneva 12 Bold. When you install or remove fonts in a Macintosh System file, however, font family members are distinguished only by size, not by style. Font styles are determined by the Style menu, whose options affect every font the same way. Thus, even though you might have only one family member installed in your System file (Geneva 12, for example), you can display that font in at least eight different styles (normal, bold, italic, underline, outline, shadow, superscript, and subscript) using the Style menu commands. (Some application programs, such as Microsoft Word, add extra styles, such as double underline, small caps, and strikethrough to the list of available style options.)

How Do You Know Which Sizes Are Available?

The Style menu always contains a selection of type styles, along with a selection of font sizes. The size selections displayed depend on the program you are using. MacWrite, for example, shows font sizes from 9 point through 24 point, while MacDraw shows sizes up to 48 point. Some other programs, like Microsoft Word 3.01, have scrollable Style menus that show all the font sizes you have installed. (The upper limit on font sizes is 128 points.) Other programs, like Write Now, can vary font sizes one point at a time.

If you are using a program (such as MacWrite, MacPaint, or MacDraw) that displays a specific number of font sizes all the time, the menu can show font sizes that you may not necessarily have installed. Fortunately, these programs help you remember which sizes in a given font you actually have installed by displaying available font sizes in a different style from font sizes that aren't available. If a particular size is available, it will be displayed in the outlined type style on the menu, while a size that isn't available will be displayed in the plain type style, as shown in Figure 4–8. Obviously, programs that display only installed font sizes don't have to use this method, because everything you see on the menu at a given time is available.

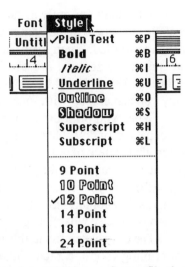

Figure 4–8. If a font size is installed in your System file, that size will be displayed in outlined style on the Style menu in certain programs. If the size is not installed in your System file, it will be displayed in the default type style.

The Macintosh's System software is shipped with various collections of fonts, but three fonts—Chicago 12, Geneva 12, and Monaco 9—are required by the system. Because these fonts are essential to your Mac's operation, you can't remove them from your System file.

Aside from the essential fonts, you can use the Font/DA Mover to decide the font families, and which font sizes within those families, you want to install. The 12-point Geneva font is the default font that appears when you work with many application programs, but there are a couple of ways to select a new default font, as we'll see later.

System Fonts, Screen Fonts, and LaserWriter Fonts

Fonts are used in three ways by the Macintosh and its printers. First of all, the System file fonts are used to display characters on the screen, and the dot patterns (or bit maps) of those fonts are reproduced by the ImageWriter when it prints a file. For the LaserWriter, built-in or downloaded fonts are used as models for printing. Let's look at the difference.

When it displays characters on the screen, your Mac uses fonts as specific patterns of dots. If you specify 12-point Geneva, the Mac makes characters in exactly that font's pattern and size. You can't specify a font family that isn't currently installed on your system (because a font has to be installed to appear in the Font menu), but you can specify a font size that you haven't installed. If you try to use a size that isn't currently installed, the Mac will use the sizes that *are* available to make a "best guess" on what the uninstalled size should be. Sometimes this guess isn't very good, which is why you can end up with fonts on your screen that look very strange.

When you print onto an ImageWriter, the Mac sends a bit map—the exact pattern of dots that makes up each text character—to the ImageWriter, where that pattern of dots is reproduced. Actually, the pattern isn't exactly reproduced, because an ImageWriter can print a finer pattern of dots (144 dots per inch) than your screen can display (72 dots per inch, or 69 dots per inch on a Mac II color monitor). Nevertheless, the font and size you display on the screen is exactly what gets printed on the ImageWriter.

The only exception to this is when you specify the Best quality setting for printing your document. In that case, the Mac actually takes an installed font *twice* the size you chose and reduces it 50 percent to achieve a denser, higher quality printed character, then sends that bit map to the ImageWriter. If you don't happen to have a font twice the size of the one you specified when you chose Best quality printing, the Mac uses the actual size font, and the print quality isn't quite as good.

This is an important point to keep in mind if you are eliminating font sizes from your System file to save space. If you want to save space, take out the odd font sizes, and try to keep the double-sizes of fonts you want to print in high quality. If you always use 12 point Geneva, you can get rid of 18 point Geneva, but be sure to keep 24 point Geneva. If you use 10 point fonts, keep the 20 point fonts and toss the 24 point fonts.

In any case, if a font looks bad on your screen, it's a good bet it will look just as bad when printed on an ImageWriter. Some fonts look particularly good when printed on an ImageWriter. Some of the best fonts for the ImageWriter are Geneva, New York, and a shareware font called Boston II, which was created by C. L. Maurer. As you come across new fonts, remember that the way they look on the screen is a good indication of how they'll look printed out on an ImageWriter.

Unlike the ImageWriter, which merely parrots what you have on your screen, the LaserWriter tries to use specific fonts, either those built into its memory or those downloaded from a disk, to print characters. When dealing with specific fonts, the LaserWriter stores fonts in families only, not in specific sizes. When you specify different font sizes, the LaserWriter scales the font to the correct size.

If you specify a font that isn't built into the LaserWriter or can't be downloaded from disk (and you have checked the Font Substitution box in the LaserWriter's Print dialog box), the printer first tries to substitute one of its own fonts that is similar (like using Times 14 for New York 12). If no substitution is possible, the font is treated like a bit map and printed accordingly, just as with an ImageWriter. Note: When the LaserWriter substitutes fonts, it substitutes only the characters, not the proportional spaces between them, which is why the spacing on documents with substituted fonts often looks weird.

Because it uses its own fonts most of the time, there's no direct relationship between what you see on the screen (which is determined by system fonts and the screen's resolution) and what you get on paper (which is determined by built-in or downloaded fonts, bit maps, and the LaserWriter's resolution of 300 dots per inch). That's why it's possible to have fonts that look terrible on the screen (such as Times Roman and Helvetica) but print out very nicely on the LaserWriter. It's also why tables and other documents with complex formats sometimes look different on the screen than when they are printed on a LaserWriter.

Downloaded Fonts for the LaserWriter

The LaserWriter sets itself up to print one page at a time. It looks at the fonts you specify for each page, checks whether it has the fonts in its memory, then downloads the fonts it doesn't have, up to the limit of its available memory. There's a difference between the fonts built into the memory and those that are downloaded. The built-in fonts are always there, while the downloaded fonts can be exchanged in and out of temporary memory.

For the LaserWriter to make use of a downloadable font, the font must be available on the disk drive where your System file is located, usually in the System Folder. (The actual location varies from one font vendor to another—check the instructions that come with each font to be sure.) Also, there must be room in the LaserWriter's memory to store the font. The original LaserWriter can store one or two downloaded fonts at a time, while the LaserWriter Plus can store three. Downloadable fonts generally don't look quite as crisp as built-in fonts, and they tend to look especially bad in the smaller sizes. If you specify more than three downloaded fonts per page, the page won't print.

The Quick Brown Fox Jumped Over The Lazy Dog.
Times

The Quick Brown Fox Jumped Over The Lazy Dog.
Helvetica

The Quick Brown Fox Jumped Over The Lazy Dog.
Courier

Τηε Θυιχκ Βροων Φοξ ϑυμπεδ Οϖερ Τηε Λαζψ Δογ.
Symbol

The Quick Brown Fox Jumped Over The Lazy Dog.
Avent Garde

The Quick Brown Fox Jumped Over The Lazy Dog.
Bookman

The Quick Brown Fox Jumped Over The Lazy Dog.
Narrow Helvetica

The Quick Brown Fox Jumped Over The Lazy Dog.
Palatino

The Quick Brown Fox Jumped Over The Lazy Dog.
New Century School Book

The Quick Brown Fox Jumped Over The Lazy Dog.
Zapf Chancery

✳✣❀ ✦✧✳✳✳ ✚❑❒❙■ ✦❑❙ ❖◆❍❏✳✳ ★✧✳❑ ✳✳✳ ★❖❚
✤❑✳✎
Zapf Dingbats

Figure 4–9. These 11 fonts are built into the LaserWriter Plus. The top 4 fonts are built into the LaserWriter.

The number of fonts stored in memory at once is the maximum number of downloadable fonts you can print on any one page. The printer flushes the unneeded fonts out of its temporary memory if you need to use other downloadable fonts on another page (and you don't need to reuse the fonts currently in memory).

The built-in LaserWriter fonts are Times, Helvetica, Symbol, and Courier. The LaserWriter Plus contains these plus Helvetica Narrow, Bookman, Palatino, New Century Schoolbook, Avant Garde, Zapf Chancery, and Zapf Dingbats. Figure 4–9 shows a sample of each of these fonts.

Like System fonts, downloadable LaserWriter fonts are available from many sources. Public domain fonts are available from user groups or electronic bulletin boards, and you can buy commercial fonts from type shops or your Apple dealer. It takes a lot of effort to design a new font, and fonts are often regarded as creative works that are copyrighted, just like novels or plays. Some commercial fonts sell for over $100. Downloadable fonts come in two separate files—a suitcase file to install in your System file for display on the screen and a standard file containing the outline font that is actually loaded on the LaserWriter.

Which Fonts Should You Have in Your System?

With all that hard disk space, you may be tempted to add every font you come across to your System file. Actually, there was a limit to the number of fonts you could install on the Font menu before scrollable menus were adopted by Apple with System 3.2. (You could not install more fonts than could be listed in a menu the length of the Mac's screen.) The new limitation is determined only by your convenience—you usually stop installing fonts when it gets to be too much trouble to scroll up and down the menu and find the one you want.

Even if you can have an amazing number of fonts in your System file, though, it isn't a good idea to do so, for several reasons. As mentioned earlier, you'll probably only use a handful of fonts and sizes in your day-to-day work, and you should be able to select these easily from the Font menu without having to scan lots of other fonts you never use. Second, each font and font size you add to your System file takes up space, usually about 10–15K, and you're better off using disk space for document or application storage than for a bunch of fonts you never or rarely use. Third, font names on a menu don't show what a font looks like, and you'll only be able to easily remember what a dozen or so fonts look like. If you have a lot of unfamiliar fonts, you'll have to try them out repeatedly to see if they're really suitable, unless you've printed out a sample page showing each font for reference. Finally, it doesn't make good typographic sense. Novice Mac users often dress up their documents with several different fonts, but using more than a couple in any document just makes the document harder to read and unattractive.

So which fonts should you have? To begin with, choosing any font is a matter of personal choice. There are thousands of different fonts, each has its own unique character, and every individual reacts to a font differently. We can't cover every one and why you should or shouldn't consider it, but we can provide some basic guidelines.

You can get away with as few as half a dozen fonts in your System file, but you may want as many as 12 to 18 for variety. Other than the standard fonts and font sizes every Mac needs—Chicago 12, Geneva 12, and Monaco 9—there are two considerations: which fonts work best for viewing and printing, and which ones give you the look you want. Let's look at the viewing and printing considerations first.

You need at least one font that is easy to read on the screen. Most LaserWriter fonts are not the easiest to read on the screen, so if you're a LaserWriter user, you'll probably end up working with a good screen font, and then changing to the appropriate LaserWriter font before you print. As an ImageWriter user, whatever looks good on the screen will look good on paper. The default Geneva font, Boston, and New York are all good choices in screen fonts, and they all look fine printed with the ImageWriter. If you're the type who gets bored looking at the same font all the time, keep two or three of these fonts around.

If you own or frequently print on a LaserWriter, you'll want to have some or all of the built-in LaserWriter fonts in your system as well. Certainly, you'll want Times and Helvetica, because these are the two most popular fonts in the world.

The Courier font built into the LaserWriter is the same font made popular by IBM typewriters. Unlike most other LaserWriter fonts, Courier is not proportionally spaced, which means each character in the alphabet takes up the same amount of space, rather than an *i* character using less space than an *m* character. Courier will make your laser printed documents look like they were produced on a typewriter—but why do that, when there are so many other nice fonts to choose from? Among the remaining LaserWriter and LaserWriter Plus fonts, Bookman, Palatino, and New Century Schoolbook are attractive fonts for business use. The other fonts—Symbol, Helvetica Narrow, Zapf Dingbats, and Zapf Chancery—are specialty fonts, and whether you use them is exclusively a matter of personal style.

When considering businesslike fonts, particularly LaserWriter fonts, think about how much information you want to get on a page and who will be reading your documents. Times is a very dense font that packs a lot of information on a page, but unless you're using a size of 14 points or larger, this font is comparatively small and may be harder to read. You can print a business report people are anxiously waiting for with Times, because you're producing a document for a captive audience, but if you're submitting a short story manuscript, you'd want a larger font that is more inviting to someone who might take your document or leave it.

As mentioned before, keep the number of fonts in one document to a minimum. Use no more than three fonts at any time, and try to use only one or two. You can add a lot of variety to a page by using different font sizes or styles without destroying the visual consistency of the document.

Along with sedate business fonts, you should keep a couple of fun fonts on hand for those times when you want something a little special. You may want to do a flyer, an invitation, or another unbusinesslike document, and fonts like Avant Garde or Zapf Chancery have the right look. If you do a lot of flyers or fun types of correspondence, you might augment your fun fonts with a picture font, which produces small pictures instead of text characters. Picture fonts include Cairo, Mobile, and Zapf Dingbats. Take a look at samples of each font, and choose the one that has the most symbols you like.

Some users with large hard disks still insist on having dozens of fonts available online. We don't feel you should burden your System file with too many fonts, but if you must have a lot of fonts available, you can use a DA called Suitcase, which lets you store an unlimited number of fonts (or DAs, for that matter) in one or more files, and then access them on the fly from the Apple menu. A full discussion of Suitcase appears in Chapter 11.

Which Font Sizes?

Aside from the required Macintosh fonts, which you may not use yourself and therefore don't need in any additional sizes, it's a good idea to install a range of sizes in the fonts you use daily. Certainly, your size range should run from 10 points up to 24 points. If you create posters or flyers, you'll want fonts up to 72 or even 128 points, and if you do a lot of technical drawings or contracts, you'll want sizes down to 4 or 6 points. The only caution is that larger font sizes (30 points and above) can take up 40 or 50K per font size. If you've limited your collection of font families to a dozen or so, it's convenient to have a good assortment of sizes for each of them. Otherwise, the day will surely come when you want a certain font size and don't have it. Then, you'll have to stop what you're doing, find the disk that has the font size you want, and install it with the Font/DA Mover before continuing.

Changing the Default Font

The default font (also called the *application font*) is the font your Mac chooses to display and print if you don't specify anything else. This is almost always Geneva, although certain application programs have different default fonts. If you find yourself constantly having to change from Geneva to a different font, you should change the default font. There are two ways to do this.

If you regularly use a particular application program, you may be able to change its default font from inside the program. Many word processing programs, in particular, can set up a standard document format that appears

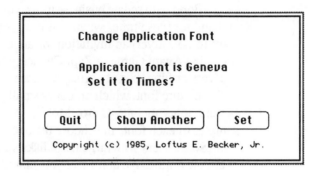

Figure 4–10. With the Chang App program, you can specify a different default font to use with new documents.

when you begin each new file. Failing that, you can always create a dummy document with the font selection you want, and save it with a name like Blank Page. Then, whenever you want to make a new file, you can open the Blank Page document and begin working with the font of your choice. (When you're done working, you use Save As... to store the document with a different name, so the Blank Page document always remains blank.)

The other remedy is to use a shareware program called Chang App, which lets you choose a different default font to be used by your Mac when you create new files. Chang App, written by Loftus Becker, presents a dialog box showing the current font and an alternative below it, as in Figure 4–10. To select the alternative, just click on it.

If you want to see the next alternative font in Chang App, just click the Next button. You can move through the fonts available in your System file simply by continuing to click the Next button. The only possible problem with Chang App is that the version available at this writing freezes up (forcing you to restart your Mac) when it tries to cycle around from the last font alternative on your Font menu to the first one. This is an easy problem to avoid—don't cycle from the last font to the first. If you pass by the font you really wanted to install, quit the program, reload it, and use the Next button to move to that font again.

Installing Fonts Directly in Documents or Applications

Every once in a while, you'll get a document from another user that looks really strange when you display it on your Mac: The spacing is off, and the font looks plain ugly. The most likely explanation is that the font used to that create the document is not one you have in your System file, and your Mac is trying to figure out a good substitute. Sometimes the substitution works well, and sometimes it doesn't.

If you're going to give a document to someone else, there are three ways to avoid this problem. Either use a standard font, send a suitcase file containing the font along with the document, or install the font you used directly into the document.

The best remedy is to use a standard font whenever you know you'll be sending a document file to another user. If you stick with Geneva, you're sure to avoid problems. Otherwise, what you consider a standard font, like Times or New York, may not be a standard font for the other user. You could always call the user up to check, but there are two ways to send the font along with the document to eliminate the problem.

The simplest method is to create a suitcase file containing the font, using the method explained earlier in this chapter. You simply load the Font/DA Mover, choose the option to create a new file, give the file the same name as the font, and then copy the font from your System file into the new file. When you return to the Finder, you'll have a suitcase file containing that font, which your correspondent can install in his or her system before viewing your document.

You can also have the font appear automatically when your correspondent opens the document by installing the font directly into the document itself. Here's how:

1. Launch the Font/DA Mover as you normally would. Your System fonts will be displayed in the left-hand list box.

2. When you click the Open... button under the right-hand list box to display files, hold down the Option key. The list box will then display all the files on that disk, instead of just folders and suitcase files.

3. Navigate to the document in which you want to install the font and select it.

4. Click the Open button. You will return to the Font/DA Mover's main screen, and the document will be displayed in the right-hand list box.

5. Select the font you want to install in the left-hand list box.

6. Click the Copy button, and the font will be installed directly in the document.

Once a font is installed directly in a document, that font automatically appears on the Font menu when the document is opened. You can install several different fonts in a document, and they will all appear on the Font menu when document is opened. When you close the document, the font (or fonts) disappears from menu.

The biggest drawback to this method is that you are placing a copy of the font in the document. If you do this a lot, you'll eat up a lot of extra space on your hard disk, because you'll have multiple copies of the same font stored in various documents on the disk.

One other possible problem is that the Font/DA mover assigns numbered spaces to the fonts it installs in the System file, and there might be a conflict for a space between a font that is installed in the System file and the one you've installed in a document. If there is a conflict, the font you installed in the document won't appear in the menu. To remedy this problem, simply use the Font/DA Mover to copy the font out of the document and into the System file itself. There, it will be assigned a valid numbered space, and it will appear on the Font menu.

You can also install fonts directly into application programs. This is the same procedure as installing a font in a document, and it has the same benefits and drawbacks.

Desk Accessories

Desk accessories (DAs) are those handy little programs you install in your System file and that become available in a list on the Apple menu. Once they are installed with the Font/DA Mover, DAs remain on the Apple menu in the Finder and in all your applications.

Because DAs are so easy to install, the development community has produced hundreds of them, most of which sell for reasonable prices, if they aren't in the public domain. There are DA games, word processors, spreadsheets, outliners, thesauruses, appointment books, communications programs, and other productivity applications, along with a huge assortment of utility programs that do things like find files on a disk, blank the Mac screen when it isn't in use, count words in a document, and so on. A partial list of DAs appears in Appendix B.

The original Mac System file came with a small assortment of DAs supplied by Apple. These were the Alarm Clock, Calculator, Control Panel, Notepad, Puzzle, and Scrapbook. Until the Font/DA Mover appeared in 1985, there was no way to alter this assortment. Over the years, Apple has done away with the Alarm Clock (by incorporating it into the Control Panel) and has added the Chooser to its standard list of DAs. Current System files being distributed also include a file-locating accessory called Find File. The original Puzzle has been excluded from current Apple-supplied desk accessories, and (depending on the amount of space on the particular disk) the Calculator and Notepad are sometimes omitted. But the huge assortment of DAs available today has tempted users to add many third-party items to the old Apple menu, and herein lies a potential problem.

It may be that Apple never foresaw the popularity of DAs or the vast assortment of them that would become available, but in any event, the Mac's design allows only 15 DAs to be installed under the Apple menu. This limit was first thought to be a function of the old nonscrollable menus, but it has continued even though menus can now be scrolled to reveal choices that aren't initially visible on the screen.

In any event, having a hard disk is an invitation to install a lot of great DAs, and the 15 DA limit is like rain on the parade. Fortunately, there are a couple of ways around the limit.

Working Around the DA Limit

There are two ways to use more than 15 DAs. The first is to use a DA extender, which you use to locate and load individual DAs as you need them, rather than having them installed in your System file and on the Apple menu at all times. There are two or three programs or DAs that let you work with DAs this way. They are covered in detail in Chapter 11.

The second solution to the problem is to conserve space on the DA menu by installing a DA in an application itself, rather than in the System file. If you have a word-counting DA, or a thesaurus DA, you probably use it only with your word processing program, not with a spreadsheet or database. Since you only need the DA some of the time, installing it directly in your word processor application is a good way to have it available only when you need it. When you install a DA directly in an application, it only appears on the Apple menu when that application is running.

You can have up to four application-specific DAs running at any one time on your system, because there are four extra slots reserved specifically for application-specific DAs in the Apple menu. When you run an application with one or more built-in DAs, and only when that application is running, these DAs appear at the top of the Apple menu. You'll probably never need to use more than four application-specific DAs for any application, so this remedy to the DA limit is a good one, as long as you can conveniently divide your DAs up among specific applications, and you don't need the DAs with other applications.

To install a DA directly in an application, you use the same procedure you would use to install a font directly into a document, as described earlier in this chapter. You hold down the Option key while clicking the Open... button in the Font/DA Mover to display all the files on a disk, then select the application file you want and open it. Then, you can copy the DA you want into the application. Like installing a font into a document, the only real danger in installing a DA in an application is redundancy. It doesn't make sense to install the same DA in several different applications, because of all the extra space you'll be using up on your disk. If you use a DA with a lot of applications, it's best to keep it installed in the System file.

There's one caution about installing DAs directly in application files. Some complex DAs have what are called *owned resources*—other resources in the system and elsewhere on your Mac that are specific to those DAs. If you install a complex DA—InBox, the electronic mail program, is a good example—that has owned resources, it may be in conflict with another complex DA with its own owned resources. The solution to this problem is to avoid installing *complex* DAs directly in applications. This is not hard to take when you think about it, because the DAs likely to be most useful in specific applications are simple ones such as Word Count.

There is one other solution to the DA limit, and that involves using one of the extra, hidden DA slots in the System file. There are 18 extra spaces on the Apple menu that have been reserved by Apple for specific uses, such as storing drivers for different SCSI devices or for network servers. We mention this option for the sake of completeness, but this is a very serious proposition that could easily cause a lot of damage to your System and hard disk. Don't try it!

If you really want to have a lot of DAs on hand, your best bet is to use one of the DA-extending programs covered in Chapter 11.

This chapter ends our coverage of basic Macintosh hard disk hardware and essential software. In Chapter 5, we'll look at various ways to use these tools to organize hard disk files for maximum efficiency and ease of use.

PART TWO

Hard Disk Strategies

5

Organizing Hard Disk Files

The whole point of using a hard disk is to store all your application programs and data files in one convenient location. But having everything in one place is more trouble than it's worth if you can't get to a file or application quickly when you want it. Most people make some use of the disk organizing tools in the Finder to arrange the contents of their hard disks, but there's a difference between sticking files in a bunch of folders and developing an effective disk organizing scheme.

Every time you have to open a window in the Finder, every time you have to open a folder to find a file, and every time you have to scroll in a window or a list box to locate a file is time away from doing your work. When your hard disk is well-organized, you can get to your files and your work more quickly. Another good reason for organizing a hard disk properly is that files arranged logically into groups are easier to back up, and actually expand the options you have for backing up your disk. (More on this in Chapter 9.)

In this chapter, we'll organize a hard disk from the ground up. We'll look at the types of files you store, the basic tools you use to organize a disk, ways files can be organized into logical groups, and methods of displaying them on the Desktop for easy access. Most of the chapter is devoted to the fundamental principles and tips involved in organizing a disk most effectively. At the end, we'll look at a few different disk layouts and discuss the pros and cons of each.

What Gets Stored: Three File Groups

Even though you could fill your hard disk with every file, application, utility, and System file you come across, it's a good idea to make some decisions about what should stay on your hard disk and what you can offload onto floppy disks.

There are three main categories of files that are stored on a hard disk: data files (or documents), application programs, and System files. *Data files* are the documents created by a specific application. *Applications* are programs, such as word processors or spreadsheets, that are used to create data files. *System files* are all the files that are contained in the System Folder. These include most of the tools, such as desk accessories and fonts, as well as some special additions, as discussed in Chapter 3.

Data

Data is all the material in the documents you create with your application programs. The official name for the Macintosh data icon is a *document,* and the icon usually looks like a piece of paper with a corner bent. It's very easy to leave every document you create on your hard disk, but you will have a serious storage problem eventually. The three types of documents you should always store on the hard disk are current projects, model documents, and new documents that you haven't decided what to do with yet.

Current Projects   The majority of documents you store on a hard disk are the ones related to a specific project. There are various ways to organize documents for your current work into different types of folders, as we'll see, but the main point here is that when a project is finished, you no longer need to keep its documents on your hard disk. Instead, copy the document(s) onto a floppy disk, label the disk, and store it in your archives in case you ever need it later. Then delete the hard disk version. If files are particularly valuable, make two disk copies and store the disks in two different locations, such as your office and your home, so a fire, theft, or other disaster won't destroy them.

It's easy to forget to purge your hard disk of unneeded documents because space seems so abundant, but eventually you'll have to pay the piper. So you can take your choice: Either spend an hour or so cleaning up your hard disk every few months, or spend a couple of minutes doing it once a month. You'll find that the more frequently you purge unneeded files the better, because eliminating unneeded files means there are fewer files to clutter up your folder windows and Open... boxes inside programs, and that means you can get to the files you do need faster.

Model Documents   One of the great advantages to computers is that you can store your work and change it, so you don't have to do similar jobs over from scratch each time. If you have regular forms you fill out or standard reports you complete regularly, it's useful to keep *templates,* or model documents for those jobs on your hard disk. Then, when you need to do a repetitive job, you can pull up the model, make the changes, and save the changed version under a different name while your model remains intact for reuse.

Model documents are useful for anything you repeat in one variation or another. The most common examples are letters that have basically the same contents and are used again and again, but other examples are spreadsheets for specific tasks, such as calculating loan amortizations or quarterly budgets. Sometimes, application software companies provide sample documents (such as letterheads) that can be used as models with their products.

Miscellaneous Documents   We often get documents from other people or companies that don't fit into the other data categories. Some examples are documentation for a new product, some notes about a new release of a product, or an electronic mail message from a bulletin board. If you set aside a folder to store these odds and ends until you figure out if you need them, you'll know where to find them. And once you look over the particular files, you can decide whether to keep them and file them elsewhere or purge them from your disk.

Applications

Most major application programs consume a great amount of disk space, so unless you have several megabytes to spare, do not store applications you hardly ever use on the hard disk. HyperCard and its related files, for example, occupy over 2 megabytes of space. If you only use HyperCard once every couple of weeks, it doesn't make sense to use that much space on your disk for it. But whether you store an application on your hard disk, and how you determine whether you use it frequently enough to justify storing it there, depends on the type of application. There are three types of programs you might want to keep on a hard disk: work applications, utilities, and games.

Work Applications   These are the programs that you use regularly to do your work—word processors, spreadsheets, page layout programs, and other workhorse applications. For these applications, a rule of thumb for determining regular use is that if you use an application once a week or more, you should keep it on the hard disk. It's also reasonable to keep less frequently used programs on the disk if they are particularly large and would require a lot of copying time to put on the hard disk when you needed them (such as HyperCard or PageMaker), or if they use more than one floppy disk and require a lot of disk-swapping to load. But it doesn't make sense to store three different word processors on your hard disk if you only use one or two of them.

Utilities   Utilities are used less frequently, but when you need them it's good to have them at your fingertips. They also tend to be smaller in size, so you don't have to give up that much space to have a collection of them handy. If you're really hard up for disk space, copy the utilities you don't use at least once a week to a floppy disk and keep it nearby. It's easier to manage utilities by storing them in their own folder, as we'll see later.

Games   Some people store a few games on their hard disks for the same ease of access they get with hard disk-based utilities and work applications. Commercial games are one of the few areas of Macintosh software left where vendors still use a fair amount of copy protection, and that may make it difficult to copy some games. There are utilities like Copy II Hard Disk (discussed in Chapter 7) that can help. Otherwise, there are many public domain games that are not copy-protected. As with utilities, games should be high on the list of things you will remove from your hard disk and place on floppies if you're hard up for space.

New Programs to Be Explored   This category of programs usually includes new public domain or shareware programs—programs you haven't had a chance to look at to decide if they're worth keeping around. It's usually best to store all programs of this type in one folder, so you can conveniently look through it to try out various programs. Such a folder will soon resemble Fibber McGee's closet if you don't keep up with the programs that you store there, however, so remember to examine the folder's contents and purge unwanted items regularly.

System Folder Files

The only group of files that you must always keep on your hard disk (if you want to boot your Mac from it) are those in the System Folder. As discussed in Chapter 3, the System Folder can contain printer drivers, Chooser resources, and Init programs, and the System file itself can store lots of fonts and desk accessories. Generally, you shouldn't consider removing files from the System Folder to conserve space. Furthermore, you can't place System file resources (printer drivers, Chooser resources, or Inits) in folders inside the System Folder, because they won't be available to the System file if you do. In short, this is the one folder on a hard disk that is likely to become somewhat cluttered, and there is little you can do to clean it up.

Basic Organizing Tools   Most file arrangements on hard disks are handled by the Finder. Within the Finder, you work with files and folders. Each folder can be opened to produce its own window on the desktop. Every time you create a folder, move a file from one folder to another, delete a file, or resize or move a window, you are reorganizing your hard disk. You can also do some reorganization from inside application programs by saving files into different folders or onto different disks. (Remember, folders only separate files into distinct places on a disk when you're using the HFS filing system, as explained in Chapter 2. This discussion assumes you're using HFS.)

Think of folders and files as organizing devices at different levels. The desktop and its windows provide a view into your hard disk's organizational structure. You can also consider the dialog boxes (called the SFGet and SFPut boxes) that appear inside application programs when you open or save a file as views of your disk's organizational structure.

Paths and Path Names   When you create files or put them inside folders, your Mac remembers each file's location by its path name. A *path name* is a written description of the route that must be taken to navigate into a disk (and possibly through some folders) to get to the file itself. If you place a file called Report inside a folder called Sales on a hard disk named Hard Disk, for example, the path name tells your Mac that it must look on Hard Disk and inside Sales to find the Report file, as shown in Figure 5–1. Internally, your Mac stores this path name as Hard Disk:Sales:Report.

To locate files in the Finder, you can simply click on folders or disks to open them, and then find a file visually. Even when you navigate to files from inside an application, you do it manually. This is rather like using a printed

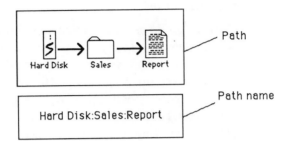

Figure 5–1. Each file on your hard disk is identified with a path name, which is the succession of disks and folders that must be navigated by your Mac to find the file.

map to find a street name. But when your Mac must find a file, it uses a path name, even though you're not aware of it most of the time. Rather than using a road map, your Mac uses written directions to find the files it needs.

The Standard File Boxes

Chapter 3 already discussed the operation of the Finder, but let's look at some tips and techniques for navigating to files from inside application programs, using file boxes. Whenever you choose the Open... or Save As... commands, application programs produce a standardized dialog box that contains a scrolling list of file or folder names, and some buttons to change disk drives, eject disks, open or save the file, or cancel the operation. The box that appears when you open a file is called the *SFGet box,* and the box you see when you use Save As... is the *SFPut box.*

For the sake of simplicity, we'll refer to the SFGet and SFPut boxes together as the Standard File boxes. The Standard File boxes help you navigate through your disk's file structure to find the file you want. Figure 5–2 shows a typical Standard File box.

For navigating a disk's file structure, the important elements of this box are the list box on the left, which contains the names of files and folders contained at the current level of your disk's file structure; the icon directly above the list box, which indicates which disk or folder directory you are viewing; and the disk name above the Eject button, which is the name of the disk you're currently working with.

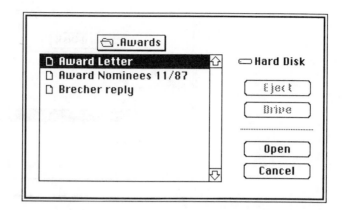

Figure 5–2. Inside application programs, you use Standard File boxes like this to locate and open or save files.

Selecting Files from the Standard File Box

As discussed in Chapter 2, disks—and folders inside disks—are specific levels of organization under the HFS system. The list box only shows the contents of one organizational level at a time: one disk or folder. A disk or folder can contain system, application, or data files, or other folders, as shown in Figure 5–3.

To select the file you want from a list box, you have to be viewing the list box that shows the contents of the disk or folder where that file is located. You use the Drive button in the Standard File box to select the appropriate disk, and you can double-click on a folder or select it and then use the Open button to see its contents. Selecting disks and moving into or out of folders are the ways you move along paths to find files.

You can navigate out of a folder whose contents are displayed in the list box by pointing to the disk/folder icon above the list box, holding down the mouse button, and dragging down to a higher organizational level, as in Figure 5–4. The menu of disk and folder names that drops down from the disk/folder icon is the path that was taken to arrive at the particular folder shown in the list box.

It's useful to see the path because you can use it to move up more than one level quickly—you could drag down to the bottom of the menu to move back to the highest level of your disk's organization, if you wanted. If you're more comfortable using the keyboard, you can move up a path one level at a time by pressing the Command key and the Up Arrow.

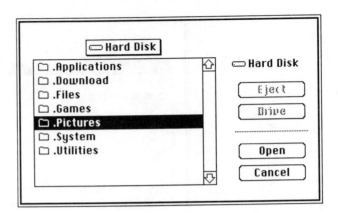

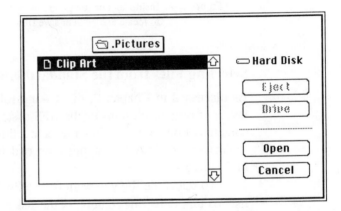

Figure 5–3. A list box only shows the files or folders on one organizational level at a time. The list box on the top shows the files and folders on a disk, while the box on the bottom shows the contents of one of the right-hand disk's folders.

File Selection Shortcuts

A file must be selected before you can open it. You can select a file either by clicking on it with the mouse or by typing all or part of its name. It's simple enough to point and click to select a file if the filename is in view in the list box, but if you have to scroll through the list box to find the filename, it's faster to type the name if you remember it.

Suppose, for example, that you want to select a file called Transactions, which is always far down the list of files and must be scrolled into view. Instead of using the mouse to scroll the list, type Tran with the list box showing. If Transactions is the only file beginning with the string Tran, it will

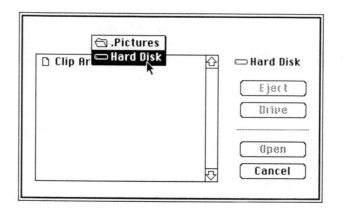

Figure 5–4. You can navigate out of the current folder in a list box by dragging the folder icon.

be selected. If there is more than one file beginning with Tran, the Mac will select the first one of the group, in alphabetical order. Therefore, if your disk or folder contains the files Transactions and Transportation, you could type Tran to select Transactions and Transp to select Transportation.

The only trick to selecting files this way with the keyboard is that you have to type the filename or the first few letters of the filename fairly quickly. If you pause too long between letters, the Mac will first select the file that most closely matches the first text string (before the pause), and it will then select a file that most closely matches the letters you typed after the pause. If you type ST, for example, the Mac will select Strange over Small. But if you pause for a second between typing S and the T, the Mac will select the first file beginning with the letter S (or the file beginning with the letter closest to S). Then it will select the first file beginning with the letter T (or the one closest to it).

To open a file once you've selected it, you can either double-click on its name, click the Open button in the Standard File box, or (if the Open button has a dark outline around it) press the Return key. The Open button is usually outlined in Standard File boxes. If you're selecting files with the mouse by scrolling and clicking on them, double-clicking is the best method, because your hand is already on the mouse. If you're finding files by typing their names with the keyboard, though, it's much faster to simply press the Return key once your file is selected.

You can also change the selection among individual files in the list box by using the cursor keys on a Mac keyboard (assuming you're using a keyboard equipped with cursor keys.) The up and down arrows will change the file selected to the one above or below it, respectively. This can be used in combination with the name-typing method of selecting files. If you typed Trans, for example, and the Transactions file was selected, you could use the Down Arrow key to quickly select the Transportation file, rather than taking your hand off the keyboard to use the mouse.

Arranging Files in List Boxes

Just as with a window in the Finder, a list box can become cluttered with too many files, so that it takes forever to scroll to the file you want to open. This is one reason why it's wise to organize files into small groups in folders. Aside from proper disk organization, however, there are a couple of tips that make using list boxes easier.

Special Characters and Document Names

Names of files and folders in list boxes are shown in a specific order. Typically, files are displayed in alphabetical order, because all of your file and folder names begin with a letter. But the Macintosh arranges names in list boxes with special characters (asterisks, periods, commas, and so on) first, numbers second, and letters last.

Normally, all your filenames start with letters, so the list appears in alphabetical order. But because the Mac places special characters and numbers before the alphabet in a list box, you can use special characters or numbers at the beginning of file or folder names to make sure those files or folders always appear at or near the top of the list. If you frequently use a folder called Transactions, for example, you would probably have to scroll it into view in a list box. But if you rename the folder .Transactions or 1Transactions, as in Figure 5–5, the name will appear at the top of the list.

If you prepare quarterly reports, you can name the files 1QReport, 2QReport, and so on, so they appear in chronological order at the top of the list. Of course, you don't want to rename files every time you want something different to appear at the top of the list, so you'll have to think about which files you use most frequently. Then, too, you'll eventually purge old files from your disk, and there will be room for new files to take their place at the top of the list box.

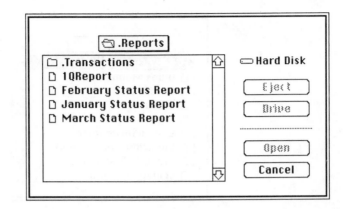

Figure 5–5. If you begin a file or folder name with a special character or a number, it will appear ahead of the alphabetically listed files in a list box.

Organizing Files in Folders

On a floppy disk system, it may be convenient enough to store files right in the root directory, or at the top hierarchical level, of a disk. These files then appear in the disk's window when you open it in the finder, or in the disk's Standard File box when you view it from inside an application.

On a hard disk, where you can easily store hundreds of files, it quickly becomes impractical to store all your files at the top level on the disk. Doing this creates a window you have to scroll through endlessly whenever you want to find something. Fortunately, you can create folders that group files so they are easier to locate.

When Is a Folder a Good Idea?

The primary use of folders is to gather the files on your hard disk so you can find them quickly. If you avoided folders completely, you would end up with so many files in one window that you'd have to spend too much time searching for the file you need, as in Figure 5–6. On the other hand, if you were to create a folder for each file and then stick each of those folders into other folders, as in Figure 5–7, you'd end up with a different kind of mess.

So how do you strike a balance between too many folders and not enough? There are three general guidelines you can use in figuring out if it's time to create a new folder. First, if you have more than about 20 files on a

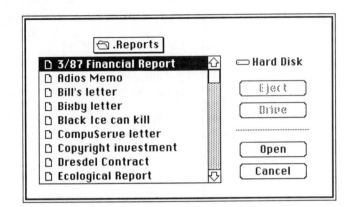

Figure 5–6. If you don't separate files into folders, you end up with a long list of files that makes it difficult to find the file you need.

disk or in a folder, it's probably time to look for some way to break up the group into a couple of new folders.

Whenever you have to scroll too much to find a file, or there are so many files that it's hard to single out the one you want, it's faster to put a related group of files inside a folder and simply open the folder. You wouldn't place one file in a new folder (unless you knew you would soon be adding other files), but ideally, folders will contain a handful of files so most of them will be in view when you open the folder's window on the desktop or view it in a Standard File box.

If possible, keep the contents of any data folder stored on your hard disk small enough so you can copy it onto a single, 800K floppy disk to back it up. In many cases, you'll be able to arrange things so a folder that itself contains some other folders can be stored on just one floppy. If you have a folder for miscellaneous work, for example, it might contain individual files for different projects, as well as a couple of folders for miscellaneous reports and memos. If you're careful to purge your disk of unwanted files regularly, you could back up the whole miscellaneous work folder onto one floppy.

The second general guideline is to consider the frequency of the material's use along with its relationship to other files as you create a new folder.

Suppose, for example, that you have a folder called Finances, which itself contains folders called Budgets, Inventory Files, and Sales. Of these three folders, the Sales folder is getting full, because in it you have tallies of

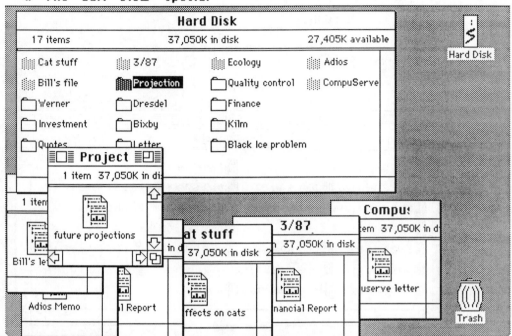

Figure 5–7. If you create too many folders, it can be just as hard to find a file as if you had no folders at all.

daily, weekly, monthly, quarterly, and year-to-date sales in three different divisions, as well as historical records of past sales, as in Figure 5–8.

You might be tempted to divide these files up into folders for Div1, Div2, and Div3, but think about it: You probably need access to each division's daily sales files every day, and if you use three different folders, you'll have to access each folder separately every day. In this case, it makes more sense to create folders according to the frequency with which you need the files, such as Daily/Weekly Sales and Historical Sales. That way, you'd reduce the clutter in the Sales folder while minimizing the steps you have to take to locate frequently used files.

A third rule of thumb is to avoid nesting folders inside one another more than three levels deep (a folder inside a folder inside a folder). If you nest folders to more than three levels, you may have to spend too much time

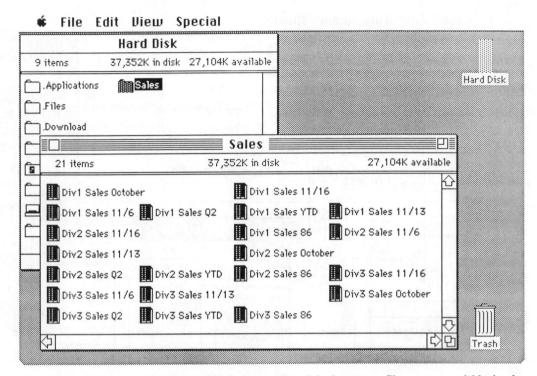

Figure 5–8. When you track daily, weekly, and quarterly activity in separate files, you can quickly develop a lot of files in one folder.

clicking on folders to open them in the Finder and navigating into and out of folders in a Standard File box. This won't matter if the deeply nested folders contain items you rarely or never use, but rather than storing files deeper and deeper in the hierarchy, think about creating new folders as the first or second levels.

Consider another example. Suppose you're a building contractor, and you have a client called Acme Development Company. You're doing a lot of business with Acme this year, and the folder you set up called Acme at the beginning of the year grew to over 40 files by March. At that point, you divided it up into folders by job: E St. Offices, Bayfront Villas, Exeter St. Garage, Bijou Drive-In, and Village Doughnuts. In July, you find that E St. Offices and Bayfront Villas each contain some 30 files of material lists, project management schedules, employee lists, budgets, and so on, as Figure 5–9 shows.

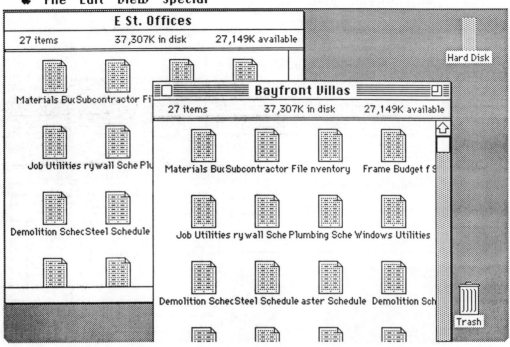

Figure 5–9. Even folders you've set up inside other folders can become crowded.

To handle this mess, you created folders inside the E St. Offices and Bayfront Villas folders to store schedules only and inventory records only, as in Figure 5–10. Now, in November, you find that the Inventory folder in E St. Offices has gotten out of hand, with some 30 different lists for plumbing, electrical, steel, concrete, tools, drywall, carpeting, and other collections of data. It makes sense to create some subfolders inside the Inventory folder called Structural, Tools, and Interior. But think: whenever you need to look at anything in inventory, you'll have to navigate the path from Hard Disk to Acme to E St. Offices to Inventory to Tools.

While it makes sense to break up all those inventory lists into separate folders, why nest them inside the Inventory folder? If the Inventory folder itself will only contain folders, why not just place the Tools, Structural, and Interior folders inside the E St. Offices folder itself? You'd have to give them more descriptive names, like Structural Inv., and so on, but you save

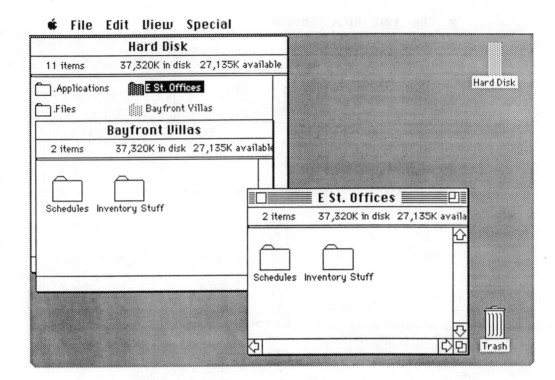

Figure 5-10. Folders inside folders can clean up the mess.

navigating a whole extra layer of folders and it only costs you three name spaces inside the E St. Offices folder.

It should be simple to avoid overnesting if you remember this. Think about what it will be like to navigate down to a folder before you create it and consider the alternative of placing its contents on a higher level.

So What Goes Where?

The specific files that go into a particular folder and where you store the folder itself is mostly a matter of opinion, but there are specific do's and don'ts, as well as some general guidelines you can follow to make things easier to find later on. First of all, the three basic types of hard disk files—System files, applications, and data files—should be in separate folders. System files must all be located in the System Folder, and that folder must be stored in the root directory of your hard disk. In other words, the System Folder must be stored at the top organizational level, rather than inside another folder. If you store the System Folder inside another folder, your Mac won't be able to find the files it needs to start up or perform other system activities.

How and where you store applications depends on how frequently you use them and how many other files are used by the application. You should store most of your applications in one or more folders, depending on how you use them (see the disk layouts at the end of the chapter). If there are a few applications you use every day or two, however, you should store them on the top level of the disk, outside any folder, to make saving files a little easier.

When you use an application, your Mac sets the folder from which the application was launched as the default storage location. If your application is in a folder called Apps, then Apps will always be the open folder when you first display a Standard File box. Because you'll probably never store applications and data files in the same folder, this means you will always have to navigate up out of your application's folder and then down into the folder where you store your data files when you load your first file of the day. But if your application is stored at the top level, you can simply move into the data folder you want.

The only problem with storing applications on the top level is with applications that make use of auxiliary files. Spell-checking programs or word processors with built-in spelling checkers or thesauruses have extra dictionary files used by the program. The word processor or spelling checker expects to find its auxiliary files in the same folder as the application file itself. Therefore, if you store an application at the top level on the disk, the application will expect to find its auxiliary files at the top level as well.

But having a bunch of dictionary files at the top level of the disk can really clutter things up. The logical thing to do is to place the dictionary and other auxiliary files in a folder, but if you do, you will always have to indicate where those files are located each time you start the application program. In other words, when you start up the application, it will look around at its own organizational level for the auxiliary files, and if it doesn't find them, it will ask you to specify where they are.

Having to tell your word processor where its dictionary files are each time you start up is a pain in the neck, but there is an alternative. You can always place auxiliary files used by application programs in the System Folder. An application program will always check the System Folder in searching for its auxiliary files if the program doesn't find them at its own organizational level. Of course, this clutters up your System Folder even more, but it beats having to locate your dictionary or thesaurus file every time you boot an application. Less frequently used applications should all be stored in one big folder, and then, depending on your preference, divided into folders inside that folder to minimize clutter. Some people like to keep all their writing tools or spreadsheets in individual folders, for example, and it's usually a good idea to keep all utility programs in a folder.

Data files can be arranged in folders by subject, client, or project, but they definitely shouldn't be separated by the date they were last worked on (because this changes each time you modify a file). Dividing data files by the application used to create them is also not a good idea, because it frequently forces you to open several different folders to work on one project.

The System Folder and the application folder should be stored at the top level of the hard disk. Depending on the number of utilities you have and the frequency of their use, you might also store the utilities folder on the top level. Otherwise, keep it inside the applications folder.

With data files, you should create folders at the top level for broad categories, then use folders inside them to organize specific projects. Here are some specific examples of the kinds of data folders you might create for yourself, and a strategy for knowing when to create them.

Start Out Simple

The idea behind storing files in folders is to make it easy to find them. But there's a balance between having everything neatly pigeonholed and being forced to navigate endlessly into and out of folders. The best policy if you're just beginning to organize your hard disk is to keep it simple. It's easy to keep using the New Folder command in the Finder to make folders, but nobody can foretell the future, and setting up a bunch of folders before you've done any work is frequently a waste of time. Somehow, all that work you planned to do for a particular project or client never materializes, or you decide you don't need to keep copies of all your memos in a file on your hard disk.

To find out which groups of files require their own folder, why not wait and see what develops? Start out with a folder called Misc. or Generic, like the one in Figure 5–11. As you begin to create lots of related files, create a new folder to separate them from the rest, as in Figure 5–12. Generally, you're safe creating a new folder if you have five or more files relating to the same project, client, or subject.

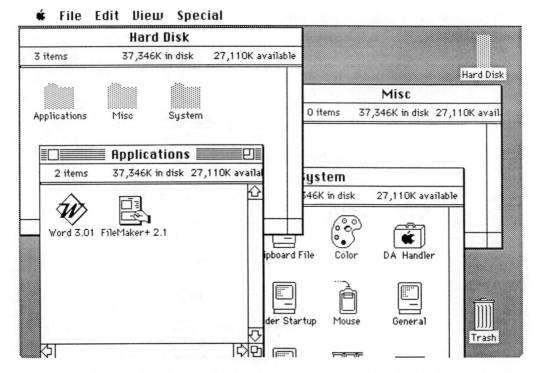

Figure 5–11. If your hard disk is new, start with just one folder for data files.

To Nest, or Not to Nest?

The level at which you store a folder depends on how frequently you access its files. If you anticipate working every day or two with a group of files, their new folder should be stored at the top organizational level for easier access. Otherwise, put the folder inside another folder. If a folder grows unexpectedly, or you find yourself working with it constantly, you can always move it to the top level on the disk.

A disk's organizational structure is like a living thing that changes over time. As you work, you'll build groups of files and you'll create folders for them. Sometimes, you'll rename folders or move files from one folder to another. The most flexible feature of folders is the ease with which you can toss them out if they don't prove useful. If you have to hunt too long through too many folders to find one or two files, think of a better place to put those files. When a list box or window becomes too cluttered with files, learn to create a new folder.

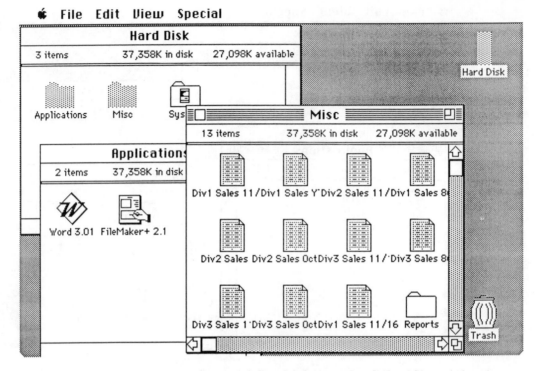

Figure 5–12. As your first folder fills up with files, break out groups of related files and place them in other folders.

Cleaning House

Just as you should periodically check your disk for files you no longer need, you should watch out for folders that have outlived their usefulness. If you've created a folder for two or three files, a practice that can clog up your disk structure, and you find over time that you haven't added any files to that folder, put the files somewhere else. Think of your disk's file structure like a tree, and do a little pruning once in awhile so you can always navigate easily to any part of the structure. Figure 5–13 shows two disk tree structures containing the same files: Which do you think is easier to navigate through?

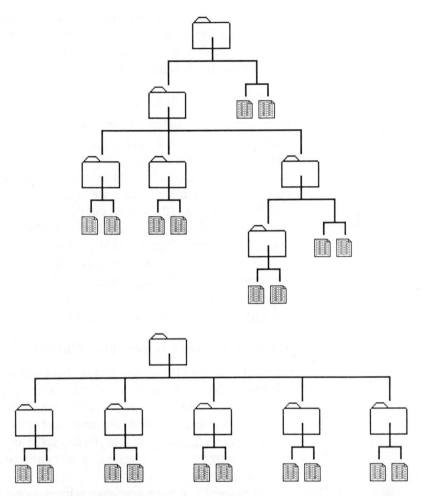

Figure 5–13. Keep your disk's file structure simple and rearrange complex structures
regularly. The fewer levels of folders you have, the simpler it is to navigate
through them.

Organizing the Desktop

A sound folder structure makes finding files in list boxes much easier, but it's
also important to arrange folders and their contents on the desktop so you can
locate things easily in the Finder. Which folders should you have open, and
how large should each folder window be?

Remembering that the whole point is to have the items you want as easily accessible as possible, try to arrange your desktop so the windows whose contents you frequently use are always open, and those whose contents you use less frequently are closed.

Storing Key Applications

Everybody has a handful of applications they use every day or so. We've already said that these should be stored by themselves on the top level of the disk so you don't have to navigate out of a folder when you want to open files from inside a program, but you can do even more. Instead of leaving these applications in your hard disk's window (where they'll be jumbled together with lots of folders), drag them out of the hard disk folder and store them directly on the desktop, as in Figure 5–14. These files will automatically be displayed as icons, since everything on the desktop is shown that way.

The applications for which this technique is best suited are those that run from individual files, such as MacPaint, MacDraw, Excel, and SuperPaint. If you have applications that use extra files, such as spelling dictionaries, store them in the System Folder.

Which Windows to Open, and Where?

One of the the most frustrating games a hard disk owner can play is the "open window shuffle." The problem with having many folders is that each of them can be opened into a window, creating a mess of windows covering other windows. Fortunately, there are rules that windows follow that make it possible to arrange things so that you can get to any window at any time. The basic rule is that windows always stay the same size and in the same place that you last left them.

The specific folders you want to have open on the desktop at all times are those whose contents you frequently need: applications and major groups of data files. The System Folder is almost never open on the desktop, because you rarely need to look at or work with these files.

There are several tricks to maximizing the number of files and folders you can view at one time on your desktop.

Arranging Data Folder Windows

For data folders, it's best to use tall, narrow windows, like the ones in Figure 5–15. You normally display data files in Name view (see Chapter 3) and you only need to see a file's name to recognize and select it, so resize data folder windows so that only the name is showing. Macintosh windows can be

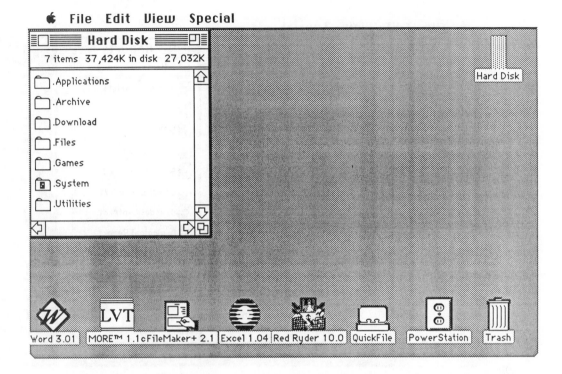

Figure 5–14. You can place frequently used applications directly on the desktop, so you don't have to browse through a window to find them.

shrunk to about an inch and a half across, which theoretically allows you about five windows across the desktop without overlapping. If you prefer, you can lay out three rows of small windows, one on top of the other. You'll find it easier to shrink windows this way if you remember two things:

- Keep your filenames as short as possible or at least put the most descriptive part of the filename at the beginning of the name. You could use a name like Report on Q3 Expenses, but you'll get more information about the file in a narrow window if you call it Q3 Expense Report instead.

- Keep folder names short as well, so the name is still meaningful when the window is narrowed. Minimum-width windows show only about four or five characters of a folder name, so use names like Apps instead of Applications, or Misc. instead of Miscellaneous.

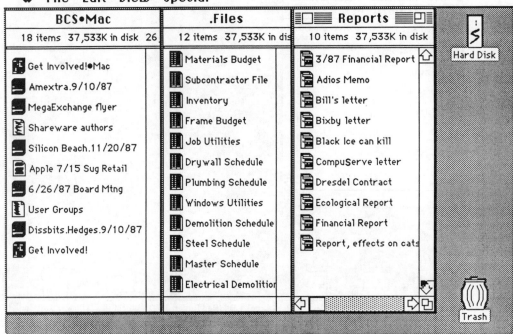

Figure 5–15. With narrow windows, you can view more windows on the desktop at once.

Use Zoom and the Hollow Icon

For your application folder, which contains icons, use the Zoom box to expand the window when you need to see more icons. The Zoom box is at the right-hand edge of the title bar. It expands the window to its maximum size. Clicking in the zoom box a second time shrinks the window back to the size and position it was last in. Be careful, though: If you resize or move the window at all when it's in the expanded mode, that new size or position will replace the minimum-sized one you had before.

If you're working with an expanded window, it will probably overlay the other windows underneath it. After you open a folder or a disk, its icon is still there, but it becomes gray or hollow. If you double-click on a hollow

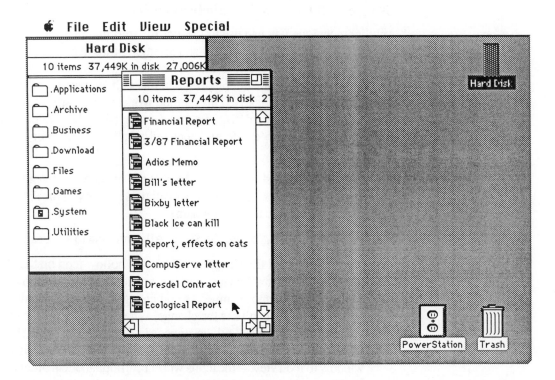

Figure 5–16. When folders contain folders, you can open an inside folder and then close the folder that contains it to preserve desktop space.

icon, its window will be brought to the front of the desktop and will become the active window.

Close Unneeded Folders

Although you must open a folder to view the files and folders inside it, a higher-level folder doesn't have to be open all the time. Suppose you have a folder called Business, for example, which contains a folder called Reports, as in Figure 5–16. Once you've opened the inside folder (Reports), you can close its containing folder (Business). The Reports folder window will remain open on the desktop, and you don't have to deal with the extra clutter from the Business folder's window.

Using Small Icons in Alphabetical Order

Another technique you can use to present file information more effectively involves using the Small Icon view and arranging files in alphabetical order. Small icons are a little easier to identify quickly, and they don't take up all the room that large icons do, but you can make them even more useful by arranging files alphabetically. This method works particularly well with the main window for your hard disk, but you can use it for other folder windows as well. Here's how to create alphabetized small icons in your hard disk window:

1. Open the hard disk window and select the Name view from the View menu, if your files aren't already displayed by name. This displays the files in alphabetical order by name.

2. Press Command-A or use the Select All command to select all the files.

3. Drag the selected files into the hard disk's hollow icon on the desktop (the icon is hollow because you've opened the disk window). This copies the files onto themselves and changes their actual order in the window, but you can't see the change. When you display files in Name view, the Finder makes them appear in alphabetical order, but they aren't actually stored in alphabetical order. (To prove this, change the window to Icon view—the icons won't be in alphabetical order because the files aren't really stored that way.) But copying files in Name view onto themselves stores the files in true alphabetical order.

4. Make the disk window as tall as possible and one column wide, so only the filenames show.

5. Change the view of the window to Small Icon. This will put all the small icons in alphabetical order in one long column in the window, as shown in Figure 5–17. (If you're using a Finder version prior to 5.5, you'll have to hold down the Option key as you choose the Small Icon command from the View menu.)

Our list of icons at this point is too long to display in the window, but we can move the ones that are out of view into a column to the right of the original column:

1. Make the window wide enough to accommodate two columns, instead of the one you have displayed.

2. Press Command-A or choose the Select All command to select all the files in the window.

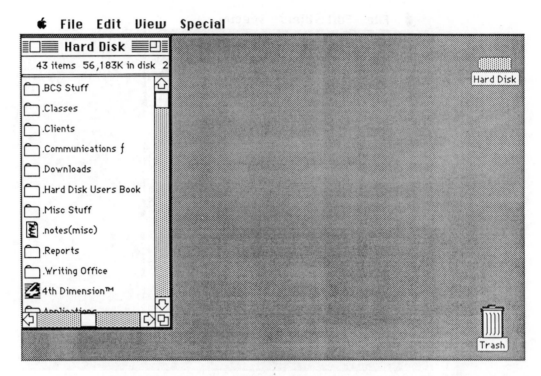

Figure 5-17.   You can make small icons appear in alphabetical order.

3. Shift-click on all but the last file visible in the window (the one at the bottom of the window). This deselects all but the last visible file in the first column and leaves the last file and the off-screen files selected.

4. Drag the selected files into the second column, lining them up with the first column. Now, you'll have two columns of small icons, which will still be in alphabetical order, as in Figure 5–18.

5. If there are still too many files to be visible in the second column, repeat steps 1–4 again, creating a third column of files.

Arranging Small Icons by Type

Having small icons arranged by name helps you locate individual files more quickly, but you can make things even easier. Instead of displaying files by Name in the hard disk window at the beginning of this process, display them by Kind instead. The Kind view arranges files first by type of file (documents

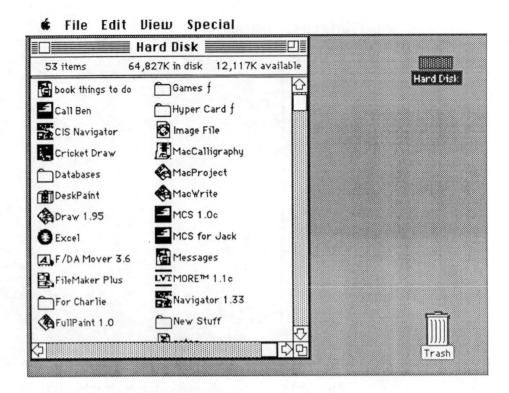

Figure 5–18. By selecting and dragging groups of files, you can create columns of icons side by side.

first, then applications, then folders), then within each kind group in alphabetical order. If you use the Kind view to begin this technique, you'll end up with a column of small icons with documents at the top, applications next, and folders last. You can then arrange each of these types of files in separate columns.

Armed with these techniques, let's look at three different strategies for arranging a desktop.

Advanced Window Dressing I—Stacked Windows

In this layout, we'll divide the desktop into three areas, one on the left half of the desktop and two stacked on the right half of the desktop. The left side of the screen will display the main hard disk window, and the right half will display folders we've opened. The idea is to have the folders in the main hard disk window visible for selection at all times, along with enough room to see

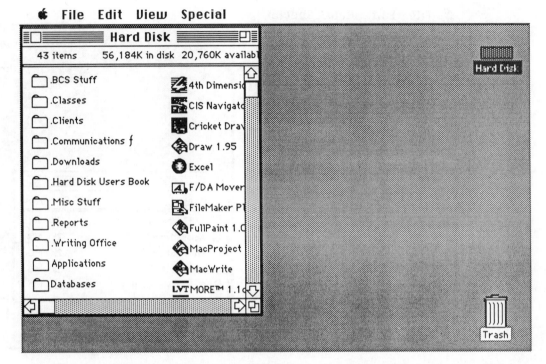

Figure 5–19. This layout uses a large hard disk window, which displays folder icons you can click to activate different data folder windows.

two opened folders at once. This layout uses the alphabetized small icon view created with the technique we just learned, so you'll want to go through that procedure before following these steps. Once the files in your hard disk window are displayed as small icons in alphabetical order, and you've arranged them in the columns you want:

1. Place and resize the hard disk window so it takes up the left side of the desktop, as shown in Figure 5–19.

2. Open the first folder in the window and resize and position it so that it is in the bottom of the right half of the desktop, as in Figure 5–20. Remember not to block the bottom row of applications (if you have applications on the desktop), or the Trash Can.

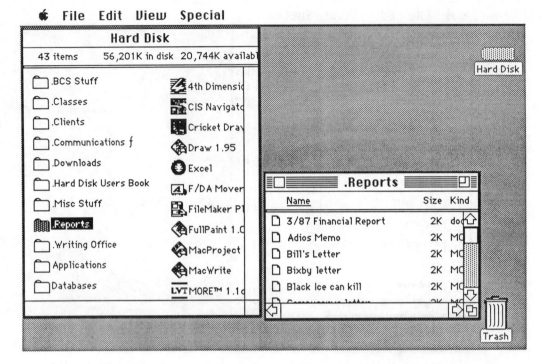

Figure 5–20. Open a data folder window and place it in the bottom half of the right side of the desktop.

3. Open the next folder window and resize it so it appears in the top half of the right side of the desktop, leaving room for your disk icons.

4. Open, resize and place the windows for the other key folders on your hard disk on top of one another in the bottom and top halves of the right side of the desktop. Now, you'll have two stacks of folder windows on the right side of the desktop.

With this arrangement, folders will overlay one another in the top and bottom halves of the right side of the desktop, but you can quickly bring any folder's window to the top of a stack by double-clicking in its hollow icon in the hard disk window at the top of the screen. This layout method is particularly useful if you need access to many windows from the Finder.

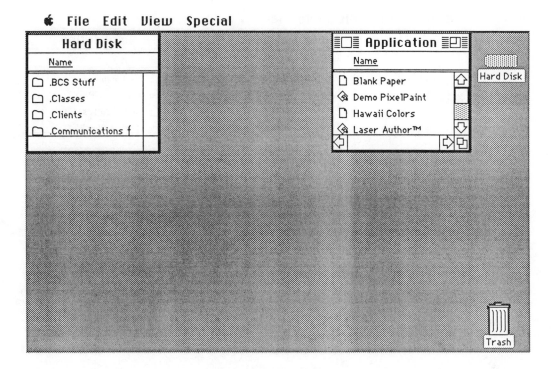

Figure 5–21. Using minimum window sizes, you can display a lot of windows on the screen at once.

Advanced Window Dressing II—Tiled Windows

Another technique is to open all the data file and application folders you need access to so they're all visible on the screen at once.

1. Open your hard disk icon to display its contents.

2. Change the window view to Name, if it isn't already set that way.

3. Resize the window so it is as small as possible and occupies the upper left corner of the screen.

4. Open your application file folder, resize it so it is as small as possible (about 1 inch square), and move the folder to the upper right corner of the desktop, as in Figure 5–21.

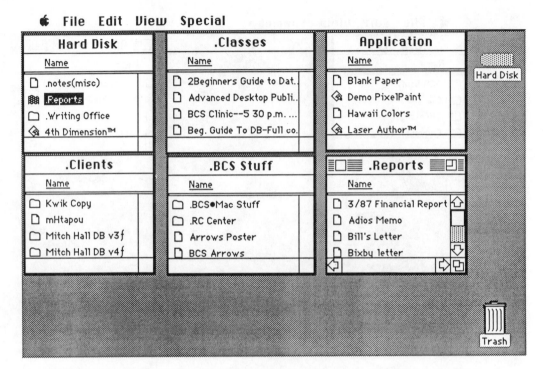

Figure 5–22. Minimum-sized windows can be laid side by side, or "tiled" across the screen.

5. Scroll your hard disk's window and open the first data file folder you want available.

6. Resize its window and place it next to the application window.

7. Repeat steps 5 and 6 until you've opened and placed every data folder window you want available. Your screen will look something like the one in Figure 5–22.

As you reach the left side of the screen, you'll have to resize and move your hard disk's window to uncover empty space for another data folder window. You can simply place the hard disk's window on top of other folder windows you've already laid out. When you're finished, you can close the hard disk window.

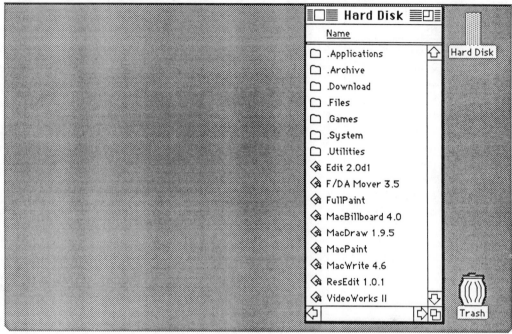

Figure 5–23. Use a long, narrow hard disk window to begin this layout.

This is another way to view a lot of folders on the screen at once. To see more inside each folder, just click its Zoom box. If you have only three or four windows open, you can make them larger, of course.

Advanced Window Dressing III—Overlapping Windows

In this layout, we'll size windows so they display a lot of filenames and overlap them so we can activate any window in the group by clicking on it at any time.

1. Open the hard disk's window, make it long and narrow, and place it at the right side of the screen, as Figure 5–23 shows.

2. Open the first folder you want to view; make its window as narrow and as long as possible.

3. Drag the window to the far left side of the desktop, as in Figure 5–24.

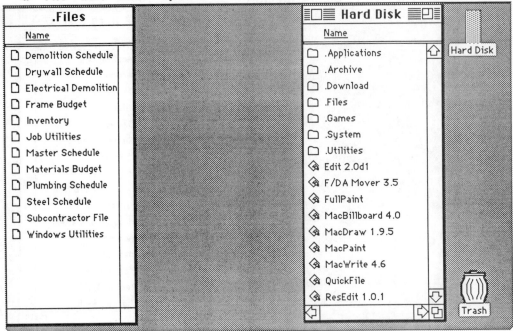

Figure 5–24. Folder windows will be arranged in an overlapping stack, beginning at the left edge of the desktop.

4. Open the second folder from the hard disk window, resize it like the first folder you opened, and drag it so it overlaps the first window, leaving the first window's title bar and about half an inch of the left side of the window sticking out, as Figure 5–25 shows.

5. Repeat step 5 for as many windows as you want to have open.

To use this layout, simply click in the title bar of the window you want to access to bring it to the front of the pile. Because each window is offset slightly from the others, a piece of every window is in view at all times, and you can always click any window in the stack to bring it to the front.

With these techniques and sample strategies, you should be well on your way to organizing your hard disk files effectively. Now, let's move on to some other specific issues in using a hard disk. In Chapter 6, we'll look at using a hard disk on a network.

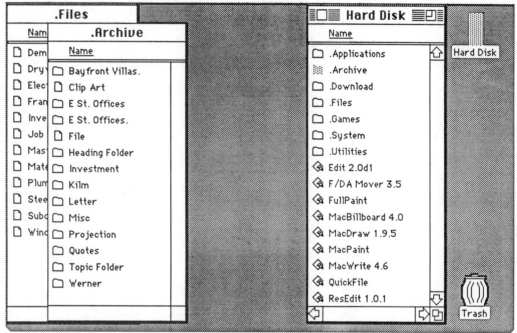

Figure 5–25 Each window overlaps the window below it so you can still see the title bar and left edge of the window underneath.

6

Networking: Sharing Files Among Hard Disks

Linking several Macs on a network is much simpler than it is with other computers, thanks to AppleTalk wiring systems such as Apple's LocalTalk and Farallon's PhoneNet Plus: You simply plug a special connector into your Mac's printer port, then lay out some inexpensive cabling. AppleTalk is frequently used so several Macs can share a LaserWriter (in fact, AppleTalk is the standard way to connect a LaserWriter to a Mac), but several software vendors have introduced programs that enable Macs to share files across a network. Usually, that means sharing the files on a hard disk.

This chapter isn't intended as a complete guide to networking with a Macintosh. Networking is a complex subject, and there are many Mac network options (special hard disks designed to work as network servers, for example) that fall outside the focus of this book. But Apple and other vendors also make software that enables you to use an ordinary hard disk on a network, and this chapter offers some advice about doing that.

Network Fundamentals

The networks that tie personal computers together are known as *local area networks,* or *LANs,* a term that distinguishes them from the larger and more sophisticated networks used by mainframe and minicomputers. Mainframe and minicomputer networks can span the globe, using telephone lines as well as cabling to make connections. They have many advanced features, such as automatic data backups, multiple levels of password protection, and automated data transmissions among several different terminals at various locations. LANs, on the other hand, are restricted to cabling between computers that are generally in the same building, and they have fewer features.

A complete LAN consists of:

- Cabling that makes a physical link between computers and peripherals (such as LocalTalk cabling)

- Network software that manages the transmission of data over the network to hard disks, printers, or other computers (such as TOPS or AppleShare)

- Application software—either programs designed for use by one computer or multiuser software that can be used by many people at once.

These are the three elements of a complete network, but you can get by with only the cabling and application programs if you don't need to transmit data to a remote disk drive or another computer. Many Apple users just use LocalTalk cabling to connect with a LaserWriter, for example, then send data to the printer over the cabling. But to use a hard disk as a common storage device on a network, you need network software that people use to load and save files on a centralized storage device.

Clients and Servers

Computers on networks are divided into two classes: *clients,* which access data from other computers' disks across the network; and *servers,* which make the data from their disks available to others on the network. With some network software, a user's computer can be both a client and a server at the same time: The user's disk or parts of it are available to other people on the network, and the user has access to data on other disks across the network. Other types of network software force each computer to be either a client or a server.

In systems where you can be both a client and a server at the same time, you can generally make your disk a server anytime you want, but to become a client, the person controlling the disk you want to access must specifically make it available to you. Depending on the network software being used, the person controlling a server can make parts of the disk available to the network at large, or he or she can control exactly which people on the network have access to specific parts of the disk.

In fact, one of the major features that differentiates brands of LAN software is the flexibility and ease with which the person controlling a server can make different groups of files available to different groups of people. With relatively sophisticated software like AppleShare, you can set a variety of access privileges for the same group of files, depending on the users. For the same folder on a disk, one person might be able to read data from or write data to that folder, a second group might be allowed to read the contents only, and a third person might be able to write data to the folder but not view the folder's contents. Less sophisticated network software offers less flexibility in setting access options.

File Sharing and Disk Sharing

The two basic methods of sharing data on a network are disk sharing and file sharing. The method you use depends on the type of network software you are using. Disk sharing is the more primitive option. On a disk-sharing system, users share data on a hard disk by dividing that disk into specific partitions or volumes, each of which is typically used by only one user, as illustrated in Figure 6–1.

Under this system, each user can write files only to his or her own partition or volume on a disk, not to the other partitions. (Users can also have their own hard disks directly connected to their Macs.) Usually, the user of a partitioned hard disk can allow other users to read files from that partition. Every user's computer is a client, but only the computer with the partitioned hard disk is a server as well. (You can have multiple servers, though.) The server disk runs specific software that makes it a server. The most popular disk-sharing software for Macs is MacServe, by Infosphere.

A disk-sharing system is primarily a way for several users to have part of a hard disk for their own (thereby saving the expense of individual hard disks), rather than a way for those users to easily and transparently *exchange* data among themselves. To modify a file in someone else's part of a disk, you must load the file and then save it to your own partition. This data-transfer method is clumsier than file sharing, the other networking method.

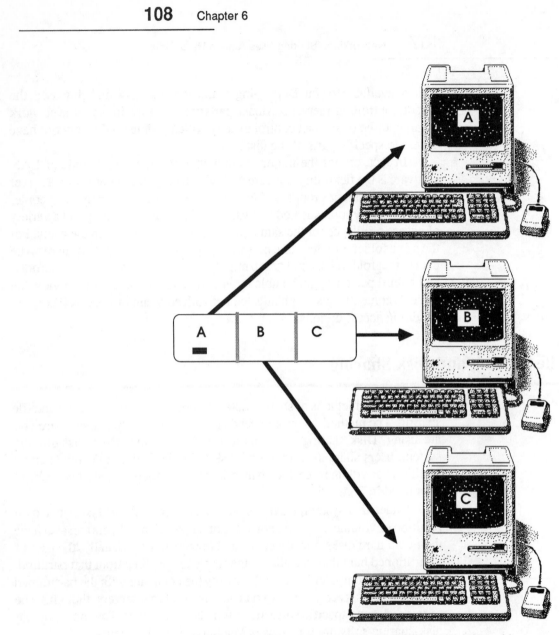

Figure 6–1. A disk-sharing network divides a hard disk into partitions.

But while disk sharing inhibits the exchange of files between users on the network, it also avoids some problems that file-sharing systems must deal with. Because each user's partition can only have one writer, it is functionally like a separate hard disk, and users of different partitions can run single-user application software without worrying about somebody else trying to run it at the same time. Each user's partition can have its own System Folder and collection of applications. On a file-sharing system, there's only one System Folder and one copy of each application, and the network must handle conflicts when two users want to run the same application or work with the same file.

A file-sharing system, as typified by AppleShare and TOPS, doesn't break a disk up into specific partitions for each user. Instead, it allows the person who controls the hard disk to make certain volumes or folders on that disk available to one or more users at the same time, as shown in Figure 6–2.

Under this system, any computer on the network can be a client or a server, or even both at the same time. Because TOPS and AppleShare are the two major brands of Macintosh network software, let's look at each one in some detail.

TOPS

TOPS was one of the first file-sharing software systems for the Macintosh, coming to market over a year before AppleShare. It's a truly distributed network system, in which any floppy or hard disk on the network can be a server, any computer can be a client, and any computer can be both client and server at the same time.

With the TOPS software, anyone can "publish" a disk volume or folder (make it a server), and anyone can "mount" a volume published on the network (become a client). Disk volumes can easily be "unmounted," or removed from network availability, without affecting the rest of the users and their published volumes. If you have published files from your hard disk, you can still use it as your personal hard disk at the same time.

Other advantages of TOPS include its low price and its ease of use. Every Mac on the network must run a copy of TOPS at $149 per copy, but that means you buy only as many copies as you have Macs. Also, because every disk can be a server, you don't have to buy an extra Mac and dedicate it as a server. TOPS installs as a desk accessory, and you can mount, unmount, publish, or unpublish volumes by selecting them in a simple dialog box. It also uses an Init file that can cause problems with some game programs, although it's possible to disable TOPS at startup in such a case.

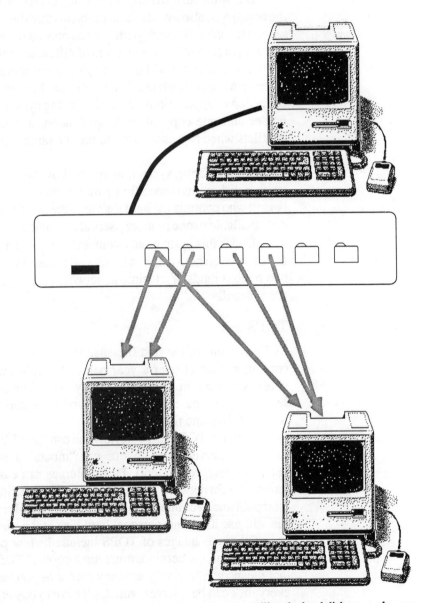

Figure 6–2. In a file-sharing system, the person controlling the hard disk can make any folder or volume on the disk available to one or more users.

Older versions of TOPS didn't deal well with conflicts between two users who wanted to run the same application from a server or open the same file, but now TOPS has improved this capability. When one user opens a file, the file becomes locked, and other users can read it, but nobody else can write to it until the original user has closed the file. This is called *file locking*. Most Macintosh applications at this point were designed to be used by one user at a time, so TOPS' file locking is an important feature if you want to use such an application on a network. But some applications, mostly relational databases and accounting programs, are designed for multiple users and have their own internal facilities that handle conflicts when multiple users access the same files.

Another complaint about older versions of TOPS was that you couldn't control access to published folders or volumes: Once a volume was published, *everyone* on the network could read it or write to it. With versions of TOPS released after the fall of 1987, you can protect individual folders or volumes with passwords, so users without the password are denied access. This security scheme still isn't nearly as flexible as AppleShare's, but it's workable.

Perhaps the best feature about TOPS is that it's easy to use. You don't need a specific network administrator to monitor activity on the network, because each person who publishes files on the network sets the access privileges for those files. The program is easy enough to install and use that you can be up on a TOPS network within an hour.

TOPS is a good solution for small offices where money and ease of use are considerations, in situations where you don't need several different levels of access privileges for your files.

AppleShare

Unlike TOPS, AppleShare uses a specific Macintosh and its hard disk as a dedicated server. This server can only be used to run the network: You can't use it as your personal machine at the same time. This means you have to spend money for a separate Mac and hard disk, along with the $795 for the AppleShare software itself (not including cabling costs), to set up an AppleShare network. An AppleShare network can have more than one server, as with TOPS.

But while AppleShare costs more than TOPS, it does more. It enables you to set lots of different access privileges for users on the network. You can publish a folder and assign read-only privileges to one user, read and write privileges to another user, write-only privileges to a third, and deny access to the folder completely to a fourth user. You can set up different passwords to give different users access. If your network has a lot of users, you can divide users into groups, set different privileges for different groups, and then customize the specific privileges within each group. You can also give users memberships in more than one group.

Like TOPS, AppleShare offers file locking to prevent user conflicts. With single-user applications, two users aren't allowed to write to the same file. Unfortunately, some programs (such as the original HyperCard) won't run with a file-locked disk.

AppleShare is also faster than TOPS at processing data traffic. When you load a file across the network on TOPS, the access speed is akin to that of a floppy disk drive, or even slower, while AppleShare's access time is more like that of a hard disk. Finally, like TOPS, AppleShare supports all multiuser software.

Along with its higher cost, AppleShare is more difficult to administer than TOPS. Because AppleShare has various access levels, it's more work to set up or change the user privileges on the network.

AppleShare will become the standard in Macintosh networking software, simply because Apple sells it. That means developers will make sure to modify their applications so they can be run on AppleShare, and new applications will automatically support it. At this writing, most major application programs will support multiple users on AppleShare, including Microsoft Word (beginning with version 3.01), More, Microsoft Excel, Microsoft Works (version 1.1 or later), PageMaker, MacWrite (version 4.6 or later), SuperPaint, Fourth Dimension, and Omnis.

AppleShare is more suited to networks on which the number of users or the applications being run change frequently, and for which flexibility in protecting network files against unauthorized access is important.

Note: For all its access privileges and passwords, the security on AppleShare can easily be defeated by simply starting up the AppleShare server with a regular floppy disk. If you don't start up the server using the AppleShare software, the network doesn't start up. AppleShare's own security facilities aren't enabled. All the files on the disk can then be accessed by the person using the server. (Because AppleShare isn't running, there will be no network access during that time.)

Managing the Network

On a network, several people may try to save and load files from the same storage device(s). Just as you might behave a little differently when traveling on a bus or airplane than you would when you're alone in a car, your file-handling methods on a network may be different than if you were merely using your own disk.

MacServe software is the easiest to adjust to, because having a disk partition is a lot like having your own disk anyway, but file-sharing systems require more thought about naming and accessing files. Here are some tips that will make your network life easier.

Use Unique File and Folder Names

Give your network-accessible files and folders distinctive names to avoid confusion for other users. If you have a budget file, for example, don't just call it Budget, because another user might have a Budget file as well. Add some personal identification to the filename, such as your initials, to stamp your files or folders as your own.

Plan the Network's Data Organization

A network hard disk is even more apt to become cluttered with files and folders, and you—and others on the network—should create folders and store files in a way that makes it as easy as possible for everyone to get the data they want. After you set up the network, sit down with the other users and plan an organization that makes sense to everybody. This will probably result in each user having a folder of his or her own to contain several folders dividing work or applications logically, as well as shared folders for everyone's use.

Protect Passwords

If you're using passwords, you probably have a good reason for them. Make sure the other network users take their passwords seriously and ensure that the passwords are stored and used securely.

Remember: The Drive Isn't Local

With a personal hard disk, you get used to speedy access to your files. On a network, though, access will be slower in any case, and it will be decidedly slower at times. If there's a lot of traffic on your network, you may have to wait several seconds to access files, and it's important to be patient. It doesn't do any good to click your mouse button or pound your keyboard if a file doesn't appear immediately.

Don't Pull the Plug

After you start your network each time, don't make any drastic changes without notifying other users. Don't suddenly unmount a folder or volume, for example, because others may be using data from that part of the hard disk. If you're using TOPS, you may well be using a server as your personal machine. If your application program crashes, inform other users before resetting your Mac, so they have time to save the files they're working on. Otherwise, resetting your machine may cause them to lose data. Certainly, you should never shut down a networked hard disk or server until you're sure you won't be disrupting other users. Ensure that either everyone else has gone home or you've unpublished all the volumes you had published.

Back Up Network Data

Once you have a network running, you have a larger responsibility to protect the network data and the system itself from failure. Backups of programs and data are even more important on a network than for your single-user hard disk. Because many people are storing files on the hard disk, the files change every day, and you should do an incremental backup of the disk every day, with a full backup at least once a week. Perform full backups even more often if you're running large database applications or if the network has a lot of active users whose files change frequently. (More on this in Chapter 9.)

Back up the network files only when other users aren't on the network, or you'll cause serious delays in file access times, or perhaps even system crashes. If you're using TOPS or MacServe, simply back up the hard disk as you would a normal hard disk, but be sure that nobody else is on the network at the time to avoid a system crash.

If you're using AppleShare, there are two ways to make backups. You can back up volumes while AppleShare is running, using its special backup software, or you can back up the entire disk without AppleShare running, using backup utility software. If you back up with AppleShare running, you can back up every folder or volume except an invisible folder called the Server Folder, which stores AppleShare setup information. To back up the Server Folder, you must shut down AppleShare and use a standard backup utility. (Some network applications, such as InBox from Think Technologies, also keep files inside the Server Folder.)

AppleShare privileges can include the ability to make backups of a certain group's files. If you're the administrator of an AppleShare network, make sure that you give yourself privileges in every group of users you create, so you can back up every volume on the network. As a further precaution, each user on any network should copy his or her important files onto floppy disks or their own hard disks as well. That way, people can continue working if the network software crashes.

If you're using TOPS, you can also protect your data by breaking it up and storing different groups of files on different hard disks. Since every hard disk on the network can be a server, it's safer to spread the files around, perhaps with accounting data on one disk, sales data on another, and personnel data on a third. That way, one hard disk failure won't completely cripple your organization.

Networks are an excellent way to share your hard disk space and make computing more productive for other users. With the right software and some basic techniques, you can create a data management environment your whole office or department can share.

7

Using File or Disk Copying Programs

Copying disks or files is a pretty simple matter on the Macintosh, but there are some special considerations for hard disk users. In this chapter, we'll take a quick look at file and disk copying on the Mac, and how you can make copies to and from your hard disk most efficiently. We'll also check out some software utilities that make disk copying easier. We'll answer such questions as:

- Is there an easy way to copy the contents of a floppy disk to a hard disk?
- Can you copy protected programs to your hard disk?
- What kinds of copy programs are there, and should you have one?
- Is there a fast way to copy floppy disks on a system with one floppy disk drive?

As a background to our exploration of the actual methods and programs used to copy files, we'll begin with a description of what happens when files are written to or read from disks.

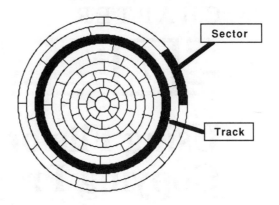

Figure 7–1. When it formats a disk, your Mac divides the disk into concentric rings, or tracks, each of which contains specific areas, or sectors.

How Files Are Stored on a Disk

In order to store and retrieve files from a disk, the Mac must maintain information about the locations of the files. The process begins when you initialize a disk, but it's slightly different for hard and floppy disks.

When you initialize an 800K floppy disk, your Mac:

- Erases any information currently stored on the disk.

- Creates a map on each side of the floppy disk consisting of 80 concentric circles, or tracks, each of which has 10 blocks, or sectors, for a total of 800 sectors per side. (On a 400K disk only one side of the disk is formatted.) Each sector can store 512 bytes of data. Figure 7–1 diagrams the concept of sectors and tracks.

- Creates a directory, a blank listing where it will later store information about the names, types, and locations of files on the disk.

- Creates a file allocation table (FAT), which is a map of all the sectors and their locations.

When you initialize a hard disk, the Mac erases all existing information, but it then divides the disk up differently, depending on the capacity of the disk. Hard disk drives contain one, two, or more individual platters that stack on top of each other on a spindle. Each platter has its own set of read/write heads. Depending on the design of the hard disk (the number of platters and heads it has), the number of sectors on each platter varies.

How Files Are Read and Written

To write a file to a disk, the Mac grabs pieces of the file out of its memory in sector-sized chunks, checks the disk directory to see which sectors are available for new files, and then places the file in some of the empty sectors on the disk. It then records the name, size, and type of the file, and its exact location by sectors in the disk's directory.

(On a new disk, a file is written to contiguous sectors and tracks. But as you write new files or change old ones on the disk, all the large contiguous groups of sectors get used up, and pieces of files are saved to different sectors all over the disk. All this sector-hunting takes time, which is why your hard disk's performance can slow down after you've been using it for a few months. In Chapter 10, we'll look at utility programs that reorganize a hard disk's files so they are once again stored in contiguous blocks, thereby improving disk access times.)

To read a file from a disk, your Mac consults its directory for the file name and sector location, checks the FAT to locate the proper sectors, and then moves its heads to that area to read the file. This is the process that occurs when you save files, load files, or copy files from one disk to another using the Finder, the Save and Save As... commands, or the sector copying option in third-party copy programs.

How Disks Are Copied

When you drag one floppy disk's icon to another floppy disk's icon in the Finder to copy a whole disk, your Mac goes through every step in the process just described, from formatting the destination disk to setting up a directory and FAT, to writing the information. It's no problem to copy an 800K floppy onto another 800K floppy—or a 400K disk to a 400K disk—because your Mac can simply create an identical FAT and directory on the destination floppy, and all the copied files go into the same places on the new disk. You can't copy a 400K floppy onto an 800K floppy by dragging icons, because the two disks are of different sizes and the FATs and directories on the two disks are different. You can, however, copy the contents of a 400K disk to an 800K disk by dragging files individually or in groups.

On a hard disk, the FAT is different from a 400K or an 800K floppy because of the disk's size, and there isn't a one-to-one ratio between the sectors on the floppy and the sectors on the hard disk. The FAT and directory are much different on a hard disk because it is so much larger. This is why your Mac won't let you copy a floppy to a hard disk simply by dragging from icon to icon.

Prior to System 4.0, you could copy a floppy's contents to a hard disk by dragging its icon into a folder on the hard disk. Because you were dragging to a folder, your Mac would simply read the files from the floppy and stick them into new locations on the hard disk, without matching two identical disk maps.

The problem with this was that in copying entire disks, users often copied the floppy disk's System Folder to the hard disk along with the other programs or data. After several floppies had been copied to the hard disk, there would be several System Folders on the hard disk, and the Mac would become confused (and usually crash), because it didn't know which System Folder to use.

System versions 4.0–4.2 don't allow this kind of copying. Now, you have to copy from floppy to hard disk by dragging files individually or in groups. It's harder to end up with multiple System Folders on your hard disk, because you would have to specifically drag those folders onto the hard disk. But while the new restriction against copying whole floppies to a hard disk is safer from the System Folder standpoint, it also requires some extra steps. Here's the simplest way to copy all of a floppy disk's files to a hard disk using the Finder:

1. Open the floppy disk's icon.
2. Use the Select All command from the Edit menu (or press Command-A) to select all the files on the disk.
3. Drag all the files to a hard disk folder.

Systems 4.2 and later simply create a folder with the floppies' names filed with the files on the hard disk. Because any System Folders are automatically at least two levels down, they pose no problem other than wasted space. There are also utility programs that make it easier to copy floppy disks to hard disks or to copy floppies on a one-drive system. The kind of program you use, however, depends on what you're copying and how you want to copy it.

The State of Copy Protection

Copy protection is a modification to a program that makes it impossible to copy a disk or that requires the insertion of a master disk to verify ownership before the program will load. (Original versions of Microsoft Word, Multiplan, and Microsoft File used the master disk system.) Most companies that sell productivity software (word processors, spreadsheets, and so on) have stopped using copy protection because of all the hate mail they received from users. Protection simply makes it more difficult to use software, either by making it impossible to run the program from a hard disk or by requiring the extra step of inserting a master disk.

If you have one of the few remaining programs that are still copy-protected, try using a utility like Copy II Hard Disk (see the description later in the chapter) to copy the program onto your hard disk. The Copy II Hard Disk manual includes a list of protected programs that it can successfully copy.

When you use a utility to unprotect software, remember three things:

1. Breaking a program's copy protection so you can give the program away to your friends is a crime. You should only copy software for your own use.

2. Vendors who use protection are constantly updating their protection schemes in an effort to stay a step ahead of the folks who make disk-copying software. If you're buying a copying utility specifically to duplicate a particular program, make sure the utility can actually copy that program before you buy the utility.

3. When you copy a protected disk with a bit or sector copier, the copy retains the copy protection. A copier simply allows you to place that protected copy on another disk.

One final thing about copy protection: Many games are still copy-protected, and copy programs are usually unsuccessful at duplicating them.

Sector Copies Versus Bit Copies

The standard file reading and writing method described earlier, in which data is transferred a sector at a time, is called, not surprisingly, *sector copying*. This is the only way the Finder and your application programs know how to copy files and disks.

Most copy-protected software can't be copied a sector at a time, however, because of protection schemes that add extra bits to sectors or create sectors that are smaller than 512 bytes. Some utility programs, like Central Point Software's Copy II Hard Disk, use modified sector copy methods that try to account for the most common types of nonstandard sectors used to protect software. If sector copying doesn't work, though, you'll have to try *bit copying*.

Instead of copying data a sector at a time, bit copiers copy individual bits (the smallest unit of data on a disk) of information from one disk to another. (There are eight bits in a byte, and 512 bytes in a floppy disk sector, remember.) You can copy many protected programs with a bit copier because it ignores sector lengths—a bit copier doesn't care if a sector is shorter than it should be, or if it contains an extra bit or two, because it is simply making an exact, bit-by-bit transfer of one disk's contents onto another disk.

The only problem with bit copying is that it takes a long time. It can take five minutes to copy an 800K disk, because the program must read and transfer individual bits, instead of 512-byte sectors. The other problem is that bit copiers only copy from one floppy to another, not to your hard disk. Nevertheless, if you want to make a backup disk of a protected program and a sector copy doesn't work, you'll have to resort to a bit copier. You should always try the faster sector copy method first, though.

Disk Copying Utilities

The Finder is all right for making day-to-day copies of unprotected files or software, but if you make a lot of disk or file copies, if you want to copy protected disks, or if you want to copy complete disks onto your hard disk, you'll need a copying utility.

Copy II for the Mac

The king of third-party copying programs is Copy II for the Mac, from Central Point Software. This $39 package includes two disk-copying programs (Copy II and Copy II Hard Disk) and a file manipulation and disk recovery program called MacTools. All three of these copying programs make copying faster by using all of your Mac's available memory to store data they've read from the disk. If you have enough memory (say, 2 megabytes), these programs can read a whole disk's information in one pass and then write it to a duplicate disk, so you don't have to swap source and destination floppies back and forth if you're copying on a single-drive system. On a one-megabyte Mac, they read about two-thirds of an 800K disk's information at once and then write it to the destination disk, so you'll have to insert your source and destination disks twice for each copy on a single-drive system. But a similar copy operation using the Finder would require 8 or 10 disk swaps on a single-drive system.

Copy II copies only floppy disks, one onto another. While a copy is in progress, Copy II displays a table that shows all the sectors on a disk and checks them off as each one is successfully copied. If it can't copy a sector for some reason, Copy II marks that sector on the sector table. The purpose of this is to enable you to make bit copies of specific tracks containing problem sectors. Typically, you start to make a sector copy, and Copy II copies most sectors of a disk and flags the problem sectors. Then, you use the slower bit copying method to copy the tracks on which the problem sectors are located. (This only works if you're copying onto another floppy, though.)

Copy II Hard Disk copies protected or unprotected floppy disks onto a hard disk. It doesn't matter what kind of hard disk you're using. Copy II Hard Disk makes sector copies only, but it has special instructions that let it copy many nonstandard sectors that couldn't be copied with the Finder. You don't get a sector table with this program—just a simple dialog box telling you the copy is being made or has been completed.

To make a copy with Copy II Hard Disk, you must place the floppy in your Mac's internal disk drive, then select the hard disk volume or folder into which you want to copy the disk. Copy II Hard Disk copies all the files or folders on the original disk into the folder or hard disk volume you've selected. It does not create a special folder to contain all the contents of the disk being copied (which would be preferable); it just shoves all the copied files into the folder you specify along with whatever other files might be there.

MacTools, the third program in the set, also includes file- and disk-copying programs. This is a regular sector-copying program, and it doesn't display a sector map during the process. But in addition to copying disks, MacTools can copy individual files. MacTools also contains a lot of other disk utilities, which we'll discuss in Chapter 10.

Disk-Specific Utilities

Some hard disks, such as the MacBottom series from PCPC, come with their own utilities to make it easier to copy disks. PCPC's Floppy Copy, for example, makes copies from one floppy to another on a single-drive system much faster. When Floppy Copy reads the source floppy disk, it reads the whole disk at once, then stores the data in a special area on the hard disk. You're then prompted to insert the destination disk, then Floppy Copy writes the data from its hard disk buffer onto the new disk.

Generic Disk Utilities

Some generic disk utility programs that perform other functions also include file-copying utilities that make single file copies much more quickly than does the Finder. One example is DiskTop 3.0, a $49.95 program from CE Software. DiskTop is a desk accessory that displays a Finder-like desktop from inside application programs, and with it you can copy files, create or rename folders, delete files, and perform a lot of other useful operations without having to quit the application you're running to return to the Finder. DiskTop also has a file-finding capability, which we'll explore more in Chapter 10.

Copying Disks Under MultiFinder

If you're using a copy program under the MultiFinder, you'll need to reset the program's application memory size for it to work properly. Copy programs assume they have a lot of your Mac's memory—800–900K—to use for storing the copy of a disk they've just read, but the MultiFinder doesn't automatically make memory available to programs. To make sure your copy program has the memory it needs to make a copy, reset the application memory size to at least 900K:

1. Select the copy program's icon in the MultiFinder
2. Press Command-I or choose the Get Info command from the File menu.
3. Double-click in the box next to Application Memory Size (K), and enter the number, 900.
4. Close the Get Info window and launch the copy program to make your copy.

Of course, if you're using a Mac Plus, SE, or Mac II with only one megabyte of memory, you won't be able to run a copy program under MultiFinder, because the System and MultiFinder themselves use up well over 100K of memory, and you won't have 900K of free memory available to allocate to your copy program.

Making Mass Floppy Copies

Small software developers and corporations that distribute program or data disks to several users sometimes need to make lots of copies of the same floppy disk. If you try to make a lot of copies of the same disk using the Finder, you'll spend a lot of time waiting for the copies to be made. If you have only one floppy disk drive, you'll be waiting so long and shuffling floppies in and out of the disk drive so much that you may soon go crazy.

You can speed up multiple floppy copying with a mass disk-copying program. Mass Copier, Disk Dup+, and PD Copy are all designed for this purpose.

Mass Copier

Mass Copier is distributed by CE Software as shareware. You can download the program from CompuServe, and you get a utility that makes mass copies of 400K disks. Of course, what you probably need is a program that copies 800K disks. CE Software sends this version of Mass Copier to you when you send in your $15 shareware fee. Mass Copier works like Floppy Copy, copying the whole disk's contents to your hard disk, but then it enables you to make multiple copies by simply inserting successive disks. Mass Copier is the fastest multiple disk copier of its kind.

Disk Dup+

Disk Dup+ is another shareware program. It copies 800K disks and verifies each disk as it is written, and its shareware fee is $10. It is slightly slower than Mass Copier, but it verifies each copy after it is written to ensure the copy was made properly.

PD Copy

PD Copy is a public domain program that copies 800K disks and verifies each disk as it is written, and keeps track of the number of disks it has copied during a session. Also, it always displays the name of the disk from which you're copying, in case you forget. This is handy if you're copying a lot of different disks at a time. This program is about as fast as Disk Dup+.

Copying files is a pretty straightforward business. With a little help from a utility program, though, you can put protected programs on your hard disk and make file or disk copies a lot more quickly.

8

Printing from a Hard Disk

As a hard disk owner, you can use some of your extra storage space to make printing faster and more convenient. All you need is a print spooler. In this chapter, we'll first describe how print spoolers work, then look at some specific products in detail.

Why Use a Spooler?

Print spoolers were invented because, simply put, printers don't work as quickly as computers. When you print a file from your Mac, the Mac can send data to the printer much more quickly than the printer can actually print it. This means your Mac can't send all its printing data out at once; instead, it must feed the data to the printer slowly, at the rate the printer can use it. When your Mac is tied up feeding data to your printer at a snail's pace, it can't be used for other things. So, whenever you print, you lose the use of your computer until the whole file has been printed—this takes anywhere from a couple of minutes to several hours, depending on the size of the file and the printer you're using.

A spooler creates a special folder on your disk, usually called a *spool folder*, where your Mac can send its printing information as quickly as it can, so you regain the use of the system much sooner. The printing data goes into the spool folder, and the spooler program feeds the data from that file to the printer at the rate demanded by the printer. In other words, the spooler program does the waiting around during a print operation, so you and your Mac don't have to. The only time you give up is the amount of time it takes for your Mac to transfer its printing data to the spooler file on your disk, anywhere from a couple of seconds to perhaps 15 minutes for the largest files.

Along with spoolers, which always create a storage space on disk, frustrated computer users sometimes turn to *printer buffers,* which are hardware devices that store printer data and feed it out slowly to a printer. Printer buffers have several advantages over spoolers, including the ability to receive printer data more quickly (because there's no disk writing involved) and the ability to print multiple copies of a document from the buffer without having to print from your computer several times. Because buffers are hardware, though, they usually cost more than spoolers—from $100 to $500, depending on their memory size and features.

For our purposes, however, we'll focus on spoolers, because those are the programs that relate directly to owning and using a hard disk.

Print Spooler Basics

Most spoolers work the same way, as far as your interaction with them is concerned. They usually come in two parts: One is either a standard application program or an Init program, and the other part is a desk accessory. If you have a spooler that works as an Init program, you place it in your System Folder, and it is then loaded automatically when you start your Mac. The spooler is ready to use after that.

Spoolers that work as application programs must be specifically launched in order for you to use them. The most convenient way to use a spooler application is to set it as the startup application, so it's the application that's launched when you start your Mac. In most cases, you can set up a second program with a spooler application (the Finder, your favorite word processor, or whatever) as the startup application as well: The spooler loads and then goes dormant, and then the second application loads. The spooler is then ready to run at all times, even though it isn't visible on the screen.

Most spoolers come with a desk accessory that you use to examine or manage the queue of files waiting to be printed. Once you've spooled a file by printing it, you can use the desk accessory to see what's in the print queue.

In most cases, the desk accessory will help you rearrange files in the queue, changing the order in which they'll be printed, setting different priority levels for different files, or pausing and resuming print jobs.

Print spoolers give you a lot of extra time on your Mac, because you don't have to wait for print jobs to finish. However, they all slow down your Mac's processing, too. While you are trying to use another application program, the Mac must divide its time between responding to your requests and processing the print file for the spooler.

From Screen to Printer: Spooler Technology

To understand a key difference between print spoolers, we need to spend a little time on how data represented on your Mac screen ends up on paper. The Mac uses a built-in graphic language called QuickDraw to represent information on its screen. All printers, on the other hand, reproduce bit maps (the specific patterns of dots that make up characters and graphics) on paper.

Between the QuickDraw description inside your Mac and the bit maps being printed, there may be intermediate steps. Most Apple laser printers, for example, use a page description language called PostScript, which is an efficient way of specifying how characters and graphics should be printed. PostScript translates the QuickDraw description from the Mac into PostScript's language and describes the specific fonts needed to print a document. Because the PostScript description of the fonts and other document elements is much more compact than a bit map, the information can be transmitted to the printer much more quickly. Once the description reaches the printer, it is translated into a bit map for printing.

Subsequently, a new breed of laser printer has appeared. It transmits page descriptions using the QuickDraw language inside the Mac. Once the QuickDraw description is ready for the printer, it is translated into a bit map for printing.

The ImageWriter, on the other hand, doesn't work with translated files. Instead, your Mac's QuickDraw screen image is internally translated to a bit map directly, and that bit map is sent to the printer.

So, no matter how a printer prints, the QuickDraw description inside your Mac must be translated for printing. This translation is known as *processing* and can include locating the fonts needed to print a file (for laser printers) and *downloading,* or transmitting, them to the printer before the actual print data is sent. Processing takes time—it's one of the big things that slows Macintosh printers down.

As-Needed Processing Versus Preprocessing

Because a spooler program takes over the job of getting data from the Mac to your printer, it also takes over the task of processing the data. But there are two schools of thought on how that processing should be done. Under the first and older method, the spooler takes the QuickDraw image of the file and sends it slowly to the printer, processing the QuickDraw descriptions into the printer's format as you're working with your Mac. We call this method *as-needed processing.*

The problem with as-needed processing is that it makes your Mac a little sluggish, because it has to switch off between receiving input from you (or doing whatever else you're having it do) and processing the printer file. The advantage is that you get control of your Mac back fairly quickly after you select a Print command. This is the method used by the Super LaserSpool spooler.

The second method, *preprocessing,* does most of the file processing up front, right when you select the Print command. It takes more time to assemble the spooler file, so you have to wait a little longer after you send the Print command before you regain control of your Mac, but once the file is assembled, your Mac is almost never interrupted for further spooler processing. This is the method used by the LaserSpeed spooler.

Both processing techniques are in use, and the total print time from spoolers using one technique or the other is about the same, but a spooler doing as-needed processing causes more pauses from your Mac as you work, while a preprocessing spooler is a little slower at spooling the file to disk when you first issue the Print command.

Laser Prep Files

Another issue with LaserWriter users is the print spooler's ability to work with nonstandard LaserWriter drivers. To work properly, your LaserWriter needs two files, a LaserWriter driver and a Laser Prep file, installed in your System Folder. The driver handles basic data transfers from the Mac to the printer and displays the LaserWriter dialog box when you select the Print command. The Laser Prep file contains the instructions used by your laser printer to convert QuickDraw routines from your Mac into PostScript or another format.

The System Folder supplied with your Mac (unless it's a very early release of the System Folder) contains a LaserWriter driver called Laser-Writer and a prep file called Laser Prep. The trouble is that some application programs, such as Aldus' PageMaker, have begun to use their own, custom prep files instead of the one Apple supplies. For example, Apple's prep file translates QuickDraw into PostScript, while Aldus' prep file translates not only from QuickDraw, but from screen elements smaller than can be described by QuickDraw, such as hairlines that are one-fourth the size of the smallest QuickDraw line.

For a spooler to work properly, it must be able to use a prep file to translate from QuickDraw into the printer's format. If it can't use a prep file itself, the spooler gives up and returns printing control to your Mac. All spoolers can use Apple's Laser Prep file, but some can't use other, custom prep files. The PrintMonitor spooler supplied with Apple's MultiFinder, for example, works only with Apple's Laser Prep file, while files created with PageMaker use their own prep file, called Aldus Prep. If you try to print a PageMaker file with PrintMonitor, PrintMonitor sees that the file needs the Aldus Prep file for processing, and then turns itself off and returns control to your Mac.

The lesson behind this is to make sure the spooler you buy will work with any custom prep files used by the programs you'll be printing from. PageMaker is the only program at this writing that uses a custom laser prep file, but others will soon follow.

With this background in mind, let's turn to specific spooler features that can affect your decision about which program to buy.

What to Look for in a Spooler

Because the whole idea behind a spooler is to return control of your Mac to you quickly, the first feature you compare among spoolers is speed. How fast does the spooler return control of the Mac to you? The popular spoolers—covered in detail later—are about the same in speed, but be careful before you buy an off-brand spooler, no matter how much cheaper it is.

A Print Queue

The second feature to look for is a print queue desk accessory that displays a list of the documents waiting to be printed. Look for a print queue facility in which you can easily change the order of the queue, remove items from the queue, pause or resume printing, and empty the cue of all files.

Prep File Compatibility

Compatibility between the spooler and the various laser prep files your application programs use is another important feature. PageMaker is the only program to worry about now, but there will be others, so check the installation instructions of your new programs to see whether they use custom prep files, and then find out if the spooler supports such files.

MultiFinder Compatibility

A second compatibility issue is whether the spooler works with the Multi-Finder. Because the MultiFinder has its own spooler (PrintMonitor), other spoolers can have conflicts with it and not run. In fact, at this writing, few of the third-party laser printer spoolers are compatible with MultiFinder. This isn't a complete disaster, because you can always use PrintMonitor for your laser printer under MultiFinder, but PrintMonitor only spools files to the LaserWriter, so make sure any ImageWriter spooler you choose will work under MultiFinder.

Crash Recovery

Crash recovery is a spooler's ability to save a print queue's status and resume printing after startup if your system crashes. Without this feature, you'll have to send all the files currently in the queue to the spooler all over again if your system crashes. Crash recovery in spoolers isn't perfect, though. The spoolers that have this feature can't remember the specific status of a file whose printing is in progress: If you have a system crash while your spooler is halfway through printing a file, that whole file will be printed again when you restart your Mac.

Other Goodies

Other miscellaneous features add value to spoolers. One is a page preview command, like the one in Super LaserSpool, which displays a miniature version of each page you'll be printing on the LaserWriter, so you can check your margins and layout before printing. Another is the ability to display an alert box in the middle of your application program if your printer has problems such as running out of paper. Finally, with some spoolers you can set a future time to actually send a file to the printer, so you can do your printing when the printer is less busy.

Now, let's see how various spooler products stack up against these criteria.

ImageWriter Spoolers

Until recently, ImageWriter spoolers for the Mac have been quite slow. Older spoolers always translated the QuickDraw description of a file into a bit map before spooling the file. Every sentence and picture was broken down into thousands of dots, so it took a lot of time to spool the file. (It wasn't uncommon for a spooler to require 60 percent of the actual printing time to spool a document—so a file that took 10 minutes to print would require 6 minutes to spool.) Today's ImageWriter spoolers take the QuickDraw image from the screen and send it directly to the spool file, where it is processed into a bit map before being sent to the printer. This change in technology has made ImageWriter spoolers 10 times as fast as before.

SuperSpool

The major spooler for the ImageWriter is SuperSpool, from SuperMac Software. It sells for $59.95, and versions of the program sold from late 1987 on are compatible with the MultiFinder.

Older versions of SuperSpool installed as an application program. You started it automatically by setting it as the startup application, and then you could set a second application to start up after the spooler loaded. The newer versions are Inits. SuperSpool comes with a desk accessory called Print Queue, which displays the order of files in the print queue.

With the Print Queue desk accessory, you can change the order of files in the print queue (as Figure 8–1 shows), pause and resume or cancel printing of a file, and remove files from the queue. Like most other spoolers, SuperSpool writes files to a spool folder, so it can recover from a system crash: The files remain in the queue during a crash, and printing will resume if you have to restart your Mac.

SuperSpool has no special features for managing files being printed by various users on a network. Everyone on a network can simultaneously use SuperSpool to print to a network-compatible ImageWriter, but you can't control the order of files printed. Each spooler sends its file to the ImageWriter, and has to wait if the printer is busy. (With the LaserWriter version of this program, you can assign priority levels to spooled documents on a network—as described later.)

On the other hand, most ImageWriters aren't on networks or aren't used by many different users at the same time if they are. SuperSpool can return control of your Mac to you in seconds, which means far more productive Mac time than if you had to wait for the printout to finish.

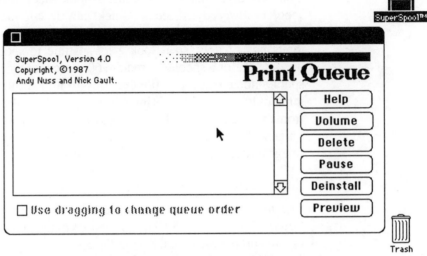

Figure 8–1. SuperSpool's print queue can be rearranged.

LaserWriter Spoolers

The three most popular LaserWriter spoolers are Apple's PrintMonitor, Super LaserSpool, and LaserSpeed. Since Print Monitor is supplied for free to use in every Mac's System Folder from version 4.2 on, we'll look at it first.

PrintMonitor

PrintMonitor works only if you're running the MultiFinder. Because it's an Apple product supplied for the System Folder, PrintMonitor interacts more closely with other System Folder tools. PrintMonitor consists of two products: an Init program called Backgrounder, which is installed in your System Folder, and the PrintMonitor application itself. You can install these resources either by using Apple's Installer program or by dragging them both into your System Folder. When you install PrintMonitor, it creates a spool folder inside your System Folder.

Once you've installed PrintMonitor, you must make sure the MultiFinder is set up for print spooling and that you have selected the LaserWriter as your printer. To do this you select the Chooser desk accessory, click on the

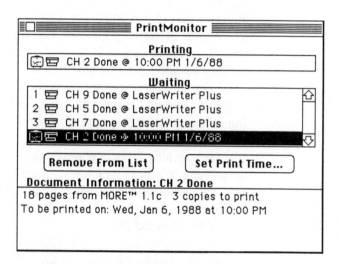

Figure 8–2. PrintMonitor presents a new dialog box after you confirm the settings in your LaserWriter's print dialog box.

LaserWriter icon, and then click the button to turn background printing on. Once you've finished these steps, you can select PrintMonitor options by selecting it from the Apple menu and displaying a window like the one in Figure 8–2.

When the PrintMonitor window appears, you can decide whether to print the file immediately, delay printing of the file indefinitely, or set a specific time and date in the future for the file to be printed. While documents are printing, you can bring up the PrintMonitor window any time by either choosing it from the Apple menu (it is listed underneath the MultiFinder at the bottom of the menu) or by double-clicking on its icon in the System Folder.

From a special File menu that appears when you activate PrintMonitor you can close PrintMonitor's window or set two preferences: whether to display the the spooler's window during printing and whether to display an alert dialog box if there's a problem with your printer.

The PrintMonitor window gives you a lot of information about the files in your print queue. You'll see the file name of each document being printed, along with the name of the LaserWriter it will be printed on. (You can print different files to different LaserWriters from the same queue just by selecting printers with the Chooser.) If a filename has a number on it, the number indicates the order in which the file will be printed from the queue. A clock icon in front of the name indicates that you've set that file to be printed some time in the future. A dash in front of a filename means that you have chosen to delay the file's printing indefinitely.

You can rearrange the files in the queue simply by dragging them to a different place on the list; you can cancel printing of a file or remove files from the queue; and you can pause or resume the printing of the current file. A handy extra feature is PrintMonitor's alert boxes that display messages when your printer is out of paper or there's another problem interfering with the printing. You use a Preferences command inside PrintMonitor if you want the alerts displayed as soon as a problem occurs, or you can have them stored in a special file so you can look at them later (although why you would want to do this is beyond us!).

PrintMonitor is a reasonably functional spooler that works well with the MultiFinder and is easy to use. It uses the same crash recovery technique as the other spoolers. It's also about as fast as the other two spoolers we discuss here. But you can't prioritize printing jobs from several users on a network with PrintMonitor, and it won't handle custom laser prep files. On the other hand, PrintMonitor comes free with System version 4.2 or later.

Super LaserSpool

This spooler from Supermac Software Technologies is very fast and offers all the necessary features plus a few extras. One key advantage it has over PrintMonitor is that it runs under the regular Finder. Super LaserSpool is an application program that you set to load every time on startup with the Set Startup command. You can specify a second application to start up after Super LaserSpool. The program also comes with a desk accessory, called Laser Queue, which you use to monitor or adjust the activity of the print queue. Super LaserSpool is sold as a single-user product for $149 or in a multiuser version (which is simply five copies of the program) for $395.

As with other spoolers, Super LaserSpool stores files you print in a spool folder. To inspect the print queue, you choose the Laser Queue desk accessory, which brings up a window like the one in Figure 8–3.

Using this window, you can rearrange the order of files in the queue, pause or resume printing of a file, or remove files from the queue. If you select a file, you can produce a page preview of any page in that file by clicking a button in the Laser Queue dialog box. The page is shown in miniature in front of the dialog box, as Figure 8–4 shows.

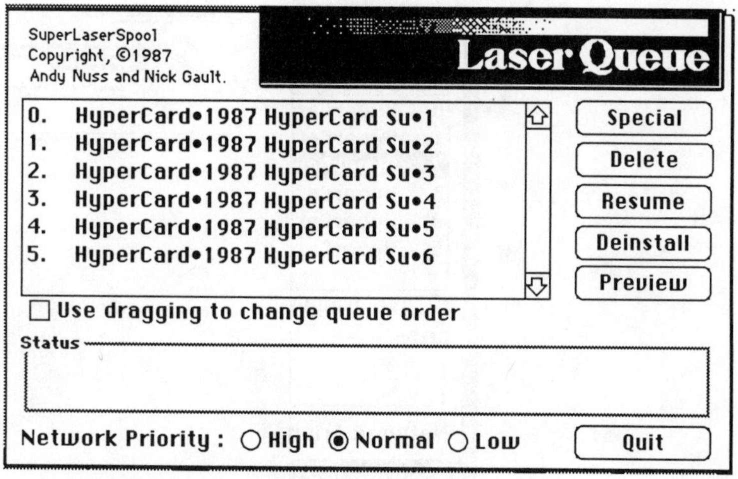

Figure 8–3. From Super LaserSpool's window you can monitor the activity of the print queue.

With Super LaserSpool you can also set the network priority of a file, so you can bypass the other jobs spooled on a network. To use it, you set a numeric priority level for your document, and if your document is set to a higher priority number than those from other users, it will be printed first. Of course, what often happens is that everyone wants his or her job printed first, and everyone sets a job's priority to the highest level. When this happens, documents are printed on a first-come, first-served basis, just as they are with other spoolers.

Super LaserSpool offers the same crash recovery feature as other spoolers, and it is compatible with the Aldus prep file. It alerts you when something is wrong with your printer, but it only beeps, instead of giving you a specific message like you see with PrintMonitor and LaserSpeed.

Super LaserSpool is the best-selling commercial spooler because it was the first of its kind and because it's slightly faster than the others. It's the most expensive spooler program of the three compared here, but you get what you pay for. It isn't compatible with the MultiFinder at this writing, but Version 2.0 of the program, scheduled for release in June 1988, will be.

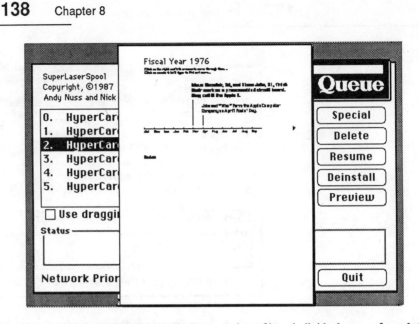

Figure 8–4. Super LaserSpool can display a preview of how individual pages of spooled files will look when they are printed.

LaserSpeed

LaserSpeed is a spooler from Think Technologies. It sells for $69, and it is sold as both an Init program and a desk accessory called LaserSpeed. You use a special installer supplied with the program to install the DA on the Apple menu.

This program covers all the basics. Once you've spooled a file, you can use the LaserSpeed DA to look at the print queue, change the order of files, pause or resume printing, or remove files from the queue. LaserSpeed is slightly slower than Super LaserSpool at spooling a file because it does preprocessing. However, that makes LaserSpeed run more efficiently in the background once your file is printing; with LaserSpeed you can switch to another application as your file prints. The overall printing speed is about the same as with the other spoolers.

LaserSpeed also has particularly informative alert boxes. If your printer is out of paper, for example, the box tells you so.

Finally, LaserSpeed has a crash recovery provision from its spool folder, and it is compatible with Aldus' laser prep file. It is also compatible with the MultiFinder.

LaserSpeed is a good, basic, and inexpensive spooler for the Laser-Writer. If you don't need the extra bells and whistles of Super LaserSpool and you want a spooler to run under the regular Finder, you can save yourself some money with LaserSpeed.

In the beginning, there were no print spoolers for the Mac. Then, early Macintosh spoolers were all buggy and inefficient. Now, there are several good spoolers to choose from, any of which will give you much more productive computing time on your Mac.

CHAPTER

9

Backing Up a Hard Disk

Computers are pretty reliable—so much so that it's easy to take that reliability for granted. You go along, merrily creating data and storing it on a disk, and then one day, you can't read the disk any more, or your computer breaks down. If your computer breaks down you can always get another computer, but if the disk where you store your data becomes unreadable, you lose your data.

If you lose your data, you've lost the hours, weeks, months, or even years it took to create it. This is an especially terrible prospect with a hard disk, because it almost always contains a lot of data. The way to protect yourself against data loss is to make a *backup*—a second copy of your data stored on tape, floppy disks, or another mass storage device. That way, you can get your data from someplace else if your hard disk goes out.

This is the most important chapter in the book. It covers the why and how of backing up the data and programs on your hard disk. Having a backup can let you keep right on working if your hard disk breaks down, while not having a backup can put you out of action. There are a lot of backup options, some of which are so painless that you don't even know you're protecting your data. But whichever backup option you choose, stick with it and do it regularly.

Why People Don't Back Up

Sad to say, most of the hard disk users out there don't have adequate backups of their programs and data. (If your hard disk went out right now, how much data and how many programs could you replace?) There are three reasons why people don't adequately back up their data:

1. *It's Not Necessary.* Even if you know backing up a disk is a good thing, you can often put it off. The reasoning is that the hard disk is working perfectly, and there's no reason to suspect that it won't work when you sit down tomorrow. Unfortunately, hard disk or computer problems usually don't announce themselves—they just happen from one minute to the next. So backups are *always* necessary, because you never know when you'll need them. If you're ever in doubt about whether you should back up or not, just ask yourself how you'd get along without the files you'd lose if your disk went out that very second.

2. *It's a Hassle.* Yes, backing up takes time. You have to run a backup program and wait while the data is copied from one medium to the other, or you have to manually copy files from disk to disk. At the end of the day, when you should be backing up your files, heading home seems a lot more attractive than watching files get copied or feeding backup disks into your Mac. Again, when in doubt, ask yourself whether you can afford to lose the data you haven't backed up. If you really can't stand staring at your Mac during backups, there are alternative backup systems that will take care of the backup problem for you when you're not looking, as we'll see later in this chapter.

3. *It's Too Expensive.* Backing up 10 or 20 megabytes of data onto floppy disks requires a lot of floppy disks, and you'll probably have to buy a bunch of new floppies just for that purpose. A box of floppy disks costs about $20. But the cost is nothing compared with the days or weeks you'll spend trying to re-create lost data that you haven't backed up.

How Do You Know You Need a Backup?

The rule of thumb about how often you should back up your files is this: Back it up whenever you would be really annoyed if you lost what you had just done. Sometimes this can be a whole morning's work, other times it can be just one sentence or spreadsheet formula. If you're like most people, even 15 or 20 minutes' work is too much to lose, so you should back up your files at least that often by saving twice—once onto your hard disk and once onto a backup floppy. That way, if your disk suddenly becomes unreadable, you can retrieve your file from the floppy and you'll only have lost a few minutes' work at most. The process of saving files twice like this is called *file backup*, but there are two other types of backups, as well.

Three Types of Backups

Each of the three different backup options has its place in protecting against data loss. These are the three options:

- A *file backup* is a copy of an individual file that you have placed on another disk.
- A *complete backup* is a copy of all the files and folders on a hard disk. It preserves the organization of your hard disk on several floppy disks.
- An *incremental backup* is a copy of the files you've changed or added to your hard disk since the last complete backup or since the last incremental backup.

Let's look at these different backup options in detail.

File Backups

A file backup is simply a copy of a file you store on another disk. When you drag a file icon from your hard disk to a floppy disk, you're making a file backup. Some application programs (Microsoft Word, for example) have a built-in backup option that automatically saves a second copy of a file. The problem with this kind of backup option is that the backup copy is saved on the same disk as the original copy, so if the disk becomes unreadable, you lose both copies.

As mentioned earlier, it's simple to make file backups as you work by keeping a backup floppy disk in your internal drive and saving each file twice—once to the hard disk and once to the floppy. This will protect most, if not all, of your important data files.

To make the process of file backups as convenient as possible, make backup floppy disks that correspond to folders on your hard disk. That way, when you're working on a particular project, all the files associated with that project will be on one floppy, and you don't have to do a lot of disk-swapping to make backups. (Some of the folders at the top level of your disk's organization may contain too much data to be saved onto one floppy. If so, create floppies that duplicate folders nested at the second organizational level, inside the top level folders.)

You should get into the habit of making file backups as you work, saving a second copy of every file, every time you save. That way, you'll always have a current backup available.

Complete Backups: Using a Backup Utility

A complete backup involves storing a complete copy of your hard disk's files and organization on another medium, either floppy disks, a backup tape, or another large storage device. To make a complete backup onto floppy disks (the most common method), you run a backup utility program and then insert a series of numbered floppy disks as the program asks for them.

You could make a complete copy of your hard disk manually, by dragging files and folders to floppy disks, but backup utility programs make the job easier in a couple of ways. First, they fill each floppy disk to capacity, so there's no wasted space. Sometimes, this means splitting large files—beginning the copy at the end of one floppy disk and finishing the copy on a second floppy disk.

Second, backup utilities create a directory of all the backed up files, and you can easily recover some or all of the files from the backup floppies by selecting them from a list on the screen. To restore a file, you use the backup utility's restore option and select the files you want to restore. To begin a file restoration, you must insert the first in the series of backup floppies, because the directory of files is located there. The utility checks the directory for the location(s) of the file(s) you want to restore, then prompts you to insert the right floppies so it can read the files.

Another good reason to use a backup utility when you make a complete backup is that the backup utility copies files to floppies much more quickly than the Finder does. Most backup utilities compress files as they save them to disk, so they can store more files on a floppy than normal and cut down the number of floppies you need for a backup.

The only possible drawback to using a backup utility is that some utilities compress files in a special format when they save them, and you must use the same utility to restore the files—you can't simply open files on backup floppies from the Finder or an application program. (Most popular backup programs don't compress files, though, or they compress them in such a way that you can still open them from the Finder.) The other problem with a complete backup is that it takes some time—20 minutes or more, depending on the number of files you're backing up and the specific backup utility you use (some are faster than others).

A faster, more convenient way to back up a hard disk is to use a tape drive system designed especially for making backups. Usually, all your data will fit on one tape cartridge, so there are no floppy disks to swap, and tape backups tend to be much faster than floppy backups. These systems are described in more detail later.

Whichever backup method you choose, you should make a complete backup regularly, anywhere from every week to every month or two, depending on the amount of new information you put on your disk during a given period. Even though you will be making file backups daily, and you'll be preparing incremental backups (described next), doing a complete backup regularly ensures that you can always restore a recent version of the complete contents and organization of your hard disk.

Incremental Backups

Incremental backups are also made with a floppy disk backup utility or a tape system, and are used to make sure you have backup copies of every new or changed file on your disk. An incremental backup copies every file that is new or has been changed since the last complete backup. Even though you make file backups as you work, there are always other files on your disk that you don't think to copy manually. These include:

- New Init, FKey, or Chooser resource files you may have downloaded from a bulletin board.
- Public domain programs or desk accessories that you copied off a floppy disk.
- Application programs and their associated files.
- Data files you made minor changes to and forgot to back up with the file method at the time.

In some cases, files like this seem too insignificant to back up onto floppy disks, and in others, you have a copy of the original program disk and assume that's good enough. But making a separate backup copy of these files after you've been using them is a good idea, because:

- You may not have another copy of the file.
- Some program files change as you use them, such as spelling checker dictionaries or preferences files in programs like Word or Excel, and you want to have a copy of the current version of these files.

- You may not remember where you put your original copy of a file, especially if it's a small program.
- You may have reused or lost the disk that once contained the original copy of a program.

An incremental backup avoids problems like this by backing up everything new on your disk since the last complete backup. You must use the same backup utility to make an incremental backup as you used to make the complete backup, because the utility reads the original backup's directory and compares it with the current directory of your hard disk, saves the changes either onto new disks or the existing disks, and then updates the backup directory. While a complete backup requires numerous floppies and takes 20 minutes or more, an incremental backup may consume only one or two floppies and require only a few minutes, depending on the number of new files to be copied.

It's hard to tell how often you need to make an incremental backup, because incremental backups are designed to archive files you've forgotten to copy. (If you had remembered to copy all your changed files with the file backup method, you wouldn't need an incremental backup at all.) The best approach is to choose a specific interval and stick with it. If you make a complete backup once a month, make an incremental backup every Friday. If you make a complete backup once every two weeks, make an incremental backup twice a week. It really depends on the level of disk activity, and the number of changes you feel you need to make to files such as application preference files, spelling dictionaries, and the like.

How Floppy Disk Backup Software Works

Most hard disks (including Apple's) are shipped with floppy disk backup software, either the vendor's own brand or something acquired from a third party. If your hard disk didn't come with floppy backup software (the program you run to copy a hard disk's data onto multiple floppy disks), you can buy it for $30–$60. There is also software supplied with tape backup devices, but we'll get to that in the section on backup hardware. All floppy backup programs perform the same functions. The differences are speed and the interface used. Let's look at the basic operations of backup software, then see how three popular backup programs handle the job.

Backup Options

Backup utilities generally give you three backup options: a complete disk backup, an incremental backup, and a single (or selected) file backup. Once you select the option you want, you choose the hard disk volume you want to back up. Some programs, like HDBackup, automatically display all the hard disk volumes you have connected to your Mac, and you choose the one you want by clicking a button. Otherwise, you select a hard disk volume by navigating to it with a Standard File box.

When you perform a complete disk backup, the software does the following:

1. Calculates how many disks (or 400K sides of disks) you will need to make the backup you have chosen, then displays the number. (The incremental and single file backup options generally don't spell out the number of disks you'll need.) That way, you can make sure you have enough disks available.

2. Prompts you to insert floppy disks, one after the other. If the disk you're using is newly formatted or has other information on it, the program tells you the contents of the disk will be destroyed during the backup. If the disk is new, you may be asked to initialize it, or the backup program will initialize it automatically.

3. Reads and verifies each disk as you insert it to make sure there are no bad sectors that might corrupt your hard disk's files. (You wouldn't want to back up your data onto a disk that has problems to begin with.)

4. Gives each floppy disk a consecutive number, usually starting with 1. If you can use two floppy disk drives, most backup programs will switch from one disk to the other automatically as a disk is filled. (This saves you from having to insert new disks so often.)

5. Verifies the copy for each backup disk to make sure there were no errors during the writing process.

During an incremental backup, you use a different set of floppy disks from those that store the complete backup. Again, you insert disks one by one. Each incremental backup you do requires additional disks, because it makes copies of the files that have been changed since the last complete backup.

A single file backup is just the backup of one file or a selected group of files. You can backup individual files using the Save As... command inside your application program, but the single file backup option in a backup utility is usually used to back up a file that is too large to store on one disk. With a large file like this, the single file backup option splits the file onto two disks.

Another use for single file backups is when you only want to back up certain parts of a disk. The complete and incremental backup options back up everything—you don't get a choice about what to copy. But sometimes, you don't want the backup program to copy certain files. If you have floppy disk versions of application programs, for example, and you know those program files never change as you use the program, you really don't need to make another backup copy. In this case, you could filter those files out of the backup process by choosing to back up individual files or selected groups of files.

File Restoration Options

Naturally, the point of having a backup is being able to use it if your disk has problems. If you run into disk trouble and end up having to reformat your hard disk (see Chapter 15), a backup will enable you to recreate all your hard disk files just as they were. Backup programs offer at least two—and usually three—different options for restoring files.

The two options found in every backup program are restoring all files and restoring individual files. The restore all files option simply copies all files from your backup floppies back onto the hard disk, recreating the same file and folder organization it had originally. To perform such a restoration, you choose the option to restore all files, then insert the backup floppies by number, as you are prompted.

When you restore files from a complete backup, you can select the destination volume where you want to restore the files. The volume can be an entire hard disk (in the event your hard disk has become unreadable and you had to reformat it), or simply a portion of a different hard disk. So you can restore a backup not only to the disk from which it was originally made, but to a subsection of a different disk. If you backed up your 20 megabyte hard disk and then had to send it out for repairs, for example, you could restore the backup to a large folder on a 40 megabyte hard disk.

If your backup software doesn't have an option to restore an incremental backup (restoring only the files changed since the last complete backup), the option to restore all files incorporates incremental backups as well. In the HDBackup program supplied with Apple hard disks, for example, the Restore Files option will ask you to first insert the disks from the complete backup, then it will ask you to insert disks from the incremental backup. Other backup utilities, like HFS Backup, have a separate option for restoring incremental backups.

The other option every backup utility has is to restore individual or selected files. With this option you can restore long files that spread over two disks or individual folders that span two or three disks.

Backup Software

Now, let's look at four backup programs in action.

HDBackup

HDBackup is the utility supplied with Apple hard disks. Actually, it comes with all new Apple System software, even if the computer you buy doesn't have a hard disk. This program was written by PBI Software and is licensed to Apple.

All of HDBackup's options are controlled from one dialog box, as shown in Figure 9–1.

The list of hard disks is great, as long as you have five hard disks or less online. The list can only contain five hard disks, and if you want to back up a sixth volume that isn't online, you have to shut down one of the other hard disks so the sixth volume's name appears in the window. For anyone with fewer than five hard disks connected to their Mac, however, this method of selecting the disk is simpler than navigating to the disk you want to back up through a Standard File box.

You'll notice in Figure 9–1 that HDBackup has three backup and two restore options. There is no option to restore incremental backups, because the Restore all files option handles restoration of incremental backups automatically.

The other thing about HDBackup is that its Back up a single file option does just that, and no more. If you want to back up a specific group of files, like those in one particular folder, you have to back them up one at a time with

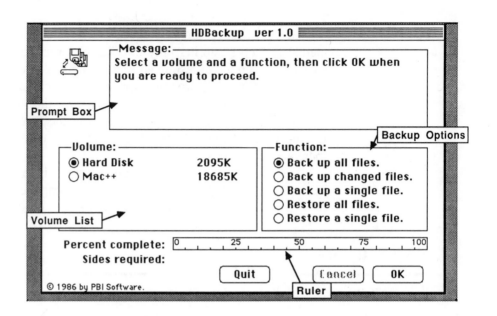

Figure 9–1. HDBackup's screen includes a prompt box, a list of the hard disks you have
connected to your Mac, buttons for various backup and restore options, and
a ruler that shows the progress of the backup.

HDBackup. The screen displays a list of files and folders on the disk, and you
navigate to individual files just like you would in a Standard File box. Other
programs let you select a whole group of files and then back them up all at
once, which is far more convenient.

HFS Backup

HFS Backup is the program supplied with MacBottom hard disk drives from
Personal Computer Peripherals Corporation (PCPC). It is also sold commercially for users of other hard disks.

Rather than displaying a dialog box when it loads, HFS Backup shows
a blank desktop with File, Edit, and Goodies menus. The File menu contains
the backup and restore commands.

When you choose the Backup command on the File menu, you see a
dialog box that lists the volumes currently connected to your Mac and
contains buttons for backing up an entire volume, backing up only the
changes on a volume, or backing up selected files, as shown in Figure 9–2.

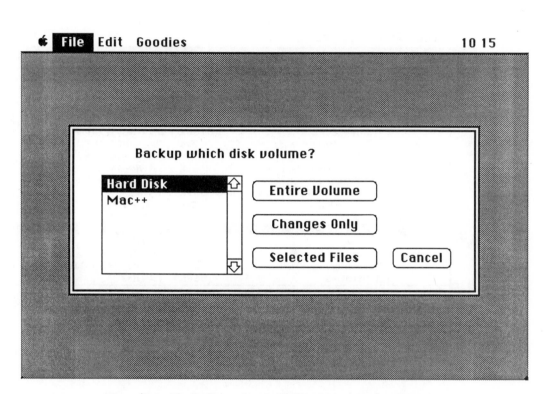

Figure 9–2. The backup options in HFS Backup appear in a dialog box.

You click on the volume you want to back up and then click the appropriate backup option button.

Once you choose the backup option, HFS Backup displays a list of all the files and folders on the disk, with the folders in alphabetical order. If you want to select individual files to back up, you choose the Display by File command from the Goodies menu to list all the disk's files (without folders) in alphabetical order, as shown in Figure 9–3.

Unlike HDBackup, HFS Backup can restore files from an incremental backup separately. The Restore Changed Files option in the Restore dialog box causes the program to search the directory from the complete disk backup and compare it with the current hard disk directory. It then restores all the files that have changed since the last complete backup.

HFS Backup comes free with MacBottom hard disks and sells for $50 retail to other hard disk owners.

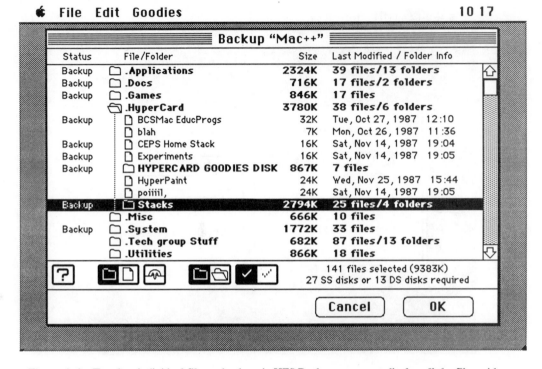

Figure 9–3. To select individual files to back up in HFS Backup, you must display all the files without folders. Files you select for backup display the word *Backup* next to the filename.

DiskFit

DiskFit is the most versatile hard disk backup program currently on the market. It's the only backup utility that you can use to back up your hard disk files to floppy disks, another hard disk, a high-capacity disk such as a Bernoulli Box or MegaDrive cartridge, a tape backup device, or any combination of these. In addition, DiskFit's backup options are a little more flexible: You can perform file, incremental, and complete disk backups, but you can also choose to back up only applications or only documents on your disk. (This is handy if you already have copies of your application programs on floppy disks.)

Another unique feature of DiskFit is that it will run in background under the MultiFinder. You can start a backup with DiskFit, then switch to another application under MultiFinder and start working. As it needs disks inserted for the backup, DiskFit will display a message asking for them.

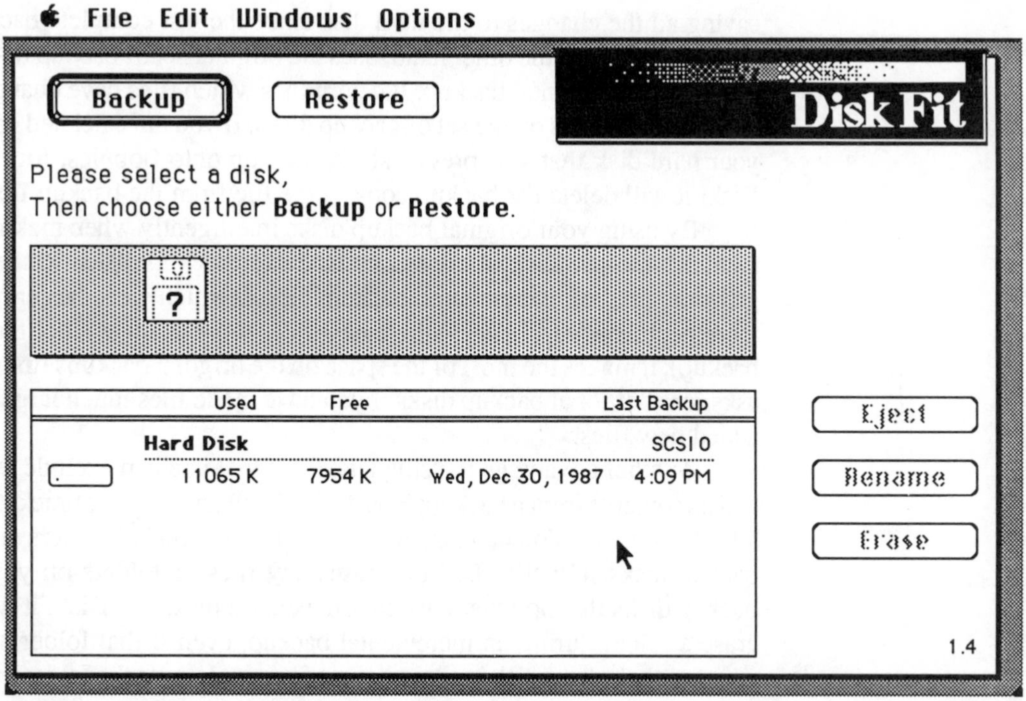

File Edit Windows Options

Figure 9–4. The DiskFit screen shows you the disks you have available for backup, how much space is used on each disk, and when you last backed up each disk.

As with other programs, DiskFit scans your source disk to determine how many backup disks or volumes will be needed, and then asks you to insert backup disks one at a time. When it's finished backing up your disk, DiskFit can automatically print a report that describes which files are on each backup disk. It all starts from the main DiskFit screen, as shown in Figure 9–4.

The DiskFit screen shows the name of each volume currently available to your Mac, along with the free and used space on each disk, and the date and time when you last backed up your disk. There's also an Options menu where you can choose to have DiskFit automatically format new backup disks as you insert them or verify disks after it has written to them. But DiskFit goes beyond other programs with some other added features.

One big difference is with incremental backups. Other backup programs, as explained before, create a separate set of incremental backup disks, saving all the changes to the hard disk since the last complete backup was made. DiskFit, on the other hand, uses the original set of backup disks when it does an incremental backup. It determines which files have changed, then changes those files on the set of backup disks. If you have deleted a file from your hard disk that was previously backed up onto floppies, for example, DiskFit will delete the backup copy of the file from the backup floppy.

By using your original backup disks intelligently when making incremental backups, DiskFit consumes far fewer backup disks. Rather than a growing pile of incremental backup disks (which gets larger for each incremental backup, because there have been more changes since the last full backup), it makes the most of the space on the original backups first and only asks for additional backup disks if you have made files much larger or have added new files.

Another advantage to using DiskFit is that you can exclude any folder and its contents from a backup. You do this by placing square brackets around a folder's name. You can also use this feature to archive folders on a set of backup disks. Usually, DiskFit erases any files or folders on your set of backup disks that no longer appear on the hard disk. But DiskFit will never erase a folder during an incremental backup, even if that folder no longer appears on the hard disk you're copying from, as long as the folder has square brackets around its name.

DiskFit stores files on backup disks in their regular Macintosh format, so you can open them with your application programs if something should happen to the DiskFit program. (The only exception is with large files that are split onto two or more disks.) When restoring files, you can only restore the complete backup or selected split files; you can't use DiskFit to restore individual files (you just drag files from the backup disks to your hard disk in the Finder to do this).

At $74.95, DiskFit is more expensive than many other backup programs, but it does a lot more by offering a choice of backup media and conserving disk space. It's also about twice as fast (about 200K per minute) as most other backup programs, and it comes with an excellent manual.

Fastback

Fastback is a backup program that claims speed as a great selling point. It can back up a hard disk onto floppy disks at an average rate of 1 megabyte per minute, compared with only 100K or 200K per minute, as with other

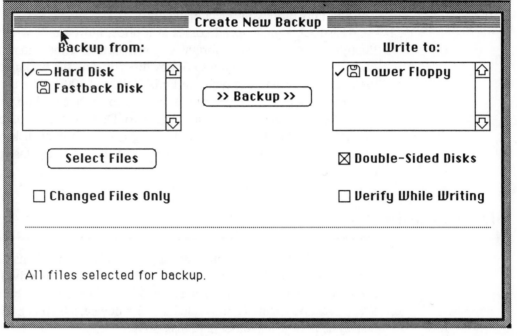

Figure 9–5. Fastback provides one window from which you can select source and backup volumes and choose other backup options.

programs. Fastback achieves this speed by reading data from your hard disk at the same time that it writes the data to a floppy disk. Other backup programs must read hard disk data first, then write it afterward.

From the main backup window displayed by Fastback you select the hard disk volume you want to back up, as well as the floppy disk drive where you want to write backups, as shown in Figure 9–5.

The window also contains options to verify each backed-up file as it is written, to back up selected files only, or to back up only the files that have changed since the last backup. The changed files option provides an incremental backup. These backups are made to additional floppy disks, as with most backup programs. The Selected Files option lets you manually select files or folders to back up, or it can automatically select files that have changed since a date you specify. As such, Fastback offers the three basic backup options: a complete backup, a file backup, and an incremental backup. When you need to restore files, Fastback can copy back all files on a disk or only those you select manually.

Fastback's great speed comes at a price, however. It writes files to floppy disks in a proprietary format, so you must use Fastback to restore files. Fastback will back up only onto floppy disks, and all the backup disks you use must be the same size; you can't mix 400K and 800K disks in a backup.

Fastback retails for $99, so it's the most expensive backup program on the market. It lacks some of the intelligence of DiskFit in terms of letting you use different media for backups or recycling space on backup disks when you perform incremental backups, but it is three to five times faster than its competitors.

Backup Hardware

If you really think backing up onto floppy disks is too much hassle (and it might very well be if you're using a 40, 60, or 80 megabyte drive), you can spend some extra money and get a dedicated backup device. This might be a tape backup system, a removable hard disk device, a high-capacity floppy disk system, or just another hard disk drive.

Tape Backup Systems

Tape backup systems back your files up onto tape cartridges. They are sold either as standalone units or in a combination unit along with a hard disk, and they cost from about $800 on up. The tapes used by these systems are either 1/8-inch cassette-like cartridges or 1/4-inch cartridges. Tape systems come with software that you use to back up and restore your files in various ways, and in some systems, you can set the software to back your hard disk up automatically at preset intervals. A typical tape backup system is shown in Figure 9–6.

Tape drives are fast and convenient. In most cases, your entire hard disk can be stored on one or two tapes, so you don't have to do a lot of swapping. You simply start the system's software, tell it to back up your hard disk, and sit back and relax. Tape drives use high-speed motors, and some of them can back up 20 megabytes of data in under 10 minutes, although most are considerably slower.

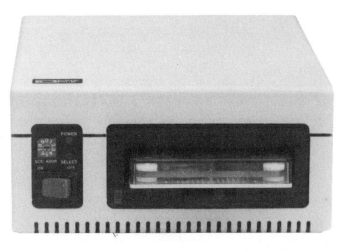

Figure 9–6. A tape backup system like this uses cartridges to back up your data.

In choosing a tape drive, you should consider four factors:

- The capacity of the tapes versus the size of your hard disk
- What kinds of backup options the system offers
- Whether you may need to run one backup tape on more than one tape drive
- Whether it will restore consistently (some tape drives are unreliable)

Try to match the capacity of your hard disk to the capacity of the tape cartridge. Tape cartridges for the Macintosh range in capacity from 20 to 60 megabytes. Obviously, you're better off having a tape drive that can back up your entire hard disk on one tape cartridge. The higher the capacity, the more expensive the tape drive, however—the price difference between a 20 megabyte backup system and a 60 megabyte backup system is about $500— so you may want to save money by buying a smaller drive and swapping a couple of tapes during the process. This strategy particularly makes sense if you don't use the full capacity of your hard disk.

Most tape systems let you back up your disk in the same ways floppy backup software offers. You can choose from image (complete) backups, incremental backups, or file-by-file backups. An *image backup* is a complete snapshot of everything on your hard disk, dumped onto tape. This is the fastest backup method (most units run at something like 3–4 minutes for every 10 megabytes), but to restore from an image backup, you must restore the entire backup—you can't restore individual files from an image backup.

File-by-file backups are more like the complete backups you get with backup utility software. Files are copied one at a time to the tape, and a directory is created on the tape so you can restore all the files or just selected files. You can automatically copy all files at once, or just individual files or groups of files.

Incremental backups are file-type backups with which you also get a directory and can restore selected files, and they back up all the files that have been changed since the last file-by-file backup. Every backup system available for the Mac offers image and file-by-file backups; fewer offer incremental backups.

Another backup option you may want to look for is *timed backups:* the ability to preset intervals at which your disk is backed up automatically. This makes your backups truly worry-free, because the system itself always remembers to make backups for you. Mirror Technologies and Peak Systems both offer backup units that have timed backups.

The last major consideration in selecting a tape backup unit is compatibility. If you're just buying a tape drive to back up your own Mac, it doesn't matter too much which one you choose. But if you work in an office where several hard disks will be backed up and where there are other tape drives, you should get the same kind of drive other people are already using. Obviously, your 1/8-inch backup cartridge won't fit in a 1/4-inch tape drive, but even tapes that are the same size usually won't work on systems from different manufacturers. This has to do with the software each manufacturer uses and the specific technology used to record data onto the tape. If there are other tape drives in use where you work, you may as well get the same type of drive. Then, if your tape drive ever breaks, you can recover your files using someone else's drive.

Tape/Hard Disk Combinations

Another hardware option is a combination unit that offers both a tape drive and a hard disk. You won't save much money over buying the two devices separately, but at least you'll have them both in the same unit, as shown in Figure 9–7. The combination unit cuts down on the desk space you have to give up for your storage peripherals.

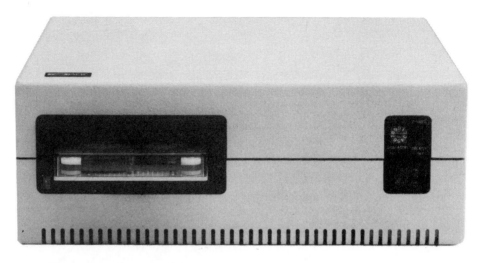

Figure 9–7. Some hard disk systems come with a built-in tape drive for backups.

The big problem with these units is that if the power supply goes out, *both* your hard disk and tape backup unit will be out of action. Unless you know somebody else with the same unit, you'll lose your ability to recover backed-up files from the tape at the same time you lose access to your hard disk.

Alternative Backup Devices

Tape drives are made specifically to back up hard disks. They're slower to recover individual files than a disk system, because the drive must advance or rewind the tape for several seconds to reach the specific file you need, while a disk's head can move directly to it. This doesn't matter much if you don't restore backed up files very often, but it can be a real pain if you do.

Alternative backup devices such as large capacity floppy disks, Bernoulli boxes, or redundant hard disks give you a backup as well as fast access to your data. In fact, you can use these for day-to-day storage as well as for backups, if you have to.

Removable Media Devices

There are now a couple of different mass storage devices with removable media. Like a floppy disk drive, you have an unlimited storage capacity, because you can keep swapping disks in and out. But instead of 800K disks, the disks on mass storage devices have capacities of 5 to 20 megabytes.

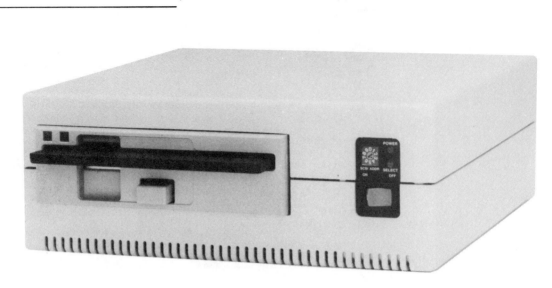

Figure 9–8. A Bernoulli box uses high-capacity flexible disk cartridges to store data.

The oldest of these devices is the Bernoulli Box from Iomega, which uses either 5 or 10 megabyte cartridges that contain what is basically a large floppy disk, as shown in Figure 9–8. (Bernoulli technology is covered in more detail in Chapter 1.) Bernoulli Boxes are expensive, however: Ten megabyte drives cost about $1300. Data cartridges cost about $60 each. Another drawback is that Bernoulli systems are noisier than other backup systems. Iomega once had a monopoly on Bernoulli systems, but now, other manufacturers, including Bering and Supermac, also sell Bernoulli-type units.

Another storage option is a high-capacity floppy disk drive, which uses the same floppy disk technology as your 800K drive, but with larger disks (about five inches in diameter) that pack data much more closely together. Jasmine Technologies sells a high-capacity product, MegaDrive, which uses 10 megabyte floppy disks, for about $1000. Disks for this unit are about $35 each. The MegaDrive's file reading and writing times are closer to those of a floppy drive than of a hard disk.

Finally, some people just buy a second hard disk and save all their data onto both hard disks, or use DiskFit to make a backup from one hard disk onto another. This option gives you the simplest recovery from a disk problem, because when one disk stops working you simply start using the other disk.

Which Backup to Choose?

Floppy backup programs and the various dedicated backup hardware options each have their place, depending on how you use your hard disk and how important your data is. Here are factors to consider.

- Floppy backup programs are generally fine for individual users doing basic productivity work on a Macintosh. It may take you 20 or 30 minutes to do a complete backup, but after that, you can make faster incremental backups for quite a while. If you're an individual user, you probably don't have that much data turnover on your disk, and if you generate an occasional complete backup, incremental backups, and daily file backups, you're perfectly safe.

- Tape backup devices are better suited for hard disks that contain a lot of important data that changes frequently. If your hard disk is on a network and several users share it, or if you are running a large database application where the data is constantly being updated, a tape backup gives you protection with a minimum of trouble. However, if your hard disk has to be sent out for repairs, you'll be stuck with the slow access times of the tape drive when you load programs and data, unless you can restore the files to another hard disk.

- Removable media storage devices are designed to work as a secondary storage system when you need to store specific groups of files or projects on separate disks, and you want reasonably fast access to them. If you use them for a backup, you can use Supermac's DiskFit backup program to back up a hard disk onto these larger removable disks.

- A second hard disk is really for people who want a second day-to-day mass storage device as much as or more than a way to back up their data.

Backup Strategies

Whichever backup method you choose, you should combine complete disk, incremental, and file backups in a regular routine to protect your data against a hard disk failure. Let's look at some guidelines for how you should use each type of backup.

Planning a Strategy

The best policy is to back up everything all the time, but few people do this. Realistically, you should consider just how important a backup is to you and your work. Before deciding how much trouble you'll go to in maintaining a backup of your data, sit down and ask yourself some questions about exactly what would happen if your hard disk was to suddenly stop working:

- How important are your hard disk files? Maybe many of them are from completed projects, and their loss wouldn't mean much.

- How many important files could you replace from other sources? You probably have floppy disk copies of the applications you're using, so a backup of those isn't crucial, but what about the data?

- Have most of your data files been printed out, so you could recover the information (however laboriously) by retyping data from printouts?

- Have you given copies of your files to other users who could provide them if needed?

- Are your important files also stored on a network server or on a larger computer somewhere else?

Give some thought to these issues, so you'll have a good sense of how important your data is, how much trouble you want to take to protect it (or restore it), and what level of data loss risk you think is acceptable. Once you've characterized the importance of your data, you're ready to implement a specific backup strategy using the options we've discussed earlier.

Three Sets of Disks

A good, continuous backup of your hard disk requires you to maintain three distinct sets of floppy disks:

- The disks containing a complete disk backup
- The disks containing one or more incremental backups
- The disks containing file backups

The complete disk backup is a set of several disks, labeled with numbers assigned by your backup program. Once you make a complete backup, you should store these disks in a safe place. Your concept of "a safe place" will depend on the importance of your data. Some people keep their complete backup disks right next to the computer with their other disks, while other people keep them in a safe deposit box. It all depends on how much risk you think is reasonable, given the data you're backing up.

Where to Store Backup Disks

If your hard disk contains files that are the life's blood of your business (accounting files, a large database, a customer list), you should store the backup disks in a different location: your house or another office site, for example. You could even use a safe deposit box, but you'd be limited to banking hours when you wanted to retrieve your disks. Keeping your backup disks in a separate location protects you against a fire, flood, or other disaster at the location where you keep the computer. With your backup stored at a different site, you would have to be very unlucky indeed to lose both your hard disk and your backup data.

When you select an alternate site, choose one that's convenient, so it's no trouble to take disks back and forth from your computer. That's why your house is a good bet. If you happen to work at home, store the disks in a separate place in your house that has better protection against fire or flood, or in a fireproof safe. (Note: There are different levels of fireproofing in safes, one for paper and one for magnetic media. Paper can handle more heat than disk media, so safes that protect disks in a fire are more expensive because they insulate better.)

If your data is less important, on the other hand, or if you could restore it from alternate sources if you had to, you're probably safe keeping your disks in the same place as your computer, or in your desk.

The disks from an incremental backup should be kept in the same place as the complete disk backups. This will not only give you the same amount of protection for your more up-to-date backups, but it will let you judge when it's time to make a new complete backup by comparing the number of incremental disks with the complete backup set (discussed next).

The file backup disks should be kept right next to your computer, because you'll be saving to them many times during each day. If you wanted to be totally safe, you might carry those disks home with you each night or else make an incremental backup at the end of each day and take its disk(s) to your alternate storage location.

When to Make Backups

A full disk backup should be done whenever you've made significant changes to your hard disk's contents or organization, or whenever your stack of incremental backup disks equals more than half the number in your full disk backup. If your full disk backup contains 15 disks, for example, and you get to the point where you have 7 or 8 incremental backup disks, it's time to make a new full backup. If you need to restore the contents of your hard disk, it's easier and faster to work from full disk backups as much as possible. (Since the incremental backup disks are simply updates to files that have already been restored by the full disk backup, you have to write some files to the disk twice during restoration.)

Using the number of incremental backup disks as a guide is an easy way to determine when you need a full disk backup. Otherwise, it can be hard to know exactly when you really need a full disk backup. You end up wondering whether adding one new folder at the top level of the disk is enough of an organizational change to merit a new full backup, for example. Incremental backups take most of the guesswork out of the process, but whenever you're in doubt about doing a backup, go ahead and do it.

As for incremental backups themselves, you should set a schedule for frequent backups and stick with it. Because you'll be using the file backup method to safeguard the data files you work with daily, you may not feel it's necessary to do an incremental backup very often. But remember, there are always files and file changes that you forget about, and that you don't protect with the file backup method. If you're a typical user working with a handful of files each day, an incremental backup once a week is probably adequate. If your files change a great deal, you should do an incremental backup once a day.

Day in and day out, your basic data protection will come from file backups. You can make these a lot easier if you create separate floppy disks that match folders you work with regularly. You don't have to be concerned with making floppies that match your application programs, unless you don't have a floppy disk copy of a particular program. Usually, though, the original program disk can serve as your backup.

If you have three hard disk folders called Jones, Smith, and Brown, for example, you should create floppy disks that match them. Then, as you work in each folder, you can keep the corresponding floppy disk in your internal drive and save onto it with the Save As... command after you save to your hard disk.

It Doesn't Work If You Don't Do It

Nobody ever recovered data lost in a hard disk crash by using backups they *should* have made. The only way to protect your data is to back it up regularly, faithfully, and completely. It's well worth a few minutes a day of extra work to avoid losing important data.

PART THREE

Supercharging a Hard Disk

CHAPTER

10

Disk Optimizing Utilities

A number of utility programs help you get the most out of your hard disk by enabling you to manage large numbers of files more easily or to protect specific files against unauthorized access. These programs fall into five categories:

- File-finding programs
- Disk cataloging programs
- Disk performance optimizers
- File compression and encryption programs
- General disk utility programs

In this chapter, we'll see how each type of program works and look at some examples of specific programs in each category.

File-Finding Programs

As you manage your hard disk's organization with HFS using folders to store other folders and files, it's easy to lose track of a specific file. You may spend a lot of time opening and closing folders and scrolling through lists of files to find the file you want. The solution is to get a file finder program.

File finders work as desk accessories or Init programs and help you locate a file when you type all or part of its name in a search window. A file finder searches through your entire hard disk (or another disk you have selected) and tells you the location of the files it finds. Most file finders can locate a file on a 20 megabyte hard disk in less than 10 seconds. (They often work faster; it depends on how deeply nested inside folders the file is.) In addition to searching a whole disk, most file finders can search only through a folder you indicate, which also speeds up the process.

You can differentiate among file finders by comparing these features:

- The number of different ways you can search for a file
- The number of disks that can be searched simultaneously
- The speed of the search
- How the path to each found file is displayed
- Whether you can open a found file from inside the file finder
- Whether you can store default folders to be searched or accessed each time
- Whether you can perform other file management functions—such as copying a file from one disk to another—from inside the file finder

File Search Criteria

If you have to resort to a file finder, it's possible you don't remember the complete name of the file you want. Most file finders search for either a complete name or for a set of characters that appear somewhere in the filename. If a file finder locates every file with a small string of characters in it, though, you may end up with a long list of found files to sort through. As an example, if you typed in the letters *cat*, the program would find the files *Cat*alog 1988, Appli*cat*ions Folder, and Black *Cat*.

It helps to be as specific with the search string as possible, but most file finders make the job easier by enabling you to search for a string at a certain position in the filename. If you remember that the file you want has a three-letter suffix, like SIT, for example, you can tell the program to find only the files with those letters at the end of the name. Most programs can search for a string at the beginning or end of a filename, as well as searching for it anywhere in the name. (It's faster to search for a string matching the beginning of a filename, because file finders search by matching the first letter in a name, then the second, and so on in sequence. If the program only has to match a few letters at the beginning of a name, it has less work to do.)

Along with searching for files by name, some of the more sophisticated file finders can search by the size of the file, the type of the file, the creator of the file (a code name that indicates which program was used to create the file), or even the date when a file was created or last modified. These extra options can help you zero in on specific files more easily, as long as you can remember the search information you need.

Searching Multiple Disks

Most file finders search only one disk or folder at a time, according to what you have selected. DiskTop, from CE Software, can search every available disk—one or more hard disks you have connected and floppy disks inserted into floppy drives. This may seem of little value (after all, you should at least know which disk the file you want is on), but it can actually be very useful in locating multiple copies or versions of the same file or searching multiple hard disks when you store data on more than one.

Performance

File finders should be as unobtrusive to use as possible, and that means they should be fast. As you'll see in the descriptions of specific file finders below, programs vary in the speed with which they can find one file. If a program has far more features than another, however, that should outweigh a minor difference in speed.

Displaying Found Files

Once they complete a search, file finders will either display the found files or tell you no files were found. Found files are displayed in a list, and depending on the program, the display may include buttons for opening the file or navigating directly to the file, as shown in Figure 10–1.

When the file list is first displayed, none of the files is selected, so no file paths are shown. To see the path of a file, you select that filename, and the path is displayed at the bottom of the screen, as in Figure 10–2.

Some first-generation file finders only show a file's location as a text path name. The file named Books in the folder Library on the disk Data would be shown as Data:Library:Books. (The path name is the technical term for the list showing which disk and folders your file is in. The left-most item in a text path name is always the disk name, and the rightmost item is the filename. In between these are all the nested folders along the way.) Most programs, however, display icons showing the disk and the folders in the file's path.

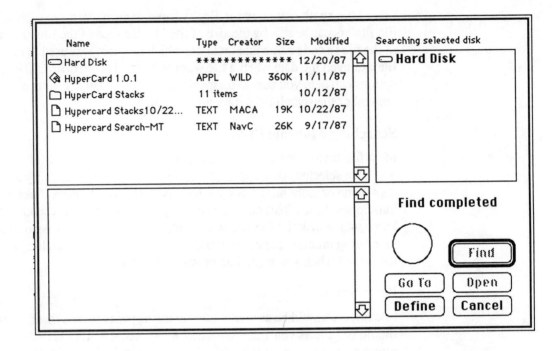

Figure 10–1. File finders show the results of a search by listing all the files that match your search criteria. In this case, the search string was "Hyper."

Working with Found Files

What you can do with a found file from inside a file finder also depends on the program. Low-end programs like Apple's Find File will only show you a file's path, and that's basically it. To actually open the file, you must quit Find File and open the file with your application program. Of course, it's far easier if you can open a file from inside the file finder's window by double-clicking on its name or clicking an Open button. Findswell, DiskTop, and HFS Navigator all can open found files from inside the file finder window, so you don't have to return to the application to do it.

With Findswell and HFS Navigator, you can only open a file if that file was created by the application you're currently running. With DiskTop, you can actually launch other application programs from the DiskTop window—DiskTop automatically quits your other application using its own Quit

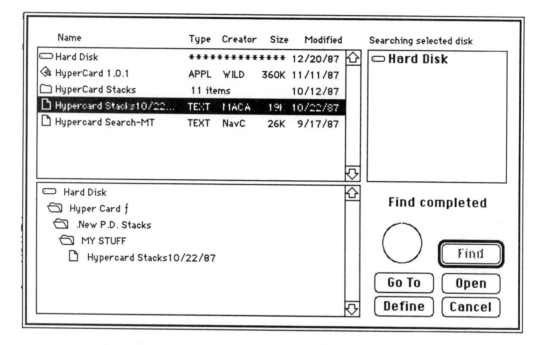

Figure 10–2. To see the path to a particular file, you select that filename in the file finder's window.

command (so you have a chance to save changed files you had open), then opens the new application.

Setting Default Folders

Another feature of the more advanced file finders is the ability to set default folders. Default folders always appear in the file finder's window when you first open the program or on a special menu that appears when you use the file finder. Being able to set default folders makes it much easier to get files from deeply nested folders that you use regularly. Rather than having to navigate to these folders manually whenever you want a file, the folders appear whenever you open the file finder, and you can open them up from the file finder's window. With default folders you can also specify a standard folder where you save files, which cuts down on navigation time during saves.

File Manipulation Features

The more advanced file finders offer extra features that you use to perform many of the Finder's tasks without leaving your application program. HFS Navigator and DiskTop, for example, can create new folders, rename files or folders, delete files, move files from folder to folder or disk to disk, or copy files. You can also use a Get Info command like the Finder's to get size, creation, and modification date, and creator information about a file. You can also see how large each file is, how large each disk is, how much space is available, and how much memory is available as well as in use. As mentioned before, DiskTop also can launch applications from its window. Having a full-featured file finder, therefore, saves you a lot of trips to the Finder.

But to really get a feel for how some of these programs work, let's take a close look at the most popular ones: DiskTop, HFS Navigator, Findswell, Find File, and DiskInfo.

DiskTop 3.0

DiskTop is currently the ultimate file finder, in our opinion. It was a shareware program available for $15 or $20 until late 1987, when version 3.0 came out and it went commercial for $49.95. DiskTop installs as a desk accessory on the Apple menu, but if you also install the DiskTop Init file in your hard disk's System Folder, you can activate DiskTop by typing a keyboard command. The default keyboard command is Command-Option-Shift-D, but you can easily change the keys to whatever you like.

DiskTop is designed to be much more than a file finder. The screen you see when you activate it is called the *disktop,* which is a desktop-like window showing disks you are using (or have been using) along with other information, as in Figure 10–3.

From this window, you can select and open disks to reveal their contents, you can erase or rename disks, and you can drag disks to the Trash Can to delete them. The Find button (you can also type Command-F) takes you to the DiskTop file-finding screen, shown in Figure 10–4, which you use to search for files using a variety of criteria.

As you can see, however, DiskTop is different from most other file finders in that you can only search by name one way, rather than being able to select which part of the filename you want the program to match. On the other hand, the other searching options enable you to do things you can't do with other file finders. If you specify 0K to 0K as Size criteria, for example, DiskTop will search only for folders. The more you narrow your search, the faster the search is.

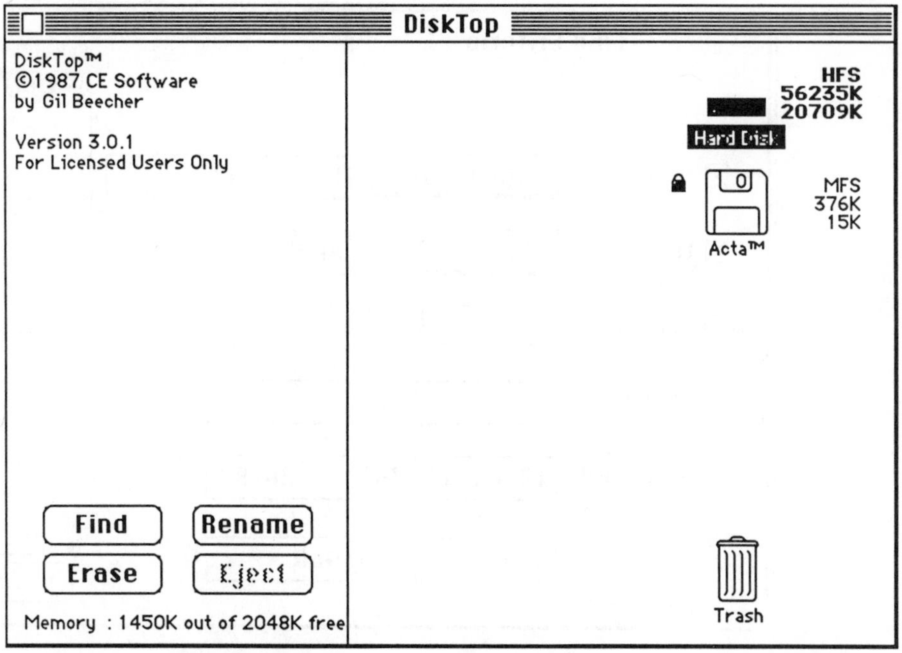

Figure 10–3. DiskTop's basic window shows the disks you have available, along with their sizes, amount of free space, and whether they're HFS or MFS disks. It also shows you how much memory your system has and how much is currently available.

When you find files with DiskTop, it shows them in a list (which appeared earlier in Figure 10–1) and then shows you the path to that file as a series of disk and folder icons (see Figure 10–2). You can open files or applications from within the DiskTop window. As you can see from the buttons in Figures 10–1 and 10–2, you can also delete, move, copy, or rename files from this screen. Another handy feature of the found files screen is that the last folder you had open is always the one that first appears when you reopen DiskTop, so you don't have to repeatedly navigate to the same folder if you use it a lot.

There's also a DiskTop menu that appears in the menu bar, and you can use it to get information about a file (like the Finder's Get Info command) or make new folders. You can also set a default folder to appear each time you

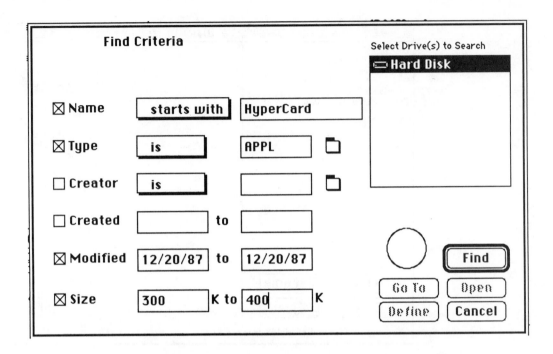

Figure 10–4. You can search for files using many different criteria with DiskTop.

use the Find command. In fact, when you set a default folder or open a specific folder in DiskTop, that folder becomes the new location in the Standard File box of the program you're using.

Being able to do all these things from inside an application is incredibly handy, and will save you a lot of time. In fact, DiskTop is actually faster at copying or moving files than the Finder is. Using only a filename to search with, the program found a file nested inside two folders on a 20 megabyte hard disk in 10 seconds, which is fairly slow, but no other program has as many features.

DiskTop Bonus Programs

When you buy DiskTop, you also get two bonus programs, LaserStatus and Widgets. LaserStatus is another desk accessory that you use to monitor the activity of a LaserWriter and download information easily. When you choose

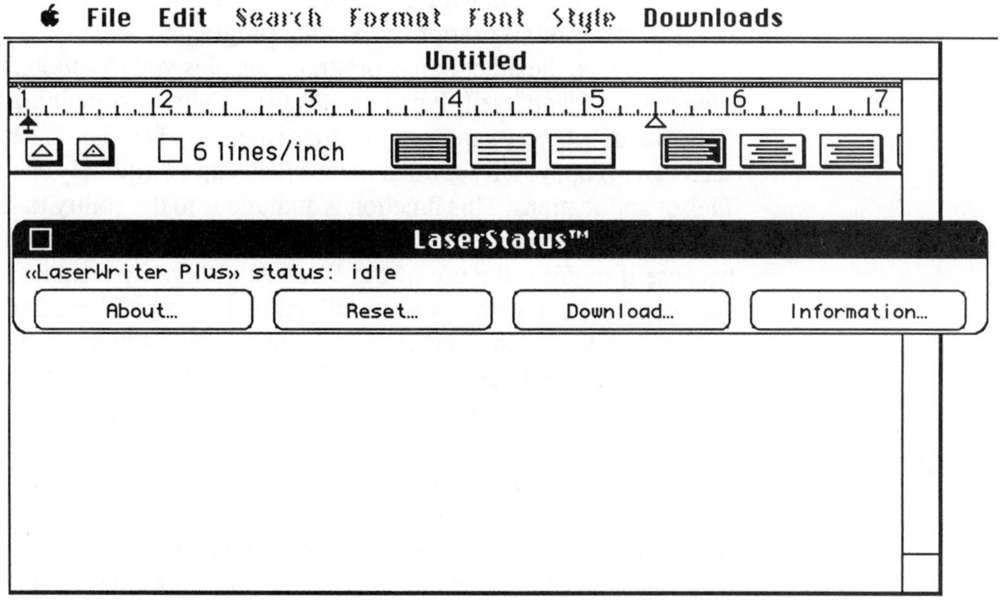

🍎 File Edit Search Format Font Style Downloads

Untitled

1.....1.....2.....1.....3.....1.....4.....1.....5.....1.....6.....1.....7

△ △   ☐ 6 lines/inch   ▤ ▤ ▤   ▤ ▤ ▤

☐   **LaserStatus™**

«LaserWriter Plus» status: idle

[About...]   [Reset...]   [Download...]   [Information...]

Figure 10–5.   The LaserStatus program included with DiskTop helps you monitor the activity of a Laser-Writer and download files quickly.

LaserStatus from the Apple menu, it presents a small window at the bottom of your screen, which you can leave visible while you work with your application program, as shown in Figure 10–5.

The LaserStatus window shows you whether your currently selected LaserWriter is in use at any time, so you can see if somebody else is printing on it if you're on an AppleTalk network with others. There are also buttons to reset the LaserWriter and to download files to the LaserWriter. The Download button lets you download new fonts or PostScript files on the fly by selecting them from a menu.

LaserStatus also has its own menu with commands to put together sets of files to be downloaded together. There's also a Get Info command that shows you which fonts are currently resident in the LaserWriter, how much memory it has and how much is available, how many total pages the LaserWriter has printed since it was new, and whether or not the startup page—the page that comes out whenever you turn the LaserWriter on—is enabled or disabled.

The big problem with LaserStatus is that it may well crash if you try to use it with a LaserWriter print spooling program.

Widgets, the other bonus program, enables you to add items to Laser-Status or DiskTop itself. It can create custom menus containing the files or LaserStatus sets you want, then add those menus to DiskTop. Then, when you select DiskTop, you'll see other menus that help you quickly choose specific files or applications. This function is analogous to the ability to store several default files or folders with other file finders, but it isn't quite as convenient, because it requires the use of the Widgets utility. By creating LaserStatus sets, you can put together custom collections of fonts and PostScript files that will appear on the Download menu in LaserStatus as individual items. So, if you always needed a certain group of fonts to print a certain report, you could store all those fonts with that report's name on the LaserStatus Download menu.

Widgets has a lot of unrelated but handy features. One is the ability to import a MacPaint graphic and use it in place of the Welcome to Macintosh screen that you see when you start your machine. It's great to see a pretty drawing or digitized photograph instead of the same old welcome notice, and you can easily swap MacPaint files at will.

You can also convert MacPaint files to the PICT format used by MacDraw, SuperPaint, and other object-oriented drawing programs, or you can convert from PICT files to MacPaint files. You can reset the date or time on your Mac's system clock. You can change the creator of a file, so that a file will open within a different application than the one that originally created it. (This doesn't work all the time, though.) You can also change the paper size used by the ImageWriter, so it can work with custom sizes of paper.

Another feature of Widgets is the ability to change the size of the System Heap. The *System Heap* is an area of memory (RAM) set aside for the operation of System files. If you use a lot of fonts, DAs, Inits, Chooser Resources, and cdevs, your System file may begin to have problems because there isn't enough room in the System Heap to manage everything properly. With Widgets, you can increase its size.

Widgets also has numerous additional LaserWriter functions, including the ability to enable or disable the startup page, as well as the functions you can get from inside LaserStatus. One particularly useful feature is *Laser Thumbnails,* which prints reduced versions of MacPaint files (up to 16 on a page), so you can create a handy graphic catalog of a disk or folder. In all, DiskTop is an incredible value.

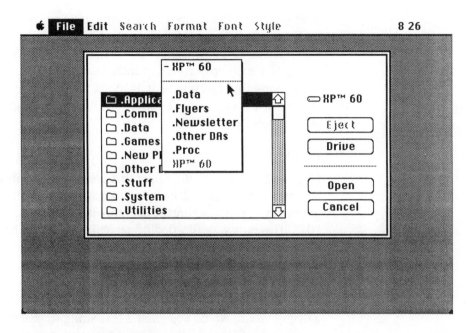

Figure 10–6. HFS Navigator installs a special menu in your Standard File boxes that helps you move to different folders quickly.

HFS Navigator

HFS Navigator is a program that makes it easy to move quickly to different folders on your hard disk, and that helps you find files as well. You install HFS Navigator by clicking on its icon. After that, you'll see a special menu that appears above the current disk or folder name when you click on it, as in Figure 10–6. You can install up to 16 different folders on this special menu, then navigate quickly to any of the folders by simply selecting them.

The other option you have in using HFS Navigator is to find files. If you hold down the Command key while clicking the current disk name in a Standard File box, the HFS Navigator menu appears. It has options for creating a new folder, finding a folder, finding a file, finding the next file, and getting information about a selected file (like the Get Info command in the Finder). You can search for files or folders by matching a whole name or a partial name, and you can limit the search to specific folders of a disk. HFS Navigator is also very fast: It found a file on a 20 megabyte hard disk in about three seconds. When it finds a file, the program automatically navigates to the folder the file is in and then selects the file itself, rather than simply showing a path name. The downside of this is that it only finds one file at a time.

It's handy to have frequently used folders on a menu, but HFS Navigator's find function isn't as robust as those in Findswell or DiskTop, and you can't copy or move files as you can in DiskTop. In addition, it's $10 more expensive at $59.95.

Findswell

Findswell is a $49.95 file finder that installs as an Init file in your System Folder. With Findswell installed, the SFGet box inside any application program you run will contain an extra Findswell button, as shown in Figure 10–7. This puts your file-finding capability exactly where you need it to be. You usually don't realize you can't remember a file's location until you use the Open... command inside a program, and when you realize you need help, the Findswell button is right there.

When you click the Findswell button (or press Command-F), you see a dialog box in which you enter a text string to search for. Findswell then searches for filenames that contain that text string and displays the files, folders, and volumes containing that string in a list window in the same dialog box, as Figure 10–8 shows.

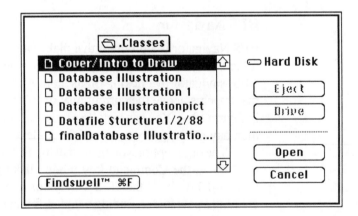

Figure 10–7. Findswell is accessed from a special button that appears in the SFGet box of any application you run.

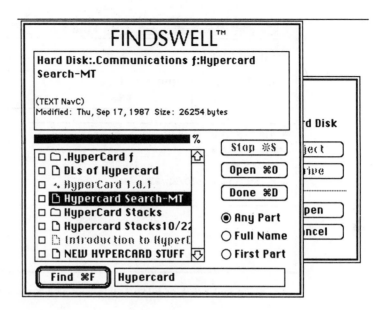

Figure 10–8. The Findswell dialog box shows found files in a list window.

As you can see from Figure 10–8, the Findswell dialog box has buttons that let you search for the text string you enter in any part of a filename, at beginning of a filename, or as only the full name of a file. When you select a file in the list window, its path name appears in the box above, as shown in Figure 10–8. Findswell displays path names as text, rather than as a set of disk and folder icons.

As with other file finders, you can double-click on folders in the list window to open them. If you double-click on the name of a file in the list window that was created by the application you're currently running, that file will open. Unlike DiskTop, however, you can't launch other applications from inside another program using the Findswell window. (If you want to launch applications, you can open Findswell from the Finder using an application called Findswell Launch. Findswell Launch displays applications and lets you launch one of them.)

Findswell also lets you set default files or folders, so they will be displayed automatically in the Findswell window each time you activate the program. This makes getting to deeply nested files or folders much simpler.

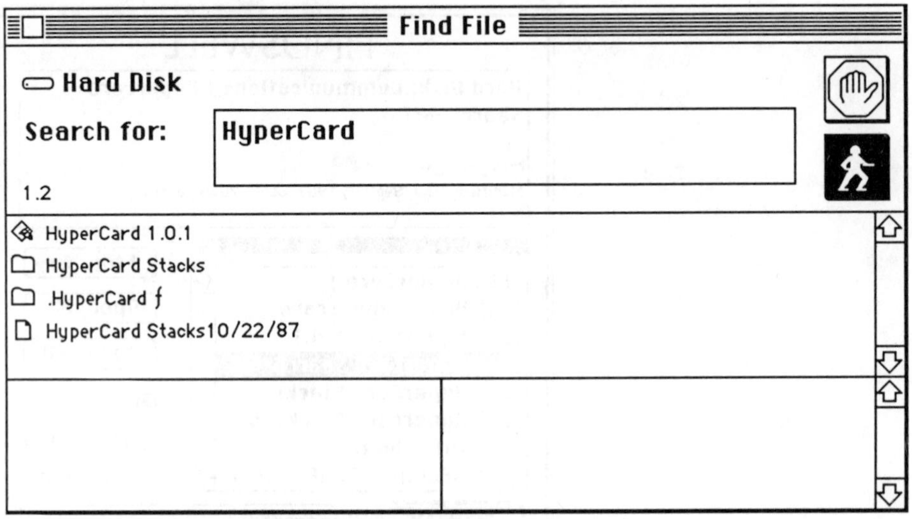

Figure 10–9. Find File uses this one dialog box to search for and display files.

Findswell is quite fast. One file on our 20 megabyte hard disk was located in slightly less than four seconds. Findswell sells for $49.95, the same as DiskTop 3.0, but it offers fewer features. Its main virtues are its ability to find files so quickly, its convenient button in the SFGet box, and the ability to store default folders in the Findswell list box.

Find File

Find File is a desk accessory that has been distributed on a utilities disk by Apple since System 4.1 was released. It's a very basic program, without a lot of the extra features other programs offer. When you choose Find File from the Apple Menu (there is no keyboard equivalent you can use to activate it), it displays a dialog box like the one in Figure 10–9.

With the Find File dialog box on the screen, you simply type the name or text string you're searching for, and then click the "walk" button (the button containing the human figure) to begin the search. Find File is fairly fast—it found a file on a 20 megabyte disk in just under six seconds. Once it finds a file or files, it displays them in a list box within the same dialog box, underneath the area where you enter search text. If you select one of the found files, you'll see size and creation information about it as well as a graphic depiction of the file's path, as shown in Figure 10–10.

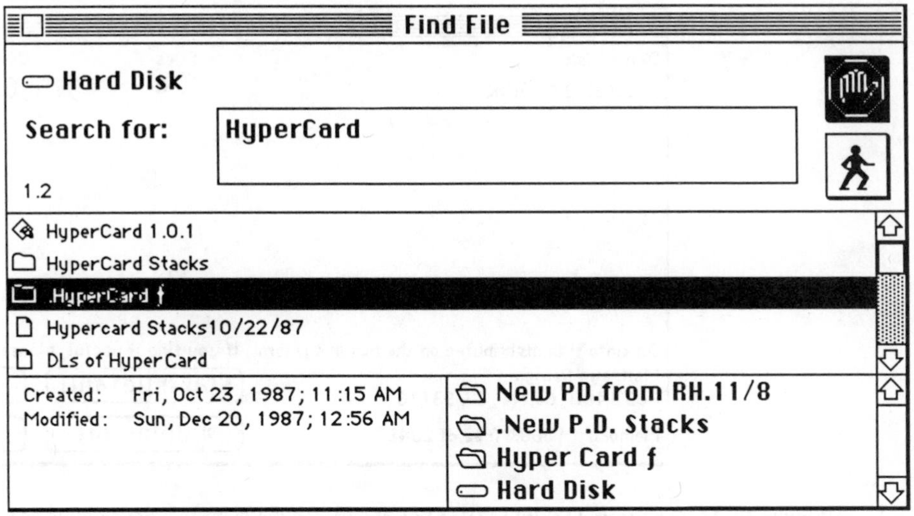

Figure 10–10. When you select a file in the Find File dialog box, it displays file information and the file's path.

You can't open a file from the Find File dialog box, and you can't perform other file management functions. The only options are available from a Find File menu that appears when you select this DA. You can search specific folders only (instead of a whole disk) by using the Search Here... command on the Find File menu; and if you have selected a file in the Find File dialog box, you can move it to the Desktop, which moves the file from the folder it was in to the top level of the disk so you can locate it more easily. (This is a substitute for the option to navigate to a found file featured in DiskTop.)

Find File is pretty basic, but it's also free. You may want to try it out for awhile, and then move to a different program if you find yourself longing for more features.

DiskInfo

Disk Info is a shareware desk accessory that has a $10 registration fee. This was one of the first programs with a file-finder feature and has gone through many versions, each adding features. When you choose DiskInfo from the Apple menu, it shows a dialog box listing the disks you currently have on-line, as well as disks you have recently ejected, as Figure 10–11 shows.

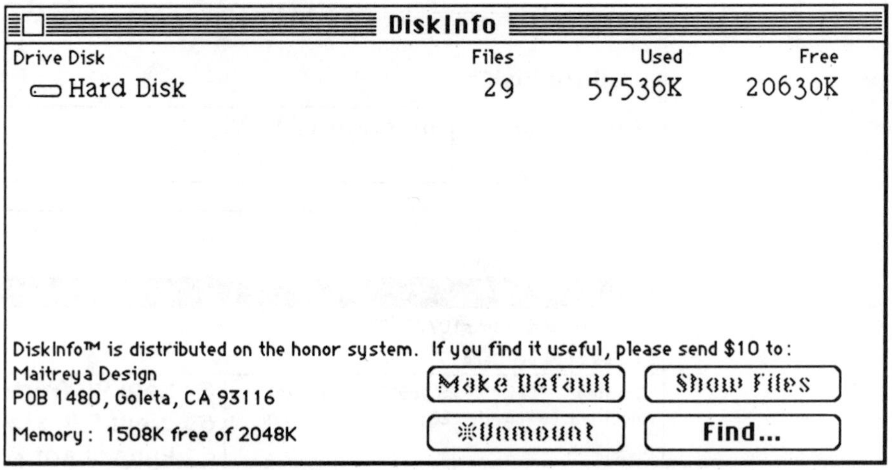

```
┌────────────────────────────────────────────────────────────────┐
│ ▣▢▭▭▭▭▭▭▭▭▭▭▭▭▭▭▭═══ DiskInfo ═══▭▭▭▭▭▭▭▭▭▭▭▭▭▭▭▭ │
│ Drive Disk                         Files      Used       Free    │
│   ⊂⊃ Hard Disk                       29     57536K    20630K    │
│                                                                  │
│                                                                  │
│                                                                  │
│                                                                  │
│                                                                  │
│ DiskInfo™ is distributed on the honor system.  If you find it useful, please send $10 to: │
│ Maitreya Design                    ┌─────────────┐ ┌─────────────┐ │
│ POB 1480, Goleta, CA 93116         │ Make Default│ │  Show Files │ │
│                                    └─────────────┘ └─────────────┘ │
│ Memory: 1508K free of 2048K        ┌─────────────┐ ┌─────────────┐ │
│                                    │ ※Unmount    │ │  Find...    │ │
│                                    └─────────────┘ └─────────────┘ │
└────────────────────────────────────────────────────────────────┘
```

Figure 10–11. The main DiskInfo dialog box shows you the disks you have online or have recently ejected, the number of files or folders on each disk, the amount of used and available space on each disk, and the amount of used and available memory.

From this dialog box, you can click the Find button to search for a file. (Early versions of DiskInfo don't have a Find button.) The Find window that appears has a space for you to enter a text string, along with buttons that tell DiskInfo to match your search string with the full name of the file/folder only, the first part of the file/folder name, or any part of the file/folder name.

As it locates files that match your search criteria, DiskInfo displays them one at a time in the Find window, as shown in Figure 10–12. Along with the name of the file, the window shows the path name of the file in text.

To see whether there are other files DiskInfo has found, you must keep clicking the Find button until you see a message that says there are no other files that match. Aside from displaying the name of only one found file at a time, the other problem is that once it searches your hard disk, DiskInfo will automatically search inserted and ejected floppy disks. You will have to insert a previously ejected floppy so DiskInfo can continue its search—there's no command to abort the search once you learn the file isn't on your hard disk. The way to avoid this problem is to unmount any ejected disk that appears in the main DiskInfo dialog box when you first activate the program.

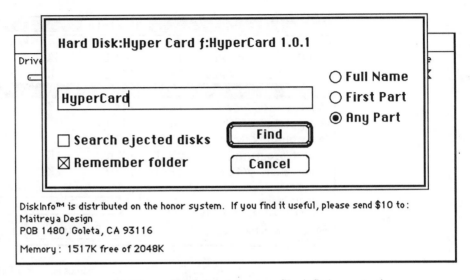

Figure 10–12.   DiskInfo only presents files it finds one at a time.

When you select a disk and double-click its icon (or click the Show Files button) from the DiskInfo dialog box, DiskInfo displays the files on the disk in a different window, like the one in Figure 10–13. From this window, you can open and close folders and rename or delete selected files.

You can't open a file from inside this window, but you can rename or delete files or folders. Using the DiskInfo menu, you can sort files in the listing of a disk's contents by name or creation date, and you can choose to display file sizes in characters or K. With one of the commands on the DiskInfo menu, you can compact your system's memory, which frees up anywhere from 3–5K to about 100K of additional memory space, depending on how much RAM your Mac has. It does this by pushing out of memory anything put there by your program that was marked as purgeable.

DiskInfo falls in the middle range speed-wise. It found a file on a 20 megabyte hard disk in about six seconds. But this program is primarily designed to simply show you the files you have on a given disk, and to show you the amount of available space on disks and in your Mac's memory. Also, you can't open DiskInfo from the keyboard. Unless you're particularly attracted by the option to compact memory or the ability to rename or delete files, you're just as well getting Find File for free.

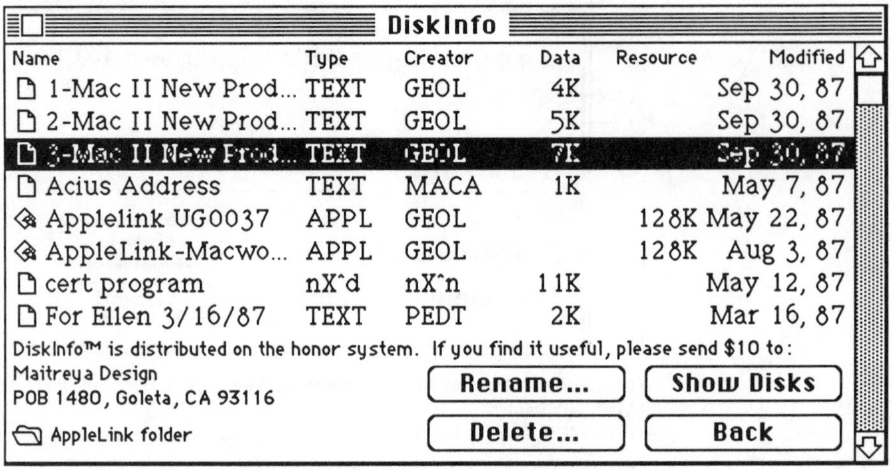

Name	Type	Creator	Data	Resource	Modified
1-Mac II New Prod...	TEXT	GEOL	4K		Sep 30, 87
2-Mac II New Prod...	TEXT	GEOL	5K		Sep 30, 87
3-Mac II New Prod...	TEXT	GEOL	7K		Sep 30, 87
Acius Address	TEXT	MACA	1K		May 7, 87
Applelink UG0037	APPL	GEOL		128K	May 22, 87
AppleLink-Macwo...	APPL	GEOL		128K	Aug 3, 87
cert program	nX^d	nX^n	11K		May 12, 87
For Ellen 3/16/87	TEXT	PEDT	2K		Mar 16, 87

DiskInfo™ is distributed on the honor system. If you find it useful, please send $10 to:
Maitreya Design
POB 1480, Goleta, CA 93116

AppleLink folder

[Rename...]   [Show Disks]
[Delete...]   [Back]

Figure 10–13. DiskInfo shows filenames and file information.

MacTree

MacTree is actually a finder alternative, and it is discussed in detail in Chapter 13. We mention it here because it is the fastest file finder available for the Macintosh. MacTree is a standalone application that displays all your hard disk files as a branching tree structure. When it loads, it reads your hard disk's entire file directory into your Mac's memory. When you use MacTree's file-finding function, it can find any hard disk file in less than one second, because the program only needs to search for the file in RAM, rather than on the hard disk itself.

MacTree searches for a file by name or by the date the file was created. You can enter partial filenames as well as whole ones to search for, and you can specify whether the partial name string you want the program to match appears at the beginning or end of the filename. To simplify searching, you can exclude application files, System files, or document files from the search. When it finds files that match your search criteria, though, MacTree shows them on the screen one at a time, with each file displayed in the window listing all the contents of the folder where the file is located.

But MacTree is only useful as a file finder if you run it with other applications under the MultiFinder. Otherwise, you have to quit your current application program to find a file. A good file finder is almost essential to using a hard disk conveniently. Whichever program you choose, you'll be better off for having it.

Disk Cataloging Programs

In some cases, it's useful to have a complete list of all the files on your hard disk. By scanning a sorted list of files, you can quickly spot duplicate files, outdated versions of files, or large files you don't really need to have on the disk any more. Disk cataloging programs produce a complete list of the files on a hard disk. (They also work with floppy disks.)

Cataloging programs find all the files on a disk and then create either a printed list or a text file that can either be used by a word processor or a database. The information they provide usually includes filenames, path names, creation and modification times and dates, file sizes, and file types and creators. The better cataloging programs sort the files in the list by these different sort criteria. You might want a catalog sorted by name if you were looking for duplicate files, for example, whereas you'd be better off with a catalog sorted by file size if you were looking for large files you could delete to reclaim disk space. Two representative cataloging programs are Cat•Mac and HFSDir.

Cat•Mac

Cat•Mac comes in two versions, or levels, and each level is distributed differently. The first level is distributed as shareware and costs $10. You can get the second level by registering as a Level 1 user and sending in $16.95. The program is the same at both levels, except that Level 1 can catalog up to 1000 files, whereas Level 2 catalogs up to 10,000 files and offers more sorting options.

This is the most flexible and powerful disk cataloging product we know of. You select the volume you want to catalog, then start the program. It took us about 10 seconds to catalog over 11 megabytes of files. Once the program is done cataloging one volume, you can tell Cat•Mac to read other volumes and add the files to the same catalog. Once it finishes reading a disk, Cat•Mac presents a list of files on the disk, as in Figure 10–14.

After the initial cataloging process, files are displayed in alphabetical order by folder, and then by filename within each folder. Each filename is shown with its path name, modification date and time, size, type, and creator code. But you don't have to leave the catalog sorted this way. In Level 1 of Cat•Mac, you can sort this listing alphabetically by volume name or file type as well as filename, and in Level 2 of the program, you can also sort by file size, creator code, or modification date and time. You can also set up multilevel sorts, so the catalog is sorted on up to five different criteria, in

 ⚜ File   Edit   File Sort   Options   Windows   Help

TYPE	FILE NAME	CRTR	VOLUME:<FOLDER:NAMES>	MOD DATE and TIME	SI
WDBN	:::December 1987	MSWD	Matilda:"The Ac:Activis	11/20/87 01:08 PM	
WDBN	:::Activist FYI	MSWD	Matilda:"The Ac:Activis	12/29/87 05:40 PM	
WDBN	:::article	MSWD	Matilda:"The Ac:Activis	01/14/88 03:03 PM	
WDBN	:::sources	MSWD	Matilda:"The Ac:Activis	01/06/88 05:33 PM	
WDBN	:::Activist 7/87	MSWD	Matilda:"The Ac:Activis	07/23/87 05:13 PM	
WORD	:::George	MACA	Matilda:"The Ac:Activis	05/21/87 10:12 AM	
WORD	:::Hi, I'm Judy!	MACA	Matilda:"The Ac:Activis	05/20/87 05:30 PM	
WDBN	:::View	WORD	Matilda:"The Ac:Activis	05/19/87 05:04 PM	
WDBN	:::What I Martha...	WORD	Matilda:"The Ac:Activis	05/19/87 05:10 PM	
WDBN	::Office Security	MSWD	Matilda:"The Ac:.......	07/22/87 03:23 PM	
WDBN	::Office Securit...	MSWD	Matilda:"The Ac:.......	07/23/87 10:46 AM	
WORD	::Three Cheers	MACA	Matilda:"The Ac:.......	03/18/87 03:50 PM	
WORD	::view	MACA	Matilda:"The Ac:.......	11/20/87 10:39 AM	

Cat•Log™ Volume Listing

Cat•Log™ File Listing

Cat•Mac™ Status

Number of Volumes Read: 1

Number of Files Read: 624

Waiting for a Disk...

Figure 10–14.   Cat•Mac displays files from a disk in alphabetical order by folder, and within each folder by filename.

order. Also, you can filter files before you begin cataloging, so only files of a certain type are included in the catalog.

Another option you have with the files display in Cat•Mac is rearranging the columns of information in the window. You can shuffle the columns around to appear in any order you want.

Cat•Mac is also very flexible when it stores and prints catalog information. You can save a catalog to disk in Cat•Mac's format or as text with spaces, commas, or tabs separating the columns of data. Each of these formats is used by different database programs, so you can load text files into a database program for further searching, sorting, or manipulation. When you print a catalog, you can print either the file list or just the list of volumes that you cataloged.

Cat•Mac does just about anything you could want as far as listing the files on your disk, and it does it all for $26.95 (if you buy both levels).

HFSDir

HFSDir is a much less ambitious program, distributed as shareware with a $15 registration fee. You simply run this program, click the option to catalog a disk, and it writes a catalog to your disk under the name you specify. Once it creates a catalog file, the program quits and returns you to the Finder. If you prefer, you can print the catalog as it is assembled, rather than creating a disk file of it, but you can't use both options at one time: You would have to run HFSDir twice to print and create a file. The catalog produced by HFSDir is sorted alphabetically by folder and then by filename. It took this program about 15 seconds to produce a disk file of our 11 megabytes of data.

HFSDir sells for a little more than Level 1 of Cat•Mac, but it does a lot less. It is almost completely automated, however, and is very simple to operate.

Disk Performance Optimizers

The next utility programs on the list are those that improve the performance (speed) of the disk itself. Performance optimizers attack two problems: the obsolete information on your hard disk long after it isn't needed any more, and files that become fragmented on the disk as you load and save them repeatedly.

Compacting the Desktop

The first problem concerns the size of the Desktop file your Mac maintains invisibly on every disk. The Desktop file stores information about the state of the desktop: the names and positions of icons, folders, and files that are needed by the Finder to present the desktop each time. The problem is that the Desktop file *retains* information on icons and files you have deleted from your disk, so it grows over time. The larger your Desktop file, the longer it takes for the Finder to draw the desktop each time.

Performance optimizers usually have an option to rebuild or compact the Desktop file, tossing out the information about icons and files you no longer have stored to reduce the size of the file. By cleaning unnecessary information out of this file regularly, you can display your desktop as quickly as possible. Apple's own System has a special command you can use to rebuild the Desktop file, but it can remove some information you still need when you use older System/Finder combinations, such as the description of program icons, so that your old program icons may be replaced by a generic application icon. The desktop file option in a disk optimizing utility doesn't cause these problems. Rebuilding your Desktop file takes two minutes or less (sometimes just a few seconds), but it can save you one or two seconds or more every time you return to the Finder.

File Fragmentation

When you first use a new disk and save files on it, those files are written to fairly continuous blocks on your disk, one after the other. But as you work, the files become fragmented, with part of a file stored in blocks in one sector, and part of the file stored in another sector. This happens because files grow or shrink as you work with them. Here's a simplified version of what happens:

Suppose you start out saving a 10K file and then another 20K file right after it. Your Mac will write the 10K file, and then begin writing the 20K file in the next free block after the end of the 10K file. If you add to your 10K file so it now consumes 15K, there's no longer room for the whole file in one place (because the original space was only 10K). In this case, your Mac saves the extra 5K of data to other blocks someplace else. Even if you have a lot of free space on the disk (as you probably do on a hard disk), files become fragmented because they were initially saved to certain areas, and after file revisions your Mac still saves those original parts of the files to the same areas. The Mac isn't smart enough to store the entire file in a continuous group of blocks elsewhere on the disk to avoid fragmentation.

The problem with fragmentation like this is that as your files are stored in increasingly numerous pieces over your disk, your Mac takes longer to find the pieces and load them, or to find the different storage locations and save the pieces of the file.

Disk optimizers *unfragment* files. In an operation akin to major surgery, they read the files on your disk and rearrange them into continuous blocks again, so that each file is in only one place. This operation takes from a few minutes to an hour, depending on the size of your disk and the number of fragmented files on it. It should be performed only after you have completely backed up the contents of your hard disk (see Chapter 9), and once you begin the optimization routine, you can't interrupt it without damaging some of the data on your disk. If your disk contains a lot of fragmented files, though, once you optimize the disk you can experience dramatically faster file-loading and file-saving times.

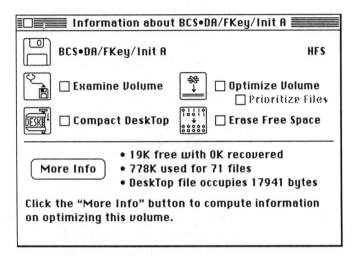

Figure 10–15. When you load DiskExpress and select a disk to work with, the software displays basic information about the space on your disk.

DiskExpress

The best program in this category currently on the market is a program called DiskExpress from AlSoft, which sells for $49.95. It has four functions: examining a disk for bad blocks or a damaged directory; compacting a Desktop file; optimizing a disk (unfragmenting files); and really erasing areas of the disk where files have been deleted.

When you load DiskExpress and click on the icon for the disk you want to work with, you get an information window that shows how much disk space is used, the number of files on the disk, and the current size of the Desktop file, as in Figure 10–15.

This screen contains check boxes for you to select which of the four different operations you want to perform on your disk. Once they're selected, you can click the Continue button to start the operations.

Clicking the More Info button causes DiskExpress to examine your disk more closely for a minute or so, then report on the percentage of fragmented files on the disk and the amount of data that would be moved during optimization.

As DiskExpress performs the operations you've selected, one after the other, it displays a scale that shows how far along the current operation is. Here's what DiskExpress does during its four operations.

The Examine Volume option reads each block on the disk to see if it's readable (for more on blocks, see Chapter 7) and that the disk directory (which stores information about the sizes and locations of files) is undamaged. This operation takes from a few minutes to half an hour, depending on the size of your disk.

The Compact Desktop option removes all unnecessary information from the Desktop file. The Optimize Disk option unfragments files and can take from 15 minutes to an hour or more.

The Erase Free Space option erases the areas of the disk where you previously deleted files. As explained in Chapter 3 and in the section on MacTools later in this chapter, deleted files aren't really erased—their names are just removed from the disk directory. This option in DiskExpress finds areas where there are deleted files and erases them. You can also have DiskExpress erase your entire disk.

If you perform the first three of these operations, plan on having your hard disk out of action for at least an hour. But once DiskExpress is finished, you should see some performance improvements. The best way to use the program is to use the More Info button to see the percentage of fragmented files on your disk. Don't bother optimizing the disk unless 30 percent or more of your files are fragmented. As far as compacting the Desktop, however, you can do that any time, because it only takes a few minutes.

File Compression and Encryption Programs

File compression programs are typically used to lower the cost of telecommunicating. By compressing files you send, or assembling a group of normal-sized files into one compressed package, you can cut down transmission time and save on telephone or online service charges. File compression programs are of interest to a hard disk user because they can also be used to archive seldom-used files on your hard disk in a way that conserves as much disk space as possible. If you finish a project, for example, you could assemble all the files relating to that project into one file compressed to be 25 to 40 percent smaller than the normal size of the constituent files. Because the project is over and you won't need fast access to the files again, it makes sense to compress them into one package.

File compression programs are pretty simple. To use one, you create a storage file for the files you want to archive, then move the files you want into the storage file. When you assemble selected files into the storage file, you have the option either to compress them or to store them at normal size. In addition, most compression programs also can encrypt the files you store, so they can't be opened without a password.

The two most popular file compression programs at this point are PackIt III and StuffIt, both of which are available as shareware.

PackIt III

PackIt III was the first popular file compression program on the Mac. It's available for a $10 registration fee. You load PackIt like any other application program, and it presents one menu, the File menu, which contains options for packing files, unpacking files, entering a password for encrypted files, accessing two screens of instructions, and quitting.

To archive or compress files with PackIt III, you first create a storage file. Storage files always have the suffix .pit so you'll know a PackIt file by its name. Once you've created a storage file, you can select files from a Standard File box and move them into the storage file. As you move files, you have the option to compress them or not, and to encrypt them or not. To uncompress files, you choose the Uncompress option from the File menu.

If you use PackIt (or another file compression program) to send files to somebody else, the recipient must use the same program to uncompress them. This is a simple, reliable program that can save you from 15 percent to 25 percent of the space you'd normally use to store files.

StuffIt

StuffIt compresses files a little more tightly than PackIt—20 to 60 percent smaller than normal, and it compresses files about 50 percent more quickly than PackIt III. (A benchmark supplied with the StuffIt documentation says it took PackIt III over 10 minutes to compress a 529K PageMaker file, whereas StuffIt did the job in just under 5 minutes.) But StuffIt doesn't encrypt files.

StuffIt offers two different file compression algorithms, which you choose from its Algorithm menu. You can apply one or both algorithms as you compress files. (The documentation supplied with StuffIt explains which algorithm is better with different types of files.) StuffIt also has a menu whose only command unpacks PackIt files—a nice feature if you've used the older program before. Unlike PackIt III, though, StuffIt doesn't let you encrypt files and protect them with a password. StuffIt's shareware registration fee is $15.

General Disk Utility Programs

General disk utility programs help you to examine and modify disks and files in various ways. The most popular disk utility program is MacTools, which is sold as part of the Copy II Mac package from Central Point Software.

MacTools

MacTools has a variety of options for working with files and disks. Some of the options are useful mainly to technically oriented users, whereas others can help you in your daily work. When you first load the MacTools program, it displays a window showing the files and folders at the top organizational level of the current disk (the disk where MacTools is stored), as in Figure 10–16.

Along with the file size, name, and modification date, MacTools tells you whether each file is protected (Prtct in the window), Locked (Lckd), or Invisible (Invis):

- A protected file is one that can't be copied by the Finder.
- A locked file can't be renamed or deleted by the Finder.
- An invisible file doesn't appear in the Finder or in Standard File boxes.

When a box in one of these columns is darkened, that means the file in that row of the window has that feature active. In Figure 10–16, for example, the file Desktop has its Invis box darkened, which means that the file is invisible: Its name doesn't appear in the Finder or in Standard File boxes. By clicking in these boxes, you can change these characteristics for each file, making a file protected, locked, or invisible. This feature is extremely useful for securing your files—an invisible file can't be seen, for example, so it isn't likely other users will have access to it (unless they use MacTools), and a locked file can't be deleted without being unlocked first.

The next set of operations you can perform with MacTools are those available from the Disk and File menus. The first four commands on the Disk menu enable you to verify, format, copy, or rename a disk. Most of these are self-explanatory, but the Verify Disk command reads the disk and reports whether all the information on the disk is readable. Verify Disk won't tell you whether unreadable parts of the disk are caused by disk damage or by problems with the actual files, however.

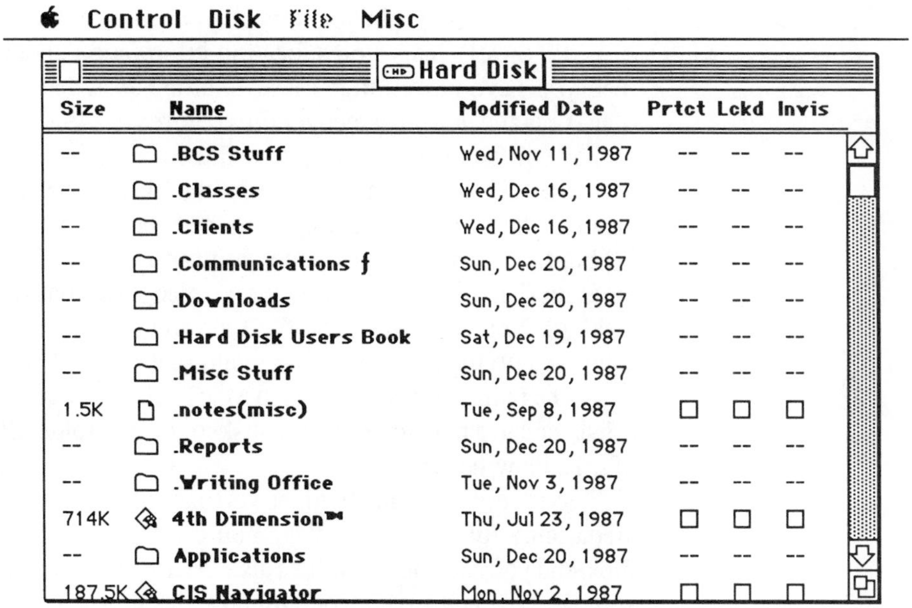

**   Control   Disk   File   Misc**

Size		Name	Modified Date	Prtct	Lckd	Invis
--	🗀	.BCS Stuff	Wed, Nov 11, 1987	--	--	--
--	🗀	.Classes	Wed, Dec 16, 1987	--	--	--
--	🗀	.Clients	Wed, Dec 16, 1987	--	--	--
--	🗀	.Communications ʃ	Sun, Dec 20, 1987	--	--	--
--	🗀	.Downloads	Sun, Dec 20, 1987	--	--	--
--	🗀	.Hard Disk Users Book	Sat, Dec 19, 1987	--	--	--
--	🗀	.Misc Stuff	Sun, Dec 20, 1987	--	--	--
1.5K	🗋	.notes(misc)	Tue, Sep 8, 1987	☐	☐	☐
--	🗀	.Reports	Sun, Dec 20, 1987	--	--	--
--	🗀	.Writing Office	Tue, Nov 3, 1987	--	--	--
714K	🔷	4th Dimension™	Thu, Jul 23, 1987	☐	☐	☐
--	🗀	Applications	Sun, Dec 20, 1987	--	--	--
187.5K	🔷	CIS Navigator	Mon, Nov 2, 1987	☐	☐	☐

Figure 10–16. The main MacTools screen.

The fifth command on the Disk menu is called ViewEdit. ViewEdit is a programmer's tool that can read specific blocks of data on a disk and display their contents in hexadecimal code (eight-digit combinations of letters and numbers used in programming). ViewEdit is of interest only to programmers.

The next command on the Disk menu is Undelete Files. As explained in Chapter 9, files are written to disk in 512 byte blocks, and the location of those blocks is stored with the filename in the disk directory. When you delete a file using the Finder or the Delete command inside an application program, the directory listing for the file is erased, so your Mac can no longer locate the file's blocks. The blocks themselves, however, remain until they are overwritten by another file.

The Undelete Files command in MacTools locates the blocks of a deleted file, assembles them, and prompts you to give them a name and store them in a new location as a new file. Storing the recovered file creates a new directory listing for it, and the file can then be loaded normally. To use the Undelete Files feature of MacTools, you must have already installed two Init programs, CPS SaveDeletes and CPS TagFix, inside your System Folder. CPS TagFix puts special markers on your files so MacTools can find them, and CPS SaveDeletes stores location information about deleted files. Only files you have saved after these Inits are installed can be recovered by MacTools and you must recover files before you write additional files to disk, or they will be overwritten by new files.

One other thing about undeleting files is that along with the file's location, the directory listing contained the file's type and creator code. Without the proper creator code, you can't open a file with an application program (because the program won't recognize that file as one of its own making). You can restore the file type and creator code using the InfoEdit command on the MacTools File menu (described in a minute).

The remaining commands in MacTools' Disk menu enable you to eject a disk, create a new folder on the disk, or open a folder displayed in the main MacTools window.

MacTools' File menu gives you basically the same options on the Disk menu, only for individual files. You can verify, copy, rename, and delete files, and you can ViewEdit files also. An extra option, called InfoEdit, stores your file type and creator code for any file. You can recreate the original file type and creator code of a file you've just recovered, or you can change the file type and creator code of an existing file. (Changing file types and creator codes is a tricky business best left to programmers.)

This description of the MacTools option provides a good example of what you can do with general disk utility programs, but there's one other utility that some users find indispensable, particularly if their data is sensitive.

Really Deleting Files

As mentioned above and in Chapter 3, when you delete a file by dragging it to the Trash Can or using a program's Delete command, the file itself isn't erased—only its directory listing is wiped out. If you work with sensitive data, you may want to make sure a file is completely erased from your disk. (This is a requirement in some government applications.) A public domain program called Complete Delete does the job. It's a simple program, stored with an icon that looks like a paper shredder. You just select the file you want to delete and then delete it. Once you delete a file this way, it's as if you erased the part of the disk where that file's blocks were stored—the file is wiped out forever.

Every hard disk user should have a collection of disk optimizing programs that includes a good file finder and a general utility like MacTools. Performance optimizers, cataloging programs, file compression and encryption programs, and deleting utilities are also extremely useful in specific circumstances.

CHAPTER

11

Font and Desk Accessory Extenders

The Macintosh is the first personal computer to offer the flexibility to install your choice of typefaces and small programs on menus, so they're available at all times. With fonts and desk accessories (DAs), you can create a custom computing environment. This flexibility has led to the development of hundreds of fonts and DAs, along with a lot of Mac owners eager to try them. But dealing with a wealth of fonts and DAs on a normal Macintosh is like having a Ferrari with a one gallon gas tank: There are hundreds of DAs to choose from, but you can only install 15 of them at once in a System file. You can install fonts in a System file to your heart's delight, but you must install and remove them with the Font/DA Mover program each time.

The wealth of available fonts and DAs has made Mac owners long for better ways to manage them. In Chapter 4, we discussed installing fonts and DAs in specific applications or documents and using the hidden DA slots as ways around the System's limits, but developers have also responded to this problem with specific font and DA management programs. In this chapter, we'll discuss the two most popular programs that make managing fonts and DAs easier. After that, we'll suggest which kinds of DAs you should keep on your hard disk, and then we'll look at some sources of fonts and DAs.

Overcoming the DA Limit

DA extender programs are the simplest and most convenient way to gain access to more than 15 DAs at a time. As explained in Chapter 4, there are only 15 spaces (or slots) available for installing DAs on the Apple menu. Font/DA extender programs install as desk accessories on the Apple menu and then provide a gateway to other desk accessories, so you have access to many DAs through the one slot occupied by the DA extender. In addition, these programs make it easy to add or remove fonts from your Font menu without using the Font/DA Mover. The two most popular font/DA extenders are Suitcase and Font/DA Juggler. If you use lots of fonts and DAs, you need a program like this.

Suitcase

Suitcase was the first program to really overcome the DA limit. An earlier shareware product called Other allows you to add four or five extra DAs to the Apple menu, but with Suitcase, your Apple menu can contain hundreds of DAs. Suitcase also handles fonts more easily.

Suitcase is an Init program that installs in your System Folder. Once installed, the program adds the Suitcase DA to your Apple menu. You can access Suitcase either by choosing it from the menu or by pressing Command-K. There are several advantages to using Suitcase:

- You can add over 500 DAs and fonts to your Apple and Font menus.
- You can set fonts or DAs to be automatically installed upon startup, or you can open them on the fly as you work.
- You can group fonts or DAs into application-specific storage files to minimize menu clutter.
- Adding DAs or fonts with Suitcase doesn't increase the size of your System file.

Once it's installed, Suitcase works in two different ways. First, if you have a folder labeled Fonts/DAs, Fonts, or DAs inside your System Folder, Suitcase will automatically open up to 12 font or DA storage files (suitcase files) stored in that folder and make them available on the appropriate menus. (As described in Chapter 4, you can create new suitcase files containing the fonts or DAs you copy there with the Font/DA Mover, or you can use the suitcase files for specific fonts or DAs from commercial or public domain

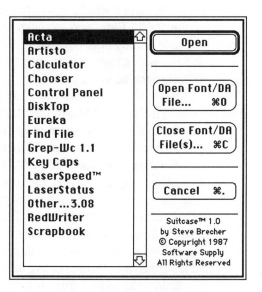

Figure 11–1. Suitcase can open additional font or DA files as you work.

disks.) Second, you can open up to 10 other font or DA files and add extra options from them to your menu by accessing Suitcase as you work.

Font or DA suitcase files can store up to 200 font sizes and 52 DAs each, so you could theoretically have Suitcase automatically place 520 DAs and 2000 fonts on your Apple and Font menus. (The limit of 2000 font sizes per file means, more realistically, that you'll only have 300–500 fonts per file, assuming you have four or five sizes per font.) When you have more fonts or DAs than can be displayed down the length of your screen, the Apple and Font menus scroll: You can bring more items into view on these menus by holding down the mouse button and dragging below the bottom of your screen.

When you choose Suitcase from the Apple menu (or press Command-K), you see a dialog box with a window showing you all the DAs you currently have installed, along with buttons that open or close additional font or DA files, as shown in Figure 11–1. You can open 10 files at once this way, in addition to the files Suitcase has automatically opened.

Along with removing the practical limit to the number of fonts or DAs you can have installed, Suitcase also makes managing DAs and fonts much easier. When you get a new font or DA, you can simply drag it into the Fonts/

DAs folder and it will be added to the appropriate menu automatically, up to the limit of 12 files. And, you can remove a font or DA by simply dragging it outside of the Fonts/DAs folder. If you get a new font or DA while you're working with an application program, you can add it to your menu with the Suitcase desk accessory.

The difference between adding or removing fonts with Suitcase as opposed to the Font/DA Mover is that the Font/DA Mover can add or remove specific font *sizes*. Suitcase only deals with font *files* (which contain the specific fonts and sizes stored in them). Once you've added a font to a menu with Suitcase, you can't add additional sizes of that font using Suitcase. Typically, though, you will create one or more suitcase files containing all the fonts and sizes you use for a given type of work.

Because you can add extra fonts or DAs to your system by choosing Suitcase from the Apple menu and opening another font or DA file, you can group them according to the task you want to perform, so your menus don't get too cluttered. It's impressive to see over 500 DAs or fonts on a menu, but in practice, the more items on a menu, the more time you'll have to spend hunting for the right font or DA when you want to select it.

It makes more sense to put DAs in application-specific groups, such as Word Processing, Graphics, Spreadsheets, Utilities, Games, and so on; and to put fonts in groups like Business, Graphics, and Leisure. Along with these specific groups, you can create two suitcase files that store the standard fonts and DAs you use every day and put those two files in the Fonts/DAs folder. This way, your basic set of fonts and DAs will always load automatically, and you can add application-specific groups of other fonts or DAs as you need them.

Adding font or DA files on the fly is easy and fast: Suitcase can add a new file of fonts or DAs to a menu within a couple of seconds, regardless of the number of fonts or DAs stored in the file. Further, adding extra fonts or DAs doesn't bloat your System file. As far as the System is concerned, only the Suitcase DA is occupying memory. While Suitcase itself uses slightly more memory if you add a few dozen fonts or DAs, the actual files you add with Suitcase only occupy extra memory when you use them.

Font/DA Juggler

The first real competition to Suitcase is Font/DA Juggler. This program offers more flexibility than Suitcase in some areas, but it is more restrictive in other areas. It retails for $49.95, compared to $59.95 for Suitcase.

Font/DA Juggler installs as a DA in your System file. When you select it from the Apple menu, you get a dialog box that you use to open or close suitcase files.

As with Suitcase, you can navigate through your hard disk to locate the suitcase files you want to open, but unlike Suitcase, Font/DA Juggler limits you to two files open at a time. Once you open a suitcase file using Font/DA Juggler, that file will open automatically whenever you restart your Mac until you specifically close it using Font/DA Juggler. This gives you the same automatic file-loading capability as in Suitcase.

Having access to only two suitcase files at once isn't as flexible as Suitcase, but because you can have up to 52 DAs in a given file, you could have 116 DAs available at once (52 + 52 + 14 in the other DA slots). Again, this is more than the practical limit. To use different sets of fonts or DAs, though, you will have to combine many fonts or DAs in large suitcase files (because you can only have two files open at a time), rather than using one of your two open file slots for a single font or DA.

One way to maximize the capacity of Font/DA Juggler is to create suitcase files that contain both fonts and DAs. To do this, you use the Font/DA Mover a little differently. Suppose you have a file called Standard Fonts, and you want to combine it with a file called standard DAs:

1. Launch the Font/DA Mover program. The left-hand list box will show the fonts in the current System file.

2. Click the Close button below the left-hand window to close the System file, then click the Open button and navigate to the Standard Fonts file.

3. Hold down the Option key and click the Open button below the right-hand list box. The list box will show both font and DA files (instead of just font files, as it would normally).

4. Select the Standard DAs file, and then copy its files to the Standard Fonts file. The Standard Fonts file will now contain both DAs and fonts.

Nevertheless, these are all extra steps you have to take to make Font/DA Juggler as flexible as Suitcase is without all the hassle. But Font/DA Juggler goes beyond Suitcase with its bonus utilities.

These utilities take the form of FKey programs (see Chapters 2 and 12) that give you keyboard access to desk accessories or other FKey programs. The first one, called Key DA FKey, installs as an FKey in your System Folder and then enables you to open any DA from a menu by typing its name. As you install Key DA FKey, you are asked to assign it an FKey combination (the Command and Shift keys along with a number key from 5 through 0).

When you press the FKey combination after Key FKey DA is installed, a menu of current desk accessories pops up (it's different than the Apple menu), and you can select a DA by typing the first few letters of its name to select it and then pressing the Return key.

Selecting DAs by name like this works just like selecting files in a Standard File box: If the list contains two very similar names, like Truck and Trucks, you would have to type the entire name Trucks to select it. You can, however, type a few letters to move to the part of the menu close to the item you want, and then use the arrow keys on the keyboard to select the correct name.

• The second bonus FKey is called Key FKey. Once you install it as an FKey, it produces a pop-up menu showing the names of all available FKey files on your disk. As with the pop-up DA menu, you can open an FKey file by typing its name (or using the arrow keys) to select it on the menu, and then pressing the Return key. The big advantage to Key Fkey is that it overcomes the FKey limit imposed by the Apple keyboard. Normally, you would only be able to install six FKeys, assigned to the number keys 5 through 0. Key FKey makes an unlimited number of FKeys available on a menu, and it only uses up one number key to do it. (See Chapter 12 for more information on FKeys.)

Whereas Font/DA Juggler's bonus programs give you keyboard access to desk accessories and FKeys, its two-file limit on open font/DA files makes it far less flexible than Suitcase overall. Still, this program is $10 less expensive, and if you don't have a large collection of fonts or DAs (and need to swap them onto and off of the Apple and Font menus), Font/DA Juggler is fine.

Which DAs to Choose?

With the ability to add more fonts and DAs than you'd ever need to your Apple and Font menus, you need to separate the wheat from the chaff. You don't want to be scrolling endlessly through hundreds of menu items looking for a specific font or DA, so you want to limit the number of fonts or DAs installed at any one time. On the other hand, you don't want to be constantly opening and closing additional font/DA files to access fonts or DAs you use frequently. We already mentioned the idea of creating application-specific groups of fonts or DAs, but here are some guidelines to help you choose the fonts and DAs you'll want to have around all the time.

Essential DAs

Two DAs supplied by Apple are essential if you want to change System information or access a different peripheral with your Macintosh. The Chooser is the DA that you use to select printer resources as well as volumes from a disk server. It is simply called Chooser, because it was designed to be open ended, to select any hard disk volume, network printer, communications server, or other device on an AppleTalk network or anything directly connected to the machine. If you are using additional Chooser resources (see Chapter 12), you can also use the Chooser to select other things such as Page Preview programs, print spoolers, and some screen dump utilities. Finally, with the Chooser you tell your Mac whether to use an AppleTalk network. Without having the Chooser installed, you can't tell your Mac to use a different printer or network device.

The Control Panel desk accessory stores and changes your setting preferences for the Macintosh, such as the mouse movement sensitivity, beep volume, keyboard sensitivity, desktop background, RAM cache size, and clock time and format. You won't be able to change any of these settings without using the Control Panel, so be sure it's installed.

Two other DAs we consider essential to hard disk users are some kind of file-finding program and a font/DA extender program. Apple supplies a simple file finder called Find File with its System software (in version 4.1 and later), but there are also commercial and public domain programs. Every file finder will quickly locate a file or folder on your hard disk by simply looking for a search string. Some of the commercial file finders also duplicate many of the Finder's file management functions, such as copying, deleting, or renaming files or folders. No matter how well organized your disk is, you won't be able to remember the location of every file, and a file finder will save you a lot of hunting. (See Chapter 10 for more on file finders.)

Even if you only want a few DAs on your Apple menu, having a font/DA extender installed makes it much easier to access additional DAs when you need them. You can open other, seldom-used DAs from inside the application program you're running, instead of having to launch the Font/DA Mover. The virtues of font/DA extenders have been covered earlier in this chapter.

There are other ways to work around the 15 DA limit, as described in Chapter 4, but a font/DA extender is a much safer, more convenient, and more flexible way of gaining access to all the DAs you want.

One last DA you should consider essential, if you have it, is a print spooler controller. If you're using a print spooler (see Chapter 8), it will have its own DA that controls printing. Without this DA installed, you can't use the spooler effectively.

If you're using a font/DA extender, you can access every other DA through the extender program: The only DA you actually need to install in your System file is the font/DA extender itself. But while these programs have proven very reliable, you should install your other essential DAs directly in the System file. Then, if your font/DA extender ever goes on the blink, you'll still have access to your Chooser, Control Panel, file finder, and print spooler controller.

Other Handy DAs

The next group of DAs are handy enough to have that they should be part of your standard DA set. Depending on how you use your Mac, some of these DAs may also be considered essential.

One of the purposes of a DA is to offer the services of an application (a graphic program, a word processor, or a spreadsheet) from inside another application you may be running. If you spend most of your time working with a spreadsheet program, for example, you can have access to word processing for quick notes with a DA word processor.

If you're using MultiFinder (see Chapter 13), you don't have as great a need to make other applications available as DAs, because you can have two, three, or more applications available at a time and switch from one to the other as you need them. Still, DA applications free up the memory you would have to use if you opened multiple applications in MultiFinder, because DAs only use memory when they're open, whereas MultiFinder applications use memory all the time, even when they're not currently active. Furthermore, there are many DAs that perform specific utility functions that aren't offered by application programs.

Number Tools

Some people think the basic Calculator DA supplied with Apple system software is useless, preferring to use the calculators they have on their desks. Most complaints about the Calculator DA have to do with its limitations. It doesn't remember numbers, it has only four functions, and it doesn't print a tape of calculations you've made. There are a number of other calculator DAs that address these problems, though. Calculator+, which is part of the

SideKick package of DAs from Borland International, has a memory function and can display and print a tape of previous calculations. Other special-purpose calculators are available for scientific and financial applications.

If you want even more number-crunching power at your fingertips, try one of the spreadsheet programs that work as DAs. One such DA is MacPlan, which comes with the SideKick package. MacPlan limits spreadsheets to 50 rows, but it has all the common spreadsheet functions and can load and save files like a normal spreadsheet.

Word-Handling DAs

Having access to a word processor at all times is also useful, and unless you're using an integrated program like Microsoft Works or MultiFinder with at least 2 megabytes of RAM, that probably means using a word processing DA. Most of the DA word processors create standard text files. They create documents without any formatting that can be read by almost any word processor, as well as other programs that can read text only files. Word processing DAs can't read or edit files created by another word processor unless that document was saved as text only by that word processor, or unless you copy text from your word processor into the word processing DA via the Clipboard. Mockwrite is the classic in this arena, although Miniwriter has been given good reviews by users.

An outlining program is also a handy, if not essential, DA if you write a lot or need to organize your thoughts or activities in a list form. Outlining DAs add this capability to any word processor you use, because you can copy from an outline window into a word processor document. Along with storing and organizing text, most outliners can store graphic files, so you could use an outlining program to store a lot of graphics and their titles. Acta is the most popular DA outliner. We used it to store and transmit the graphic files for this book, creating one Acta outline for each chapter.

Other word tools, such as spelling checkers and thesaurus programs, are also available as desk accessories. With a DA spelling checker like Thunder, from Electronic Arts, you can access a spelling dictionary from most of the applications you run—spreadsheet and database programs as well as word processors.

Other DAs can give you word-handling capabilities most normal word processors don't offer. Word Count is a DA that counts the words in text files as well as files created by the more popular word processing programs,

Microsoft Word and MacWrite. McSink is another DA that does a lot of text-manipulating chores, such as changing text to all uppercase, capitalizing the first word in every sentence, or removing carriage returns at the end of each line.

Graphic DAs

The Apple-supplied Scrapbook, or a commercial equivalent, is essential for anyone who uses a lot of graphics in his or her work. With the Scrapbook, you can store graphics created by MacPaint or other programs, then paste the illustrations into other documents. The Scrapbook limits the size of the graphics you can store, and you have to scroll through it to find the particular graphic you want. Also, all the graphics you put in the Scrapbook are stored in one file, which can become unwieldy.

Scrapbook alternatives make things easier. One popular program called SmartScrap, from Solutions, Inc., can store larger graphics and gives you a table of contents that you use to move directly to any graphic you have stored, eliminating the usual scrolling. It also lets you create multiple scrapbook files and load or save them as you need to.

Several other DAs prove to be very useful if you work with graphics a lot. Cheap Paint, from Macromind, is a commercial desk accessory version of MacPaint. It doesn't have all the functionality of MacPaint, but it's wonderful for cleaning up drawings quickly once you've put them in a document or for adding a border to a graphic. Cheap Paint can't save multiple graphic files—it just saves the last item you worked with in the Cheap Paint file—but you can copy graphics from Cheap Paint into a scrapbook file or outlining program file for storage there.

Art Grabber is a shareware DA that opens any MacPaint style document, "grabs" a section of that document, and copies it to the Clipboard to be pasted into a document.

Dialers

If you use the phone a lot, and the numbers you call with your computer are frequently busy, a dialing accessory can be very handy. One such dialer, called QDial, dials a telephone number repeatedly until it answers, and then signals you (by honking and blinking the Apple icon in the menu bar) when the call has gone through. This action happens in the background, so you can run another program while it's happening. Once QDial beeps you, you have time to start up your telecommunications program and connect to the remote system.

The SideKick collection of DAs also contains a telephone dialer called MacDialer. It doesn't redial numbers automatically, but it logs the time of each call, and can automatically code calls with a particular client name and billing rate at the click of a mouse. SideKick also has a DA communications program called MacTerm.

Utilities

Dozens of utility DAs serve useful functions:

- Screen saver DAs black out your Mac screen (so you can cut down on the wear on your monitor screen when you're out to lunch without turning down the contrast knob).

- Clock DAs present a variety of different clocks showing the current time, from a facsimile of Big Ben to a world time clock that shows times in four or five international zones.

- Game DAs give you instant access to different diversions.

- Programmer's aids calculate hexadecimal addresses or pinpoint memory locations.

- Amortizers calculate payments on different loan amounts at different rates.

- Security DAs help you to prevent access to your Mac system by anyone who doesn't have a certain password.

This only scratches the surface of the variety of DAs available. To really get an idea of just what's out there, you have to go hunting for yourself. (See Where to Get Fonts and DAs at the end of this chapter.)

Which Fonts to Choose?

As discussed in Chapter 4, fonts are a matter of personal choice for the most part, and the fonts you end up using will often be the ones you personally like. To recap Chapter 4:

- Your System file must contain the fonts Chicago 12, Geneva 12, and Monaco 9, because these are used by the Mac to display icon names, window names, and other necessities.

- You should choose at least one font that's easy to read on the screen, such as Geneva, New York, or Boston.

- If you use a LaserWriter, you'll want some or all of the LaserWriter's built-in fonts to be available. The two most popular built-in fonts are Helvetica and Times, and the others (if you're using a LaserWriter Plus or the newer LaserWriter IINT or IINTX) are Helvetica Narrow, Courier, Bookman, Palatino, New Century Schoolbook, Symbol, Zapf Dingbats, and Zapf Chancery.
- For less serious documents (invitations, flyers, and so on), have one or two less businesslike letter fonts such as Avant Garde or Zapf Chancery, along with one or two picture fonts like Cairo and Mobile.

When you install fonts, you don't have to worry as much about menu clutter. Unless you're a graphic designer, you will probably change fonts less than you'll access various DAs, so you won't spend as much time scrolling the Font menu if you include dozens of fonts as you would looking for different DAs you might use frequently as you work.

Where to Get Fonts and DAs

You can learn about commercially available fonts and DAs from friends or from reading Mac magazines, but the least expensive and most varied collections of fonts DAs are available from Mac user groups. Most Mac user groups maintain disk libraries of public domain and shareware software, and fonts and DAs make up a respectable part of any such library.

The two largest Mac user groups are the Berkeley Macintosh User Group (BMUG), and BCS•Mac, the Boston Computer Society's Macintosh Group, both of which have large disk libraries containing hundreds of fonts and DAs. You can buy a disk containing about 40 or 50 fonts or DAs for about $3–$4. (See the Appendix for BMUG and BCS•Mac user group information). Otherwise, there are local Mac user groups all over the country that offer many of the same public domain and shareware fonts and DAs themselves.

There's one caution about shareware and public domain DAs, however: Most of them are written by individual programmers who don't test them nearly as thoroughly as a commercial developer would. The more popular DAs, like those mentioned in this book, have been in use long enough that they have proven reliable. But lesser-known DAs may have problems, and you should be aware of the risk. (Of course, commercial programs can have bugs too, it's just that the bugs in commercial software tend to be less severe.)

Extending your access to fonts and DAs is one of the most productive things you can do as a hard disk user. In Chapter 12, we'll look at some other ways to expand your Mac's resources.

12

Using Chooser Resources, FKeys, and Inits

As mentioned in Chapter 2, there are some special kinds of System files that expand the capabilities of your Macintosh. In this chapter, we'll take a closer look at Chooser resources, FKeys, and Inits. After a description of how each type of program works, we'll look at some specific examples.

Chooser Resources

A Chooser resource is a small program that, when placed in the System Folder, causes an icon to appear in the Chooser window when you select the Chooser desk accessory. Chooser resources are always programs, or drivers, that tell the Mac how to send data to (and from) an external device such as a printer, a network server, or a network modem.

To install a new Chooser resource, you simply drag it into your Mac's System Folder. The resource must be *directly* inside your System Folder, not inside a folder inside the System Folder. Once you drag the resource into your System Folder, it immediately becomes available in the Chooser window: You don't have to restart your Mac first, as you do with Init programs.

If you have a typical Mac system, your System Folder probably contains Chooser resources for the ImageWriter and the LaserWriter, so those resource icons appear on the left side of the Chooser window when you select the Chooser from the Apple menu, as in Figure 12–1.

213

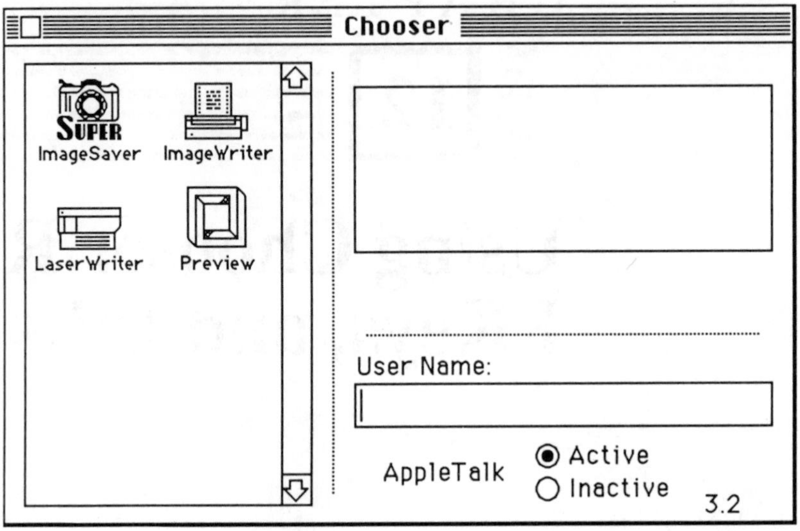

Figure 12–1. Chooser resources appear in the Chooser window as icons.

If you've installed custom drivers for non-Apple printers in your System Folder, icons for them will appear as well. If you're using a network file server and have placed its driver in your System Folder, an icon for that file server will also appear. Finally, there are products that act as printers, but are not, such as Preview and Glue (described later). You can add as many Chooser resources to your System as you like, and their icons will appear in the Chooser window. If you add more resources than can be displayed, the list of icons in the window becomes scrollable.

Of the three types of System files discussed in this chapter, Chooser resources are the least troublesome. They're simple programs that are supplied by commercial hardware or software vendors, either as utility programs or so your Mac can interact with their specific products. Even if a Chooser resource isn't working for some reason, your System won't crash—you just won't be able to use the device represented by that resource in the Chooser window. Now, let's look at some different Chooser resources.

Preview

Preview acts as a printer Chooser resource, except it prints to your Mac's screen instead. Preview is a shareware program with a $10 registration fee. When it prints a document to the screen, you can see what the document will look like when printed on paper. (Some application programs don't print exactly the same way they look on the screen.)

Many productivity applications such as Excel and Microsoft Word now include on-screen previews as a built-in feature, but if your favorite program lacks a preview feature, you can use the Preview Chooser resource.

To use Preview, you simply select it in the Chooser and then print your file normally. Instead of going to your printer, your file will appear on the screen in miniature, as Figure 12–2 shows.

Preview displays one page of your file at a time. To view more pages, you click the Next button. Preview is also distributed with an FKey (described later) that you can install to access the preview function without

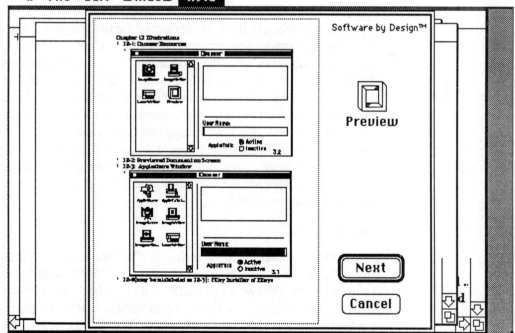

Figure 12–2. The Preview Chooser resource prints a miniature version of your document to the screen exactly as it will appear when printed.

having to select the icon in the Chooser window. Instead, you install the FKey under the number key 6, and then press Command-Shift-6 to activate the preview. To switch back to your regular printer driver, you press the FKey combination again.

Along with displaying a page in miniature, Preview has a zoom feature. By clicking the mouse as you point to a miniature page, you can display the page in normal size. This helps if you need to read something on a page, because the miniature pages contain type too small to read.

SuperGlue

SuperGlue is another Chooser resource, an $89.95 product from Solutions, Inc., that you use to print formatted files or graphics to a disk file. To use SuperGlue, you select its icon in the Chooser window. After that, the file you print will go not to your printer, but to a special Glue file on disk. You're asked to name the file and select the disk or folder in which you want to store it before the file is actually printed.

Once you print a file to disk with SuperGlue, you can open that file, resize it, and copy it into another document without having to use the application program that originally created the file. So, you can use it in lieu of a specific application program when you want to share a file with somebody who doesn't own the application. If you have an Excel spreadsheet you want to share, you can print it to disk (either as a Glue file or as a scrapbook file) with SuperGlue and send it to another user, who can open it with SuperGlue or the Scrapbook and then view it, all without having to know a thing about Excel. If you were contributing to a sales report, for example, you could print an Excel spreadsheet to disk as a Glue document and send it to the report's author. Without using Excel software, the report's author could open the spreadsheet file, resize the spreadsheet, and paste it into a word processor document.

Printworks

Printworks is the name of a series of Chooser resource products from Softstyle, Inc., with which you print from your Mac to non-Apple printers. There are three Printworks products: a daisy wheel printer version, a dot matrix printer version, and a laser printer version. Each package comes with a collection of drivers (Chooser resources) for various printers. You simply drag the driver for the printer you want to use into your System Folder, and that printer's icon appears as an option in the Chooser.

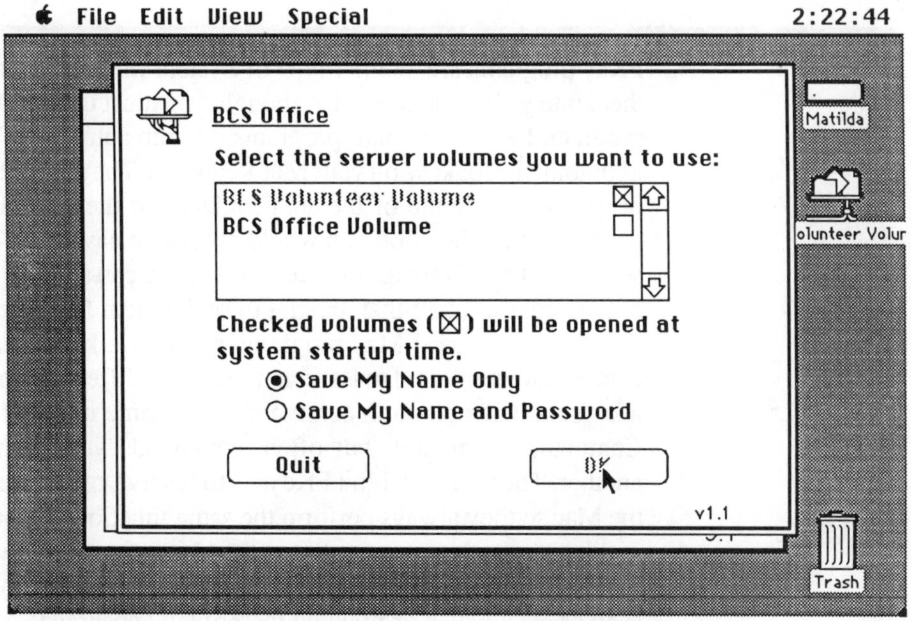

Figure 12–3. You can use the AppleShare Chooser resource to log onto an AppleShare network.

PrintWorks for daisy wheel printers ($95) comes with drivers for Brother, Diablo, IBM, NEC, Qume, and Apple daisy wheel printers. The dot matrix version ($75) supplies drivers for Apple, Brother, Epson, Hewlett-Packard, IBM, NEC, Star Micronics, Texas Instruments, and Toshiba printers. The laser printer version ($145) has drivers for HP LaserJet, Canon, NCR, and Xerox laser printers.

One last example is the Chooser resource that comes with AppleShare. To join an AppleShare network, you install this resource in your System Folder, then select the icon in the Chooser window. When you select the icon in the Chooser window, you'll see a window from which you select a file server and log onto the network, as shown in Figure 12–3.

These examples give you an idea of the types of Chooser resources available. As printing, communications, and networking options expand for the Mac, new Chooser resources will appear.

FKeys

FKey programs are another type of System file. Instead of simply dragging them into your System Folder, though, you must install FKeys with a special program. FKeys are small programs that run automatically when you press a combination of keys on your Mac keyboard. They are either small accessory programs, like some of the smaller DAs, or they're utility programs that perform a Mac function you would otherwise have to do by making a menu selection. The advantage of FKeys is that you can activate them with a couple of keystrokes, rather than having to select them from a menu.

If you've used Mac programs at all, you know that many keystroke combinations are used to issue commands in different programs. Sometimes a keystroke combination command is the same in many programs, such as Command-Q for quit, but often, commands vary from one program to another. The notion behind FKeys is to reserve certain key combinations on the Mac so they always perform the same function, no matter what program you happen to be running. Since these functions are always available, the functions themselves tend to be tasks you might need to do from any program, such as eject a disk or preview the printed appearance of a document.

Apple set aside the number keys, 1 through 0, in the top row of the keyboard as function keys. These keys just produce numbers (or symbols when you press them with the Shift key), but when they are pressed in combination with the Command and Shift keys, they perform specific activities from any program. Apple has programmed keys 1 through 4 for its own use, as follows:

- Command-Shift-1: Ejects the floppy diskette from the internal disk drive.

- Command-Shift-2: Ejects the floppy diskette from the external disk drive (or the second internal disk drive on a Mac SE or Mac II).

- Command-Shift-3: Creates a MacPaint image of the screen in a file on disk and labels it Screen0. (You can create up to 10 screen files on disk at a time, and they'll be automatically labeled Screen0 through Screen9. If you want to create more screen files after that, you must rename the first 10 screens so your Mac can use the Screen0–9 filenames over again.)

- Command-Shift-4: Prints the current screen on the ImageWriter. (This command doesn't work if you've selected the LaserWriter with the Chooser, unless you've installed a special FKey (called LaserKey) under Command-Shift-4 instead of the normal Apple FKey—as described later.)

These FKeys are installed in your System file when you get it from Apple. Try pressing Command-Shift-1 or Command-Shift-2 to eject a disk if you want to see an FKey in action. But the other six function key spaces (under number keys 5 through 0) are available for you to install your own FKey programs.

Installing FKeys

There are currently three methods of installing FKeys: using the Resource Editor, using a program called FKey Installer, and using a program called FKey Manager. Let's look at each method.

The Resource Editor The Resource Editor (also called ResEdit) is an Apple developer's utility that wasn't designed for use by a typical Mac owner. With it you can tinker with the System file in many ways, including changing the names of menus or menu commands, assigning keyboard combinations to menu commands, and installing FKeys. Using ResEdit properly requires a sound technical knowledge of the System file, and if you don't have such knowledge, you're much better off using an alternate method to install FKeys. The Resource Editor has a lot of powerful features which, if used improperly, can screw up your System file beyond repair faster than you can say "Oops!"

If you're familiar with the use of ResEdit, here's the basic procedure for installing an FKey:

1. Start ResEdit and use it to open your System file.
2. Select the resource called FKey.
3. Open the file containing the FKey you want to install, copy it to the Clipboard, and paste it into the FKey list in ResEdit.

FKey Installer The second way to install FKeys is with a public domain program named FKey Installer. FKey Installer was the first application program designed specifically for installing or removing FKeys. To install an FKey, first launch FKey Installer. You'll see a list of the FKey slots 1 through 0, as Figure 12–4 shows.

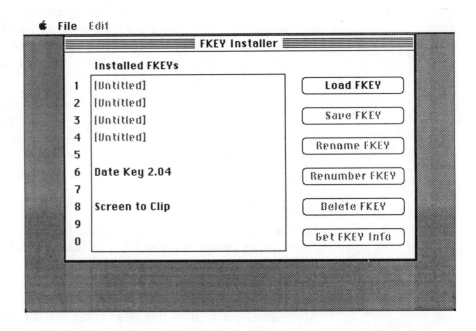

Figure 12–4. FKey Installer shows you which FKeys you currently have installed, and which FKey slots are available.

As you can see in Figure 12–4, the window also contains buttons you can use to install or remove FKeys, or quit the program. When you click the Install button, you'll see a Standard File box, in which you can navigate to the folder or disk containing the FKeys you want to install. FKey Installer only shows FKeys in this dialog box that were created in the FKey Installer format (the common format these days), so if you have especially old FKey files that don't seem to be appearing in the dialog box, that's probably why. (The old files were designed to be cut and pasted with the Resource Editor.)

If the FKeys you want to install don't appear in the Standard File box under FKey Installer, it's likely that you'll be able to find a more recent version of those FKeys. You're better off getting the most up-to-date version of any FKey you install.

When you install them, many FKeys try to grab a particular number key as their own, if they can. (Preview tries to grab key number 6, for example.) If that number key is unavailable (because another FKey is already using it),

FKey Installer will give you the option to choose a new number yourself, or to let it choose a number for you.

With FKey Installer, you can only keep installing FKeys until you've used all the other available number keys. Because there are only six available number keys to begin with, you can fill them up quickly. But once you install your six new FKeys and start using them, you may find yourself hungry for more. If so, you'll want the product called MasterKey. When you use MasterKey, you get a Standard File box through which you navigate to and open other FKeys from your disk, one at a time. This is a good way to overcome the 10-FKey limit if you only use one or two additional FKeys during a session with your Mac. If you want to have *lots* of extra FKeys available more easily, though, read about the program reviewed next, FKey Manager.

FKey Manager   FKey Manager is a public domain program written by Carlos Weber, MD. The FKey Manager package does several things. The FKey Manager itself is a tool for installing or removing FKeys or listing the FKeys you have installed. FKey Manager also lets you create sets of FKeys in groups, so you can manage them more easily. (This is a little like storing a lot of fonts or DAs in the same suitcase file. See Chapter 11.)

But FKey Manager also comes with two bonus programs. One, called FKey Pad, enables you to use the numeric keypad number keys as function keys instead of the number keys in the top row of your keyboard. The other program, Pop-Keys, creates custom menus of FKeys that can contain (and thus give you access to) more than the 10 FKeys stored under your number keys. Let's look at these programs individually.

FKey Manager works a lot like the Font/DA Mover. The basic FKey Manager screen shows you the contents of the FKey slots you currently have, along with a list of FKey files you've selected from a disk, as shown in Figure 12–5.

Along with a simpler interface, the other big advantage to FKey Manager over ResEdit or FKey Installer is that you can assign key numbers greater than nine to FKeys. These FKeys won't be available from the keyboard, but they can be made available from a pop-up menu using the Pop-Keys program (described later).

Before FKey Manager, there really wasn't a way to back up the particular set of FKeys you had installed in your System file. If you had to replace your System file, the installed FKeys would be lost (except the Apple

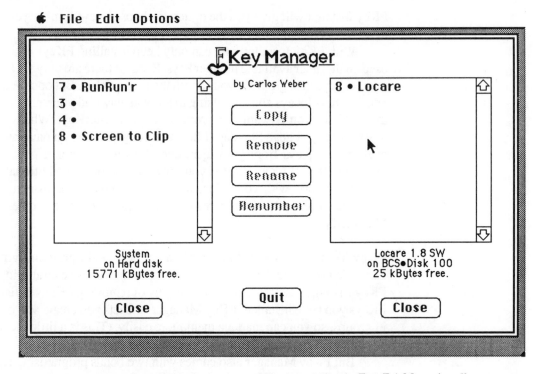

Figure 12–5. FKey Manager installs or removes FKeys much like the Font/DA Mover installs or removes fonts or desk accessories.

ones, which are included with every System file), and you would have to locate and reinstall all your custom FKeys one at a time. The FKey Manager has a menu selection that specifically saves the currently installed FKeys as a set, with a name that includes the current date. You can restore all your FKeys from this one file if the need arises.

FKeyPad   It's nice to have FKeys at your fingertips, but many people think there are too many fingertips required. Typically, you have to type three keys: Command, Shift, and a number key, to activate an FKey program. FKeyPad is an Init program that helps you reconfigure number keys on your keyboard so you can activate FKeys without pressing the Command and Shift keys at the same time.

If you have a Mac Plus, Mac SE, or Mac II, your keyboard has two sets of numbers on it—the numbers on the top and the ones on the numeric keypad. Most people tend to use one or the other most or all of the time. FKeyPad turns the set of number keys you don't use into dedicated FKeys, so that they'll activate your FKey programs when you press them individually, rather than in combination with the Command and Shift keys. With FKey Pad installed, you can simply press the number key 1, for example, to eject the disk in the internal drive, rather than pressing Command-Shift-1.

Pop-Keys FKey programs can be very handy, so handy that you may wish for access to more than six of of your own programs at once. This is where Pop-Keys comes in. Pop-Keys gives you access to a pop-up menu that contains a list of all your installed FKeys for you to scroll through. Once you've used FKey Manager to install a series of FKeys, you can use Pop-Keys to produce a menu so you can select the program you want.

Pop-Keys is an Init program that installs in your System Folder. Once it's installed, you can bring up the Pop-Keys menu in two different ways: You can assign a keystroke combination to Pop-Keys, then invoke the menu by typing that combination and clicking the mouse at the same time; or you can simply move the mouse to a specific place on your screen and click the button. If you use the keystroke-mouse click combination, the menu appears at the current location of the insertion point in your document. If you assign a specific area of the screen to activate the menu when you point to it and click, the menu will appear in that area, as Figure 12–6 shows.

All these options are controlled from inside the FKey Manager. Install Pop-Keys in the System Folder, then they become available to change. Once you've installed Pop-Keys properly, you decide how you want to activate it through a screen in FKey Manager, guided by instructions shown in Figure 12–7.

Pop-Keys, FKey Pad, and FKey Manager are the standard FKey tools these days. Although they're public domain programs, they've been around long enough and have been refined enough by their author so they're almost completely reliable. (Which isn't bad, when you consider that nothing is totally reliable on a computer.) At this writing, however, Pop-Keys isn't compatible with the Macintosh II.

The problems you're likely to run into with FKeys is with the FKey programs themselves. These are small utility programs that are offered as shareware or are in the public domain. Most of them were written by amateur programmers, as were most public domain and shareware DAs. This means

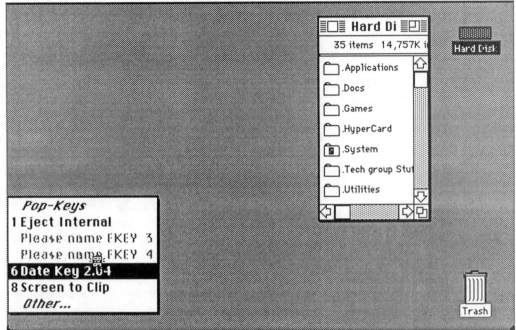

Figure 12–6. With Pop-Keys you can create a custom menu containing many FKeys.

they may not have been tested as thoroughly as commercial programs, and they may crash. If a desk accessory program crashes, you simply restart your Mac and get rolling again. But FKey crashes can sometimes corrupt your System file, and you can end up replacing your System. The most popular FKey programs have proven quite reliable, but to protect yourself, try new FKeys on a floppy disk System file first. That way, you won't have to replace your hard disk's System file (which can contain lots of laboriously installed fonts and DAs) if there's a problem.

Here are some examples of tried-and-true FKeys.

MenuSelect is an FKey that helps you create more accurate screen dump files when you use Command-Shift-4 (see the earlier description of this FKey). With System versions after 3.2, the Apple screen dump FKey (Command-Shift-4) no longer captures a menu from the screen if you were using the mouse to display that menu at the time. If you want a screen dump showing the File menu's contents, for example, pressing Command-Shift-4

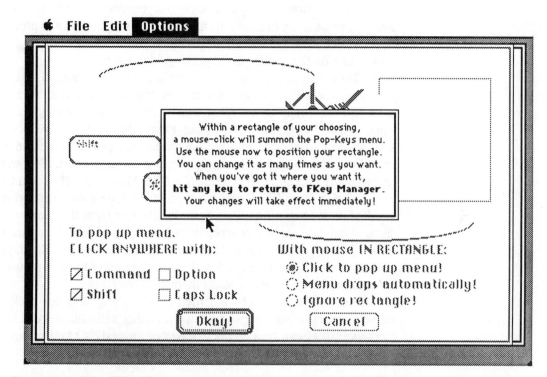

Figure 12–7. Using FKey Manager, you can decide where you want the Pop-Keys menu of FKeys to appear and how you want to activate it.

prints a MacPaint file to disk all right, but when you open that file, you'll see that the File menu isn't displayed. If you have MenuSelect installed, however, you can capture menus in screen dump files as well. All you do is press the MenuSelect FKey, pull down the menu you want, and then press the Option key.

ScreenToClip is a handy FKey if you work with graphics a lot. When you activate this FKey, you get a selection rectangle (like the one in MacPaint or other paint programs), and you can select a portion of the image on the screen and copy it to the Clipboard. You can grab pieces of screen images and save them without having to use a desk accessory.

DateKey is a simple FKey that prints the date (as stored by your Mac's internal clock) at the current location of the insertion point when you type it. This is very useful if you type a lot of letters or make a lot of database file entries requiring a date.

Sleep is a simple FKey that blacks out your screen and keeps it that way until you press a key or move the mouse. This is a good way to protect your Mac's screen from burned-in images when you're going out for an hour or two, or to hide that game you're playing from the boss.

ClipperKey places carriage returns at the end of standard text files, so you can upload them to other computers more easily. MCI Mail, for example, is an electronic mail system that won't accept messages containing lines longer than 78 characters. If you use a text editor DA like MockWrite or MiniWriter, carriage returns aren't automatically placed at the end of each line. But ClipperKey automatically places a carriage return after every 78 characters in a text file, so systems like MCI Mail won't choke on them.

DA Key is an FKey you can type to produce a menu showing your installed desk accessories. This menu is different from the standard Apple menu in that you can select accessories from it by typing all or part of their names, just as you can select files in a Standard File box. DA Key helps you activate DAs a little more quickly, because you don't have to remove your hands from the keyboard to select them with the mouse.

FKeys have long been regarded as something only for hackers and active members of user's groups, but with today's installation and management tools, they can be a productive part of anybody's Mac system.

Inits

Inits are small programs that run automatically whenever you turn your Mac on. You install Inits simply by dragging them into your System Folder and then restarting your Mac. (An Init isn't activated until you start your Mac, so those you drag into the System Folder won't work until you restart.) To remove an Init, just drag it out of your System Folder and restart your Mac.

Because Inits install in your System Folder and interact with your System file, they can cause problems. If you have a lot of different Inits in the System Folder, incompatibilities caused by the combination of Inits can cause your System file to malfunction. If this happens, you can remedy the problem by removing the Inits from the System Folder one at at time until your System works normally again. (See Chapter 15.)

Inits fall into three basic categories: *utility Inits* that perform a specific function, *program Inits* that facilitate the operation of application programs, and *fun Inits* that make your Mac look or sound more interesting. Let's look at some examples.

Program Inits

There are a number of program Inits that work with programs we've already discussed in this book.

- Findswell, the file-finding program covered in Chapter 10, uses an Init to install a special button in the Standard File boxes of your application programs.

- PrintMonitor, Apple's print spooler that runs under MultiFinder, uses an Init called Backgrounder to activate the PrintMonitor program automatically.

- Suitcase, the DA extender and manager covered in Chapter 11, uses an Init to install the Suitcase DA on the Apple menu and to start the program each time you turn on your Mac.

- Font/DA Juggler, another DA extender covered in Chapter 11, also uses an Init to load the program automatically.

Utility Inits

Utility Inits are usually shareware or public domain programs that add value to your Mac in a specific way. Following are some examples.

J-Clock, one of the first public domain Inits, installs a digital clock in the upper right corner of your menu bar, so you always know what time it is. To make the clock disappear, you point to the clock and hold down the mouse button for a few seconds. J-Clock has been refined many times by various other programmers. Newer versions present the time in either 12-hour or 24-hour formats, and with or without seconds (as well as hours and minutes). The original J-Clock didn't automatically disappear if it was obscuring a menu title (for programs that have menus going all the way across the menu bar), but newer versions do. J-Clock is free.

AutoBlack is a screen saver that automatically blacks out your screen if you don't press a key or move the mouse for five minutes. When it goes into action, though, your screen isn't completely black; instead, you'll see an analog clock (which shows the correct time as maintained by your Mac's internal clock) jumping slowly around the screen. You can black out your screen immediately by pointing to the upper right corner of your screen and clicking the mouse button. AutoBlack always blacks out your screen after five minutes, even if you're receiving a telecommunications transmission. This can be annoying if you want to monitor something on your screen without actually moving the mouse or pressing a key, so AutoBlack has an option to cancel the automatic screen blanking for two hours: You just click in the lower left corner of your screen, and AutoBlack goes out of action for two hours. AutoBlack is shareware and costs $5.

Modem Init

Ever dialed a friend and had the scream of a modem answer the phone instead? If you have a modem attached to your Mac, you've likely done that to one of your friends. The problem is that every once in a while you use a program that gives your modem instructions to answer the phone for you and then forgets to tell the modem not to do that anymore when the program is finished. Modem Init is a public domain program that sends a message to your modem not to answer the phone, so it won't answer the phone until you specifically tell it to with a communications program.

Fun Inits

Fun Inits are Inits that change the way your Mac looks and sounds.

Startup Screens is an Init that automatically uses a MacPaint image you specify as the background for the startup screen on your Mac. Instead of the typical box that says "Welcome to Macintosh," you'll see a MacPaint drawing instead. To use Startup Screens, you use a utility supplied with the program to convert a MacPaint file into a startup screen file, and then name the MacPaint file StartupScreen and place it in your System Folder. There are hundreds of MacPaint graphics you can get from a variety of sources that can be used as startup screens.

SoundInit is like Startup Screens, except it plays a bit of sound when you start up your Mac. There are many sound files available from user groups or bulletin boards. With SoundInit installed, you name a sound file StartupSound, and that sound will play whenever you start your Mac. Some of the sounds available include classical or rock music, voices, and a variety of beeps, boings, clangs, and clatters.

BeepInit is another sound Init; it plays a particular sound instead of the typical beep you hear when you make a mistake with your Mac. To use a sound to replace the normal system beep, just name it Beepsound and place it in your System Folder. One of our favorite sounds for replacing the beep is a digitized recording that says, "I try to think, but nothing happens."

Randomizer is an Init that automatically changes the Startup Screen, startup sound, and beep sound at random by selecting them from a file of possibilities you place in the System Folder.

Inits invite experimentation because they're so simple to install and because you don't have to lift a finger to use them once they are installed. They're a hard-working, unobtrusive addition to your System file, whether for serious work or just for fun.

CHAPTER

13

Using Finder Alternatives

The Finder is usually the first program you see each time you start up your Mac. It shows you the contents of your disks and folders, and it enables you to perform a variety of file management functions explained in Chapter 3. But the Finder is just an application program, like a word processor or spreadsheet, and if you don't like the way the Finder performs, you can use an alternative application instead. In this chapter, we'll look at a few different Finder alternatives—how they work, how they surpass or fall short of the Finder, and why you might want to use them.

A *Finder alternative* is an application program that partially or completely replaces the Finder as a file managing tool on the Macintosh. You install a Finder alternative by making it the Startup Application on your Mac, so it appears upon startup instead of the Finder. Finder alternatives fall into two categories: those that have fewer features than the Finder, but are faster and simpler (we'll call these SubFinders), and those that offer more features than the Finder (which we'll call SuperFinders). SubFinder and SuperFinder aren't common terms to describe these different programs; we've coined these monikers to make describing the different types of programs easier. Let's look at each type of alternative more closely.

SubFinders: The Speed Demons

The Finder is a great program, but it has a lot more functions and keeps track of a lot more information than you need most of the time. A SubFinder replaces the Finder with a smaller, more efficient program that offers basic file manipulation options with much better performance than the Finder. If you think about the way you work, you usually don't care how big a file is or when it was created or last modified—you just want to start your Mac, find a file or program quickly, and get to work. Because it keeps track of a lot of information you may not use every day, the Finder can be slow at finding and opening files. Further, because the Finder does so many things, it's a large program (version 6.0 consumes 99K) that takes several seconds to load whenever you quit an application program.

A SubFinder might display filenames only, rather than their sizes and modification dates, but because it stores less information, it can load and operate much faster than the Finder. (The SubFinder PowerStation, for example, uses only 56K.) Whenever you quit a program, you have to wait perhaps 20 seconds for the Finder to load. Once you've returned to the Finder, you must navigate your way through various folders to find the program or file you want. There are Finder techniques that help you minimize file-finding problems, as well as desk accessories (discussed in Chapter 10) you can use to load new files or programs without returning to the Finder, but you will still find yourself returning to and using the Finder at least once a day.

With a SubFinder, you can quit an application program and return to the Finder substitute much more quickly, and files can be easier to locate because there's less information about each file to sort through—typically a displayed list of names or a group of buttons, rather than a display of lots of overlapping windows, as with the Finder.

But a SubFinder probably won't replace your Finder completely. Some of the Finder commands, like Set Startup, aren't duplicated in any SubFinder. Further, it sometimes helps to view the contents of your disk in the large, detailed windows the Finder provides: It's like getting an aerial view of a city instead of a guided tour. Because the Finder is an application program just like a word processor or spreadsheet, you can make it an option under your Finder alternative's program selection menu so you can load it and use its extra features easily.

SuperFinders: Beyond the Finder

On the other hand, maybe the Finder's slowness doesn't bother you. Perhaps, instead, you're annoyed at the Finder's ability to present only one program on the screen at a time. Maybe you'd like to have several programs and the Finder itself all loaded into your Mac's memory at once, and to switch to any of them with only a mouse click or a keystroke. Those who like the Finder's approach to file management and simply want instant access to several programs at once can turn to a SuperFinder, such as Apple's MultiFinder.

Now that we've sketched the outlines of SubFinders and SuperFinders, let's examine them in more detail.

Using SubFinders

The most important thing a SubFinder does is launch applications or documents quickly. It should load more quickly than the Finder would when you start up your Mac and when you quit an application. Most Finder alternatives present one or more screen "pages," each of which contains a group of icons or buttons labeled with the names of the application programs or documents that you use most often. To load a document or launch an application, you simply click on the appropriate button or icon. One SubFinder's screen is shown in Figure 13–1.

Obviously, you wouldn't want to create a special button for every application or document on your disk, so SubFinders offer a special button you can click to produce a Standard File box, which lets you navigate through your folders and disks to load other files.

While they make finding specific files and applications easier, SubFinders omit a lot of functions you get in the Finder. The SubFinder you use may not have features like the Get Info command (which shows you more detailed information about a specific file), the Duplicate command that copies a folder quickly, the New Folder command, the Print Catalog command, the Set Startup command, or the Erase Disk command.

Making Up for Lost Features

Because much of the advantage of having a SubFinder would be lost if you had to return to the Finder all the time to get these extra functions, SubFinders are best used in conjunction with a desk accessory that offers some or most of the missing Finder commands. As described in Chapter 10, there are DAs

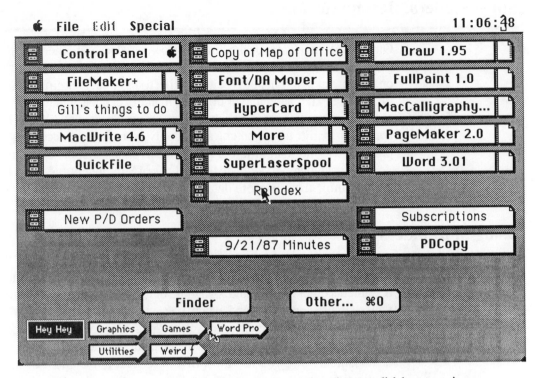

Figure 13–1. SubFinders load programs or documents when you click buttons or icons.

such as DiskTop and DiskInfo that include the New Folder, Get Info, and Erase Disk commands, so you can replace many of the missing Finder's extra functions without resorting to the Finder itself.

Most people use SubFinders along with a file-handling DA that replaces the missing Finder functions. With a combination like this, you may only have to use the Finder if you want to change Startup Applications. Otherwise, you can perform the Finder's functions more quickly and conveniently with a combination SubFinder and desk accessory setup.

Now, let's look at four programs that were designed as or can function as SubFinders: the MiniFinder, HyperCard, PowerStation, and MacTree.

The MiniFinder

The first widely used SubFinder was Apple's MiniFinder. The MiniFinder became an extra feature available from inside the Finder beginning with Finder version 4.1. As with other SubFinders, the MiniFinder was designed to give users faster access to programs and files than is possible with the Finder.

When installed, the MiniFinder becomes the Startup Application on your Mac and displays a window containing icons for specific programs or documents you have specified, as shown in Figure 13–2. You can load one of the programs or documents by clicking on its icon. Whenever you quit an application, you return to the MiniFinder window instead of the Finder.

Along with the icons, the MiniFinder window contains buttons for opening other programs that haven't been installed in the window, returning to the Finder, ejecting disks or changing disk drives, and shutting down the Mac.

To install the MiniFinder, you select the applications and documents you want to appear in its window, then select the Use MiniFinder... command from the Special menu in the Finder. You then click the Install button, and

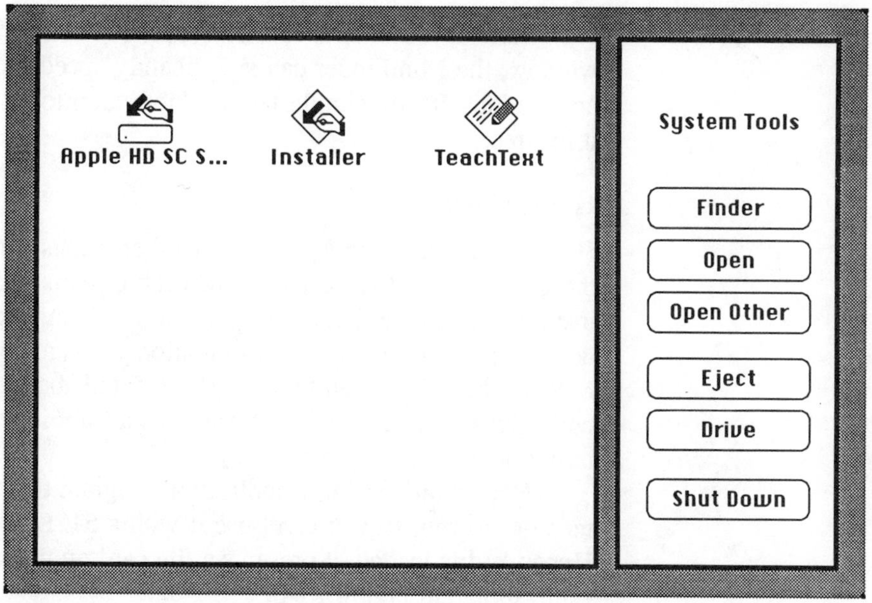

Figure 13–2. The MiniFinder opens documents or applications when you click on icons in its window.

the next time you start your Mac, the MiniFinder will appear instead of the Finder. To remove the MiniFinder, you click the button to return to the Finder, choose the Use MiniFinder... command again, and then click the Remove button.

The MiniFinder is fast and simple, but it has some serious limitations. It was designed before the HFS system was introduced, and it was really meant either for floppy disks or for small partitions of hard disks. As a result:

- You can only install up to twelve applications or documents in the Mini-Finder window.
- To install documents or applications, they must all be in the same folder or disk window.
- If you move an application or document to another folder after you've installed it in the MiniFinder, you won't be able to open it from the MiniFinder any more.
- You must use the mouse to load applications or documents—there are no keyboard commands.
- While the MiniFinder window is displayed, you don't have access to desk accessories on the Apple menu.

Still, if you keep a few key applications in the same disk or folder window, the MiniFinder can significantly speed the process of launching applications. It's the simplest of the SubFinders to set up and use, and you get it for free.

HyperCard

HyperCard is another Apple product that comes free with every new Mac these days and that you can use to select programs or documents with buttons instead of using the Finder. HyperCard is a complex product that is mostly used to generate complete information management applications on the Macintosh, and we won't go into much detail about that part of the program here. But to understand its potential as a SubFinder, we'll describe some basics about this program.

HyperCard is a large application program that requires about 700K of memory to run, so you can't use it with a 512K or 128K machine. When HyperCard is loaded, it presents a file card on the screen called the Home Card, shown in Figure 13–3.

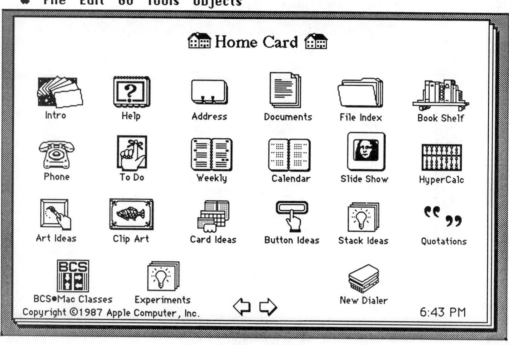

Figure 13–3. HyperCard can work as a SubFinder if you install special buttons on one of its cards.

Every screen in HyperCard is a card like this, and cards can contain labels, pictures, sounds, places for entering data, and buttons. Cards are arranged into groups, called *stacks*. HyperCard is a totally programmable application; with it you can design cards containing the labels, graphics, sounds, data entry fields, and buttons of your choice. The buttons on cards can enable you to use HyperCard as a SubFinder.

Buttons are typically used to navigate quickly to other cards containing data in a HyperCard stack, but you can also create buttons that navigate to documents or application programs on your disk and then open them. To use HyperCard as a SubFinder, you could create one or more cards filled with buttons grouped by application type or project, each of which navigates to and launches a different document or application program when you click it. Such a card might look like the one in Figure 13–4.

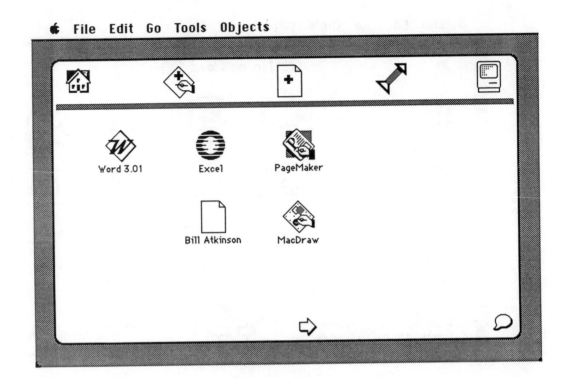

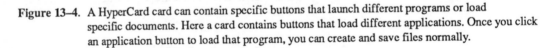

Figure 13–4. A HyperCard card can contain specific buttons that launch different programs or load specific documents. Here a card contains buttons that load different applications. Once you click an application button to load that program, you can create and save files normally.

If you set up program-launching buttons in HyperCard, you can load those programs just by clicking a button. When you quit such a program, you're returned to HyperCard, and the card containing the button you used to launch the program originally is displayed on the screen. Buttons in HyperCard are extremely versatile, so you could create buttons that duplicate other Finder operations such as Shut Down, Erase Disk, New Folder, and so forth. Creating such buttons requires an understanding of HyperCard's programming language, HyperTalk and the use of external commands.

You probably won't use HyperCard exclusively as a SubFinder, because the program is so large and takes so long to load. But if you're using HyperCard as your main application during the day (say, as a personal information manager) it will be handy to create a SubFinder card in a HyperCard stack, so you can launch other programs as you need them from inside HyperCard.

PowerStation

Finders and Finder alternatives aren't the exclusive domain of Apple Computer. The most popular third-party SubFinder is PowerStation, a $69.95 product sold by Fifth Generation Systems. PowerStation is a more powerful and complete version of an older public domain program called Waystation.

PowerStation carries the notion of using buttons to find and load files and programs to a high level of sophistication. PowerStation presents a screen filled with buttons, each of which contains the name of an application or document, as Figure 13–5 illustrates. As you can see, you always have access to the Apple menu's desk accessories from inside PowerStation, along with options on a File and Special menu (the options on the Edit menu are dimmed [not available] when PowerStation is running). The File menu's one command finds all the installed documents in PowerStation. If you have installed programs or documents in PowerStation and then moved those files to different locations on your disk, the Find All Installed Files command on the File menu determines and stores the new locations for those files so PowerStation knows where they are.

The Special menu offers commands to clean up a PowerStation page (you can clean up so buttons are alphabetized in either rows or columns), restart or shut down the Mac, black out the screen with a screen saver (see the discussion of Inits in Chapter 12), display a list of the Command-key shortcuts in PowerStation, and access a Preferences window where you can set different options in PowerStation. Most of the screen is occupied with buttons you can define to launch documents or application programs, and there are two standard buttons toward the bottom of the screen for returning to the Finder or launching other programs.

Setting Up PowerStation Buttons   To set up PowerStation, you simply load the program and click in a blank space on the screen. There are 24 spaces, or button slots on one screen, and you can define up to 16 screens (or pages) full of buttons. You can give each page a name, so you could group your applications or documents onto different pages with names like Spreadsheets, Graphics, Word Processing, and so on. When you click in a blank button space, you'll see a Standard File box that shows you the applications

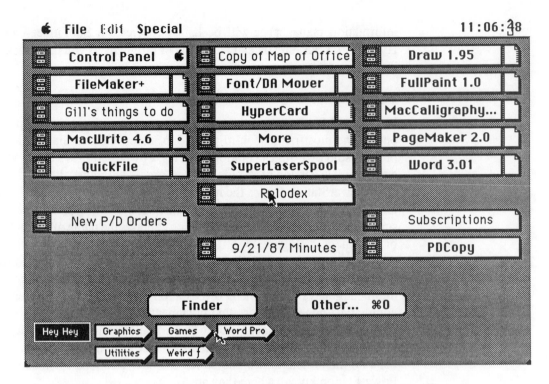

Figure 13–5. PowerStation presents documents or applications as buttons on its screen. There are
16 screens, or "pages" that can store buttons, each of which can be displayed by clicking
1 of the arrow buttons at the bottom of the screen.

in the current folder or disk directory. You can navigate to other folders or
disks from this box or select an application to install.

You can drag buttons around the screen to move them. You can cut and
paste them between screen pages or rename them. Once you've set up a
button with an application or document, you can activate the button in three
ways:

- Click on the button
- Type the first few letters of the button's name to select it, then press the
  Return key
- Select the button using the arrow keys on your keyboard, then press the
  Return key

Of course, you probably wouldn't want to define a button for each and every document or even application on your hard disk, so PowerStation gives you the ability to open other files on the fly. If you want to open an application that doesn't have its own button, you can use the Other... button at the lower right of a page to display a Standard File box, from which you can navigate to and open other applications. If you want to open a document, each of the 24 user-defined buttons on each page has commands that either access specific groups of documents you've stored under a particular button or display a Standard File box from which you can open any other document that was created by the application stored under that button. To see how this works, we need to look more closely at the extra functions of PowerStation buttons.

Each button in PowerStation contains special areas, indicated by icons, to the left and right of the button itself. The area on the left-hand side of the button shows a small menu icon. Clicking on this icon produces a pop-up menu with options for cutting or copying that button, or renaming it, as in Figure 13–6.

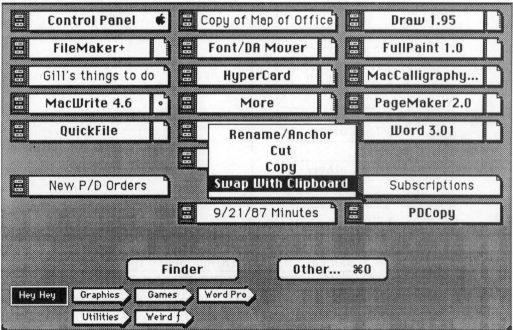

Figure 13–6. You can always cut and paste PowerStation buttons or rename them using commands on a pop-up menu to the left of each button.

These commands remove a button from a page (by cutting it to the Clipboard), paste a button into an empty slot, rename the button, or anchor the button to its location so it won't be moved when you use PowerStation's Clean Up command.

Using Documents Boxes   At the right of each button is a document icon. If you click on the icon, one of two things will happen. If you haven't yet identified any specific documents to store under that button, you'll see a window with file-finding and printing options, called the Documents Box, as shown in Figure 13–7. If you haven't installed any documents in the Documents Box, the list of installed documents at the right of the box is empty. If you have installed documents under that button, as in Figure 13–7, you may see either the Documents Box or a pop-up menu, as explained in a moment.

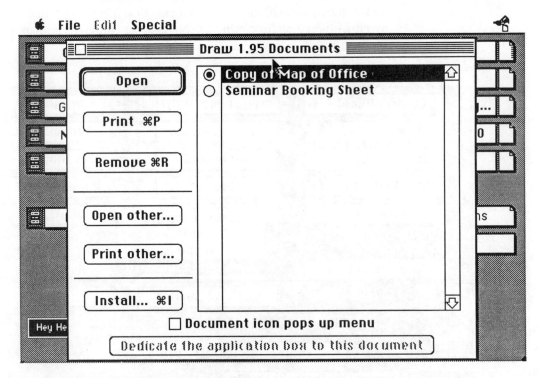

Figure 13–7. You can store a specific list of documents on a menu under any application's button in PowerStation.

Using the Documents Box, you can find and install specific documents so they'll always appear on the list in the box. When you look for files from a Documents Box, you see a Standard File box, but it only shows documents that were created by the application whose button you are using. If you are using the Documents Box from a MacWrite button, for example, you'll only see MacWrite documents.

By installing some of an application's documents in the Documents Box, you can display the list and open documents easily. If you always use MacDraw to work on an office layout, for example, you could store the office layout file in the Documents Box under the MacDraw button. That way, you could always find the layout file without having to navigate through folders to get it. In fact, if the layout file were the only file stored in the Documents Box, you could set an option that would automatically load the layout file whenever you clicked the document icon next to the MacDraw button.

But the Documents Box has lots of other features. You can install as many documents as you want on a scrolling list in the box. You use the Open Other... button to locate a document you want to install on the menu, and then use the Install button to install it there. The Print Other... button prints documents you navigate to. The Open and Print buttons are for opening and printing documents already listed in the box.

Once you've installed a document in the Documents Box, you have the option either to display the Documents Box automatically whenever you click the document icon, as before, or to present a pop-up menu. The options on the pop-up menu are Open Other..., just like the button inside the Documents Box, or Show, which displays the Documents Box. The advantage to using this menu is to go directly to the Open Other... command's Standard File box when you know you'll want to open documents not stored in that Documents Box.

By storing frequently used documents in a Documents Box, you can access them faster. No matter which folder a document is located in, you can store the document in the Documents Box and save yourself the trouble of navigating to it when you want to open it. And, because PowerStation can handle more than one button for a particular application program, you could have several different buttons for the same application, each with its own special document menu containing a different group of documents.

One last tip about PowerStation: You may spend quite a bit of time setting up PowerStation the way you want it, and it would be a shame to lose all that work if you have a disk problem. Remember to back up the PowerStation file just as you would any other important application program once you're finished customizing it. When you save the PowerStation file, you'll be saving all your custom buttons with it.

PowerStation manages to be very capable and easy to use at the same time. By just pointing and clicking, you can install all the applications you want under buttons, then install the documents you want easy access to in Document Boxes under each application button. You can use the keyboard to handle all of PowerStation's options, from selecting buttons or documents to moving from one page of buttons to another.

PowerStation is the most flexible of the SubFinders, but like the others, it isn't a complete replacement for the Finder. It lacks a Get Info command, a New Folder command, and other file management commands you get with the Finder. But if you combine PowerStation with a file-handling DA like DiskTop, you may well be able to retire the Finder until you want to change the Startup Application with the Set Startup command.

MacTree

MacTree is a Finder alternative whose major strength is showing you the organization of your entire hard disk graphically. MacTree is a breeze to set up. You simply load the MacTree application, and it automatically reads your hard disk directory and then displays the disk's folder and file organization as a branching tree structure. Figure 13–8 shows a sample tree of a hard disk.

Once this tree structure is displayed, you can click on folders to open or close them, select folders to copy or rename them, drag folders to new locations in the hierarchy, or drag folders to the Trash Can to delete them. A Zoom command displays the tree structure in four different sizes, so you can view the entire structure of a particularly large disk directory on your screen.

When you open a folder, MacTree displays a window that shows the files and folders it contains in any of the standard Finder views: Name, Kind, Size, Date, or Icon. MacTree usually adds small icons in front of each filename to help you distinguish different files, unless you choose to display the files as icons only. When you locate the file you want, you can double-click it to open the file (MacTree automatically launches a document's program if you double-click on a document).

One file-handling shortcut is the Open All Files command, which displays a window showing every file on your disk in alphabetical order by name, date, kind, or size, depending on which option you select. This command is very handy for locating and deleting duplicate files on a disk—because all the files are alphabetized, duplicate files show up next to each other on the list if you sort by filename.

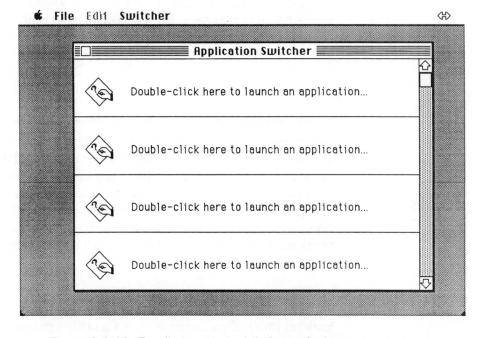

Figure 13–8. MacTree displays your hard disk's organization as a tree structure.

MacTree performs most of the Finder's functions. What it lacks are a Get Info command and a permanent Shut Down command. Instead, there's a Quit command on MacTree's File menu, and you can change that command to Shut Down by holding down the Option key when you select Quit.

While not billed as a file finder (because it runs as a separate, standalone application), MacTree is the fastest file finder available on the Macintosh. It maintains your entire hard disk directory in RAM at all times, so it can locate any file on disk in less than one second. The search window in MacTree can search by whole or partial filename, or by dates of file creation, and you can click boxes to exclude application programs, System files, or regular documents from the search. Unfortunately, MacTree locates only one file from a search at a time, rather than displaying all the files that match the search criteria in one window. You must click a Resume Search button to move to the next file found, and the next, until the search is complete.

Nevertheless, MacTree's main benefit is showing you the organization of your hard disk at a glance. Being able to see how deeply nested your folders and files are can lead to restructuring your hard disk so you can find programs, folders, and files more efficiently.

Using SuperFinders

SuperFinders augment the functionality of the Finder, enabling you to open and select from more than one application at a time. Today's SuperFinders assume you are happy with the basic functions of the Finder and want to continue using them, plus extra features. The most common feature is the ability to load and quickly move between several applications, but other features include multitasking (the ability to run more than one program at once) and print spooling. We'll look at two such programs, Switcher and MultiFinder.

Switcher

Switcher isn't really a SuperFinder. It's actually a program selector that can run several applications in memory at once. Because one of those applications can be the Finder, however, Switcher effectively adds a multiprogram selection capability to the Finder.

Switcher is an application program that Apple once distributed for free through user groups and developers. Now, it's sold as Switcher Construction Kit with a manual for $49.95. You load Switcher from the Finder, and it presents a screen from which you can install up to eight applications, as Figure 13–9 shows, assuming you have enough memory in your Mac. Once the applications are installed, they are loaded into memory and they stay there. You can move from one application to another by clicking the mouse or pressing a couple of keys.

When you select each application to work with under Switcher, the program automatically sets aside a specific amount of your Mac's memory for that application. If you prefer, you can set the amount of memory for each application yourself. One of Switcher's options is to have the Finder as one of the applications in memory all the time. You can also set Switcher so that the Clipboard's contents are maintained when you switch from one application to another. This is very handy. With MacPaint and Microsoft Word both

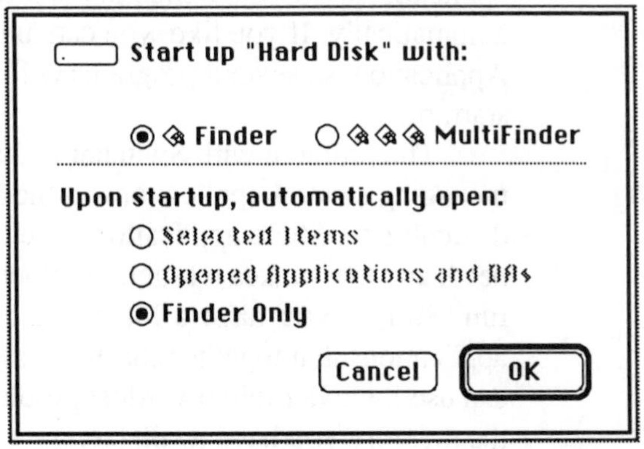

Figure 13–9. Switcher can load up to eight applications into memory at once.
The application names are the same as the program filenames on your disk.

installed in Switcher, for example, you could cut a section of a MacPaint drawing to the Clipboard, switch to Word, and paste the graphic into a document there.

Once you've set up applications in Switcher, you switch from one to the other by clicking an arrow button at the right edge of the menu bar, or by pressing the Command-[or Command-] key combinations. When you switch to an application, it occupies the entire screen, and it looks as if that's the only application running, except for the arrow icon in the upper right corner. Applications are installed in Switcher like horses in a carousel: When you switch to the next application, the current one slides out of view to the left or right and the next one in the list slides into view behind it. The applications are always in the same order. As mentioned before, you can have the Finder in rotation along with your installed applications, and you can have the Switcher configuration screen in rotation, as well. You have access to the desk accessories on the Apple menu from any screen.

The advantages of Switcher are its ease of use and its ability to move from one application to another when you press a key or click the mouse button. Rather than quitting one application and starting another, you can click an arrow icon in the upper right corner of the screen and bring another application and its currently opened file into action. This is extremely handy if you are viewing or moving data between two or three applications at one time. You can even create *Switcher sets,* which are specific groups of applications and their memory configurations that Switcher will install automatically. If you like, you can make a Switcher set your Mac's Startup Application, so several programs will automatically load under Switcher on startup.

The problem with Switcher is that it crashes a lot, because the task of managing several applications in the Mac's memory at the same time is a difficult one. Some applications like to hog more memory than they really need, and that makes it tough for other applications to have enough room to run. Still, if you have a lot of memory and are using only a couple of applications that together consume less than half of your total memory, you can use Switcher reliably. Most problems arise when you try to use most of the memory you have available.

As a Finder alternative, the only feature Switcher adds is multiprogram selection. With the Finder in a Switcher set, you can return to it quickly—you don't have to wait for the program to load from scratch each time. Other than that, however, you still deal with the Finder and its options as you would normally.

If you want to try working with a couple of different applications at once and you don't own MultiFinder, you might try Switcher. But with the release of MultiFinder (discussed next), Apple isn't really recommending Switcher as an option for those with a megabyte of RAM or more. We mention it here because there are a lot of copies of Switcher out there, and it really does work in certain situations.

MultiFinder

The first real SuperFinder released was Apple's MultiFinder, which can replace the Finder on your Mac. Every Macintosh shipped since the summer of 1987 comes with both the Finder and MultiFinder, so you have a choice. You have a choice, that is, if you have at least a megabyte of RAM. The MultiFinder won't run with less.

If you think of the Finder with Switcher built into it, rather than as a separate application program, you have a good basic idea of how the MultiFinder works. As far as file handling goes, the MultiFinder works almost exactly like the Finder. It displays the same file information in disk and folder windows, and it has the same menus. The main difference is that MultiFinder can load as many applications as your Mac's memory allows, then switch between them with a click of the mouse. The MultiFinder also features a built-in print spooler, called PrintMonitor, which was discussed in Chapter 8.

To use the MultiFinder, you set it as the Startup Application, just as you would another Finder alternative. When you set the MultiFinder as your Startup Application, though, you have the option to set other documents or applications to start up along with the MultiFinder. The Set Startup dialog box that is part of System 4.2 software (which includes the MultiFinder) gives you three ways to select various Startup Applications or documents with MultiFinder, as shown in Figure 13–10.

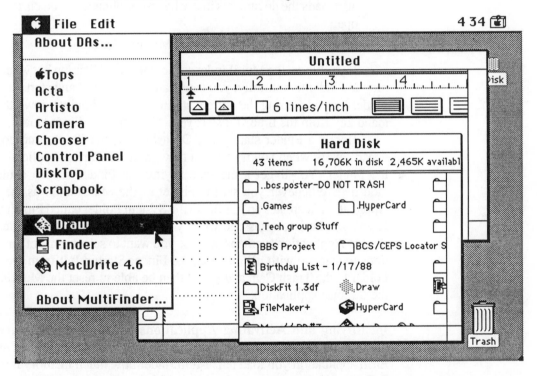

Figure 13–10. The Set Startup command under System 4.2 software produces a dialog box with three options for programs to open during startup.

Set Startup offers these alternatives for the MultiFinder setup:

- You can select several documents or applications from the same folder (as you might when using the MiniFinder), choose Set Startup, and then choose the option to start up with the selected items in the Set Startup dialog box. You can only use this option to start up selected items from the same folder, however.

- You can run MultiFinder, open a series of applications and DAs, and then use the Set Startup dialog box option to start MultiFinder the next time along with the currently open applications and DAs. This option also loads the documents in use by any applications you currently have open.

- You can choose to start up with MultiFinder only.

If you've set the MultiFinder as the startup application but would rather run the Finder temporarily, you can change your mind and start up with the Finder instead (during the current startup only) by holding down the Command key from the time you start your Mac until the Finder loads.

Here's a Finder startup tip. Occasionally, the Set Startup command doesn't work when you try to set a new group of Startup Applications with the Finder. You'll get a message saying the Finder startup couldn't be modified. Whenever you set the Finder or the MultiFinder as the Startup Application, it creates an Init file in the System Folder called Finder Startup. If you get the error message when you try to reset the MultiFinder as the Startup Application (perhaps because you want to select some other applications to start up with it), just drag the Finder Startup Init from the System Folder to the Trash Can, and you'll then be able to reset the MultiFinder as the Startup Application.

Identifying and Activating Applications Using MultiFinder, you can select and load application programs as you like, until you run out of memory. Each application you load tells MultiFinder how much memory it requires, and that amount of memory is reserved for that application. When you reach your memory limit, you'll see a message that says you don't have enough memory left to load the application you've selected. Up to that limit, however, you can load programs one after the other.

Unlike Switcher, which displays each program individually on the screen in separate windows that rotate, MultiFinder stacks applications on top of one another. You can easily tell which applications you currently have loaded by checking the bottom of the Apple menu: MultiFinder takes over a

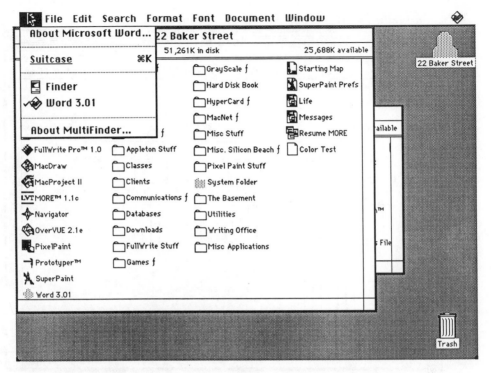

Figure 13–11. At the bottom of the Apple menu the MultiFinder lists itself and any applications you have running.

special area at the bottom of the DA menu, where it lists itself and any other applications you have opened under it in order, as in Figure 13–11.

With the programs listed on the menu, you not only see what you have loaded, but you see which program is currently active—it's the one that has a checkmark by it on the menu. Further, you can activate any of the programs by selecting its name from the menu. This is the surest way to select an application program, especially when you don't have any documents open in several of your loaded programs, because the stacked-application operation of MultiFinder can make it difficult to tell at a glance which application is active at any given time.

If an application normally displays a blank desktop with only a menu bar when it doesn't have a file open, that blank desktop will be transparent in the MultiFinder, and you'll see another application's screen underneath it. Suppose you have Microsoft Word, Excel, and MultiFinder running at the

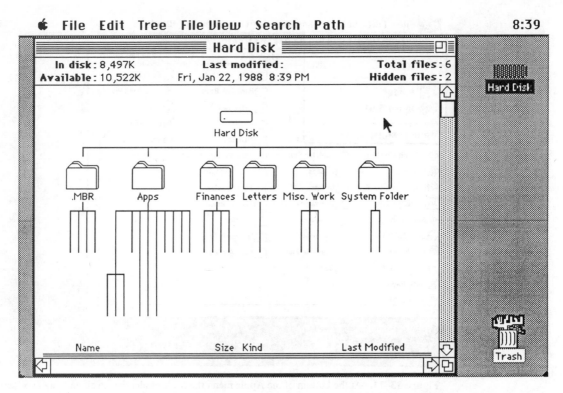

Figure 13–12. With stacked applications in MultiFinder, it can be hard to tell which application is active.

same time, for example, and you don't have files open in either Word or Excel. Your screen could look like the one in Figure 13–12.

Which of the three applications is active here? You see the MultiFinder's windows on the screen, but look at the menu bar—it contains Excel's menus. Excel is the active program at this point, but because there's no file open in either Excel or Word, you "see through" both of their desktops to the MultiFinder desktop underneath.

Actually, if you don't look to see which application name is checked on the Apple menu, you can tell which program is active in two other ways. You can look at the menu bar to see which program's menus are showing, or you can check the icon at the far right side of the menu bar. The icon is a miniature version of the icon representing each application in the Finder, and the currently active application's icon is always displayed. In Figure 13–12, you can see that Excel's icon shows at the right side of the menu bar.

To activate different applications, you can select them from the Apple menu, you can click repeatedly on the icon at the right side of the menu bar until the icon for the application you want comes into view, or you can click inside that application's hollow icon in the MultiFinder, just as you would to bring a hidden folder's window to the top of a stack of folders (described in Chapter 5).

Being able to see more than one application on the screen with transparent desktops takes a little getting used to, but if you learn to use the Apple menu and click on the menu bar icon, you can find your way among different programs easily enough after awhile.

Under MultiFinder, the Clipboard always transfers from one application to another, so it's easy to cut from a document in one program and paste into a document in another program. The other advantage is that MultiFinder is easy to set up: You can just load applications as you normally would, except you can load more than one.

Memory and Compatibility Problems   MultiFinder suffers from many of the same memory management problems as Switcher, or at least it looks that way when you try to load several programs at once. Each application stakes out a certain amount of memory for itself under MultiFinder, but sometimes a program hasn't asked for enough memory. If you want to work with a particularly large file with an application, for example, you may get a message from the program that you're running out of memory. This is particularly annoying if you have 2 megabytes or more of memory in your system and you're only trying to run one application under MultiFinder. After all, you can see that there's lots of memory available, but your program can't seem to locate it.

But once an application asks for a certain amount of memory under MultiFinder, that's all the memory MultiFinder gives it access to. As far as the application is concerned, that's all the memory available in your Mac. The only remedy to this situation is to enter a number in the Application Memory Size box that is larger than the normal allocation. To do this:

1. Activate the MultiFinder and select the application whose memory size you want to increase.

2. Choose the Get Info command from the File menu. An information window will appear.

3. At the bottom of the information window, there's a box called Application Memory Size (K). Click in the box containing the amount of memory, and enter a new value. (Add enough extra memory to the current value to handle the file you want to run. Try adding 64K or 128K extra.)

4. Click the close box to close the window.

The Application Memory Size for that application will now be larger the next time you run the program. If you're having problems, close the file you're currently working with in that program, quit the program, and then restart it so the new Application Memory Size is in effect.

This remedy will take care of many problems with applications running out of memory, but that's only one of the problems you can have. Here are two other common problems:

- Some desk accessories expect a certain amount of memory available to them. The MultiFinder has a smaller amount of memory reserved for DAs than the old Finder did, and some DAs will crash or refuse to run under MultiFinder. (Unfortunately, DiskTop version 3.0 has this problem.) Most DAs with this problem should be modified to work properly by the summer of 1988.

- Some programs that access other information files, such as spelling checkers, won't run properly under MultiFinder, because they have trouble locating the files or they run short of memory in which to run the files once they find them. (Spellswell version 2.0 doesn't get along with the MultiFinder very well.)

These problems arose when Apple changed some of the rules about memory use with the MultiFinder, and there was the usual lag before developers caught up with the new rules. The MultiFinder is a complex program, so you can expect it to become more trouble-free as time goes on.

SuperFinders like the MultiFinder will become more and more common during the next year or two. Apple will enhance the MultiFinder so it can perform true multitasking—the ability to actually run two or more programs at the same time, rather than simply being able to maintain two or more programs in memory at once. With multitasking, you'll be able to download data with a communications program at the same time you're editing a report with a word processor. As multitasking arrives and compatibility problems diminish, the reasons for having the MultiFinder or another SuperFinder will multiply. Eventually, it will become a must for almost every Mac owner.

At this point, the problems of using the MultiFinder may outweigh its advantages. If you don't have any trouble running the applications and DAs you want under MultiFinder, it's an attractive alternative to the Finder or SubFinders because it gives you instant access to many programs and the Finder's file-handling features. If you do have problems with your programs under MultiFinder, you're better off using an alternative SuperFinder (or a SubFinder and file-handling DA together) until the developers sort things out.

Finder alternatives can help you load your programs and documents more quickly, and minimize your wait between quitting one program and running another. Used with a good file-handling DA, SubFinders offer speed and simplicity. At the other end of the spectrum, SuperFinders offer quick access to multiple programs and documents as well as to the Finder itself without sacrificing speed, but compatibility problems may cause trouble. But if you've grown tired of waiting for the Finder to load when you quit a program, there are a lot of alternatives to explore, and one of them probably works the way you want it to.

PART FOUR

Troubleshooting and Maintenance

14

Preventive Measures for Your Hard Disk

A hard disk is a precise mechanism that operates within very close toler-ances. The distance between a disk's read/write head and the surface of its recording medium is measured in thousandths of an inch, as are the lateral movements a disk's head positioning mechanism makes to place the head where it can read the data you're after. But despite all this precision, hard disks are pretty sturdy and reliable devices. They have to be; hard disk manufacturers are devoted to selling as many of these beasts as possible, and if hard disks were still as delicate as they were when they were first invented, they would never have found their way into tens of thousands of personal computers.

If you set up your hard disk properly and pay attention to some simple precautions, you should get years of problem-free operation out of it. In this chapter, we'll look at how to avoid problems from the moment you unpack your disk to the time you take it on the road.

Starting Out

Proper unpacking and setup is the beginning of a happy relationship with your hard disk. If you haven't yet unpacked your hard disk, make sure everything's in order before you prepare to store your files and programs. You wouldn't store important papers or books in a room where the roof might be leaking, and you shouldn't think of putting a hard disk to use until you know it's working properly.

Unpacking

Before you unpack your disk, clear away the area where you plan to set the disk up. Nothing makes you feel dumber than dropping a new hard disk because you tried to balance it on your knee while you made room for it on your desk. While your attention will be focused on removing the disk case and its cable from the box, make sure you aren't overlooking small parts such as a terminator block or a wire jumper that you might need to set the disk up.

The best way to be sure you have all the parts you need is to check the user's manual. The manual's setup instructions will list all the parts your disk should have come with.

Before you connect the disk, inspect the drive itself by looking at the case, cable, and connector for signs of physical damage. If the case is dented (which isn't very likely), return the disk to the place you bought it for an exchange. More likely (although still far from commonplace), the connector pins on the cable may be bent. Be sure to check the pins and straighten them with needlenose pliers before plugging in the connector. If you plug in a hard disk and all the pins don't connect, you could seriously damage the disk or your Mac.

When you're sure you have everything you need and all seems in order, you can proceed to the actual setup after you do one more thing: *Save the box.* Computer hardware boxes tend to be bulky, and we are often tempted to relieve congestion in our attics, garages, or living rooms by tossing out boxes after we set up equipment. But the box for your hard disk was specially designed to transport the disk safely, and if you ever have to send the disk off for repairs, you'll need the box. Having the original box makes it easy and safe to ship your hard disk; not having the original box makes shipping a big gamble.

Setting Up

The first and best way to set up a hard disk is to carefully read the user's manual. The manual will suggest where to place the hard disk, where to plug it in, and how to check out its sound and indicator lights for possible problems. Of course, most people never read hardware manuals, so here are the basics.

Put the disk on a solid, level surface. Hard disk platters rotate on a shaft that is connected to an electric motor, and they're designed to be operated on level ground. If you place the hard disk on a slant, you'll be putting extra stress on the shaft bearings and drive mechanism. This doesn't mean you should run out and buy a carpenter's level to make sure your disk location is completely flat, but avoid running the disk at an obvious angle.

Also, make sure the surface is stable. Don't use a wobbly shelf or table, and don't prop the disk up with books, matchbooks, or other items. If you take a chance and use a wobbly surface, Murphy's Law will ensure that at the very moment you are saving a month's worth of work, the surface will shift or collapse, the jolt will cause a head crash, and your data will be history. Even if somebody simply bumps a table while the disk is reading or writing and causes the disk to shift, you could be in for some data loss, so it pays to find the most stable surface possible.

Once you've found a good shelf or table, set up the disk the way the manufacturer intended. Some disks operate horizontally, such as the Apple, Jasmine, Mac Bottom, and Micah drives, and others operate vertically, like the DataFrame series. Don't change this orientation. A disk that's designed to run horizontally should never be run vertically, and a vertical disk should stay that way. Otherwise, you're likely to have problems with read/write head positioning accuracy and drive mechanism reliability.

Protected Air Space

Hard disks also require adequate ventilation. Whether it's sitting underneath your Mac, standing beside it, or off on a shelf somewhere, make sure there are at least two inches of air space around the ventilated sides of your hard disk. Spinning a bunch of metal platters at 3500 rpm generates heat, and if the heat isn't properly dissipated, the disk media or heads will surely deteriorate.

Ventilation is an important requirement when you first set up your disk, but keep it in mind as you use your disk. In your day-to-day work, you may want to stuff books beside your computer or on top of it, or perhaps even use the Mac and a vertical hard disk drive as a couple of bookends. Don't do it! Consider the air space around your Mac and hard disk as a part of the Mac and hard disk themselves.

The Power Connection

One final aspect of your setup should be power. Power spikes or surges (fluctuations in the amount of volts coming out of your wall outlet) can damage a hard disk just as they can damage a computer, so plug your disk into a power strip to isolate it a little from possible fluctuations. If you live in an area with a particularly unreliable power source, or where frequent thunderstorms might cause severe power fluctuations, invest in a bona fide surge protector from an electronics or computer store. Otherwise, a common multiple-outlet power strip from the hardware store will do the job—look for one with a built-in circuit breaker.

A power strip also gives you the opportunity to place the on/off switch for your hard disk in a more convenient place. Rather than having to reach behind the hard disk whenever you want the power on, you can flip the switch on the power strip, which can be fixed to a nearby wall or to the side of your desk.

The only caution here is not to make the power strip's switch too available. If you put the strip on the floor or on the wall in a high traffic area, you run the risk that somebody will accidentally bump the switch into the off position while you're working. It might seem a good idea to attach the power strip to the inside of your desk, next to your legs, but you might actually bump the on/off switch there.

Incidentally, you may very well have a power outage at some point while you run your hard disk. A hard disk that is simply running when an outage occurs is safe—cutting the power is like turning the switch off, and the read/write heads automatically move to a safe area of the disk so no data is lost. This isn't the ideal way to turn off a hard disk, but it probably won't cause any problems.

A more likely cause of problems is a power outage that occurs while the disk is reading or writing. Unfortunately, you can't anticipate power outages, and you'll have to rely on luck to see you through. If it's any consolation, most hard disks used by individual personal computers spend less than 3 percent of their time reading or writing.

If your hard disk is being used on a network, and especially if it's being used for a multiuser database application that requires ongoing disk accesses, you would be wise to invest in an uninterruptible power supply that will keep your computer and disk drive running long enough for you to shut them down properly if the power goes out. Uninterruptible power supplies sell for about $300 and up, depending on the length of time they will maintain power to your system and the amount of power they can supply.

If your power goes out while you're working, the best thing to do is turn off your equipment immediately. Frequently, electricity cycles on and off one or two times as the power company tries to restore it, and this cycling isn't good for either your computer or your hard disk. It's best to shut your equipment down and wait until the power has come back on for good. It's hard to tell when the power is back on for good, but wait at least two or three minutes after power is restored before starting up your computer again.

Checking the Basic Operation

With the disk set up and plugged in, turn it on, watch, and listen. Every disk whines a bit when it starts up, and many have a noticeable whine or hum in normal operation, but listen for noises that seem out of place: Grating, grinding, or screeching are usually not good signs. If you hear something you don't like, the least you can do is call the place where you bought the disk (or the disk maker's technical support people) and describe the symptoms. It could well be that the noise you hear is normal, but it's best to be sure before you store your data on the drive.

Also, check the user's manual to learn about the disk's indicator lights. Most hard disks have one or more indicator lights you can use to judge the disk's condition. If there are two lights, one indicates that the power is on and is lit all the time, while the other lights up only when the disk is reading or writing. If a disk has only one light, the light usually goes on temporarily when you start up the drive, and then it lights up during disk read or write operations. In some cases, the indicator light is on whenever the power is on, and it merely blinks or changes intensity during read/write operations.

Your disk user's manual will tell you exactly when you should be seeing the indicator light or lights. If a light is on when it shouldn't be, or if it won't go on, call the manufacturer's technical support line and clear the problem up. If the indicator light isn't working, return the disk and get another one. And in any case, don't store anything on the disk until the indicator light problem is cleared up.

A Clean Slate

Once you're satisfied that the disk drive mechanism and indicator lights are working properly, it's time to turn your attention to the media itself: the disk surfaces where your data will be stored. The best way to check out the condition of a disk's media is to format it. Formatting erases anything that was on the disk previously, locates areas of the disk (called *bad sectors* or *bad blocks*) that can't be used for storage, and then marks the unusable areas so the disk won't later try to write to them.

Most hard disks are preformatted at the factory these days, which means you can begin storing data on them right out of the box. That makes things more convenient, but if there was any damage to the disk and bad sectors were created during shipping, the disk drive probably won't be aware of them until it simply stumbles on the problem area. Because the disk was formatted before the damage, the new problem areas haven't been identified. And naturally, drives with unidentified bad sectors usually find them just as you are trying to save important data.

The utility software supplied with most hard disks includes a program that verifies the disk, checking it for bad sectors. (There's also usually a program that reformats the disk, as well.) If the disk you buy comes out of the box with System and utility software already installed on it, as many disks do, you could use the verification utility to check the disk for bad sectors. These utilities may not identify every bad sector on the disk, though.

To be absolutely sure you find all the bad sectors on a disk, reformat it before you use it. If your disk comes loaded with some software, copy the software onto floppy disks (you can use the backup program supplied with the hard disk to make this simpler), then erase the entire disk and start over.

To reformat the disk, start up your Mac with a floppy and use the format utility supplied with the disk's software (which you will have copied to a floppy), or use the Erase Disk command on the Special menu in the Finder. Once the disk is reformatted, you can store your data with confidence.

Operating Do's and Don'ts

Hard disks are more susceptible to damage when they are running than when they aren't running, and they're particularly vulnerable during read/write operations. Here are some tips:

- Avoid bumping the shelf or table where the hard disk is located whenever it's running, and never bump the shelf or table during a read/write operation.
- Avoid turning off your Mac as a way to restart it. Use the Restart command on the Special menu instead, as this shuts your disk down in an orderly fashion.
- Avoid covering the ventilation holes in your hard disk's case.
- Never reset or turn off your Mac while the hard disk is reading or writing. This could damage data on your disk.

- Never turn off your hard disk while it is reading or writing. This could damage data on your disk.
- Always use the Shut Down command on the Special menu before you turn off your Mac and then turn off the hard disk at the same time or after you turn off your Mac.
- Always back up your hard disk files onto floppy disks. (See Chapter 9.)

The Traveling Disk

External Mac hard disks are small enough so you can carry them with you when you travel. Some people have a Mac at home and one at the office, and transport their hard disk back and forth between the two. Others put the hard disk right inside their Mac's case when they're on the move. If you plan to transport your hard disk, there are a few things to keep in mind.

First of all, remember that despite its apparent ruggedness, the hard disk is still a precision device. Most hard disks are designed to withstand being dropped from a height of anywhere from several inches to a couple of feet onto a concrete floor, but that doesn't mean you should play basketball with your data. Remember, it is *your* data you're trying to protect, and it took a long time to create it and store it on the disk.

So, when you carry the hard disk, make sure it's protected and avoid bumping it or subjecting it to any type of jolt. Treat the disk like you would an expensive camera. It will help if you carry the disk in a protective case.

If you're commuting on public transit with your Mac and your hard disk, for example, carry the hard disk inside the Mac's case, if possible. Mac cases are well padded, and any Mac Plus or Mac SE case is tall enough to accommodate any under-the-Mac hard disk. If you're just transporting the disk itself, keep it in a shoulder bag (where you can protect it with your body from serious jolts), or in your briefcase. But whenever you carry the hard disk in a briefcase or shoulder bag, remember that you've got a hard disk in there, and be extra careful.

If you're transporting the Mac in your car, it may be just as easy to use the original box. You can store the box in the trunk of your car, and the disk inside will be as safe as it can possibly be. If you do travel in a car, try not to leave the disk in the trunk for hours in very hot or very cold weather, and don't leave it exposed to direct sunlight for long periods. The heat can cause your disk's metal platters or the magnetic coating on them to expand, which invites read/write errors in the future. In extreme cold, the platters or magnetic coating will contract.

When you travel on an airplane, don't put the disk through the airport metal detector, no matter *what* the sign says about how safe it is. It's almost never a problem, but it's better to be safe than sorry. Unless the security person drops your disk while examining it, you'll be better off having the disk "hand searched" than risking exposure to magnetic fields inside the metal detector.

That's about it for safety precautions. Your hard disk is a pretty tough animal, and if you follow the advice in this chapter, you may never have a mechanical or media error problem with it. You can even overlook a precaution now and then and you'll probably still be okay. Unfortunately, though, jolts, dust, power surges, and magnetic fields are only the external problems that can affect a hard disk. More likely, your hard disk will develop problems because of a software bug or incompatibility. In Chapter 15, we'll look at some techniques you can use to recover from software-related problems.

15

Troubleshooting and Repairs

There's no sinking feeling worse than the one you get when your hard disk won't work. You think your data and application programs are gone forever. You wonder if the problem has affected your computer. You know it will take weeks to get the problem fixed, and in the meantime, you'll have to work with those tiny, slow floppy disks. Well, hard disk problems are sometimes this severe, but sometimes they aren't. In some cases, you can repair the hard disk yourself enough to gain access to all your files with only a few minutes' troubleshooting. In this chapter, we'll explore some troubleshooting techniques, and we'll look at some specific hard disk problems and their solutions. *Troubleshooting* is pinpointing a problem by applying specific tests, and then trying solutions one at a time, both to verify the problem and to solve it. You can think of the process as following a path like a tree diagram or a flow chart: You consider Problem A, then test the device to see if that might be the problem. If it definitely isn't the problem, you consider Problem B. If it might be the problem, you probe further. If it definitely is the problem you try the first of several remedies.

The Purpose of Hard Disk Repairs

The purpose of troubleshooting and repairing a hard disk is to gain access to the files on the disk, so you can save them safely onto floppy disks and then reformat the disk or have it repaired. Hard disk problems related to software are often complex, and once you start having trouble, the best course is to wipe the slate clean by reformatting the disk and starting over.

So, if your repair efforts are successful during any point in the process described in this chapter, don't assume everything is fine and begin using your hard disk again. Once you've gotten your disk to the point where you can boot from it and access files, make backup copies of all the files (see Chapter 9) and then reformat the disk. Reformatting will totally erase the disk, and it will mark any trouble spots on the disk so your Mac will avoid them when storing files in the future.

The remedies suggested in this chapter should only be considered temporary measures that will give you access to the disk so you can get your files off of it.

A Troubleshooter's Tool Kit

Hard disk problems don't announce themselves in advance; they just happen. And when they happen, you're sometimes left without a way to access the files on the hard disk. Because of this, make sure you have made some floppy disk copies of the programs you'll need to diagnose and attempt repairs on your hard disk. Let's look at some of the common disk-repairing software tools.

The System, Finder, and Installer Programs

Your Apple should have come with disks that contain the System, Finder, and (if you bought your Mac after the beginning of 1986) the Installer programs. As explained in Chapter 2, the Installer replaces the System and Finder files (as well as some printer drivers) on any disk you specify. Since one of the first remedies you'll try when troubleshooting a hard disk will be to replace the System files, keep these files safe on a floppy disk somewhere.

If you're a typical user, you'll take your original Apple System and Utilities disks and stick them somewhere, never to look at them again. When a new version of the System comes along, you'll update your hard disk, but not the original floppies. It's important to update your floppy copies of

System files whenever you update your hard disk, so the two System files will be compatible if you ever have to repair your disk. Otherwise, you'll be forced to replace a newer System file with an older one, and you may have compatibility problems that will prevent your program files from working with the older System.

You can restore System files by simply dragging them from a floppy disk to a hard disk, rather than using the Installer, but if you do, all the DAs and fonts you installed in the hard disk's System will be replaced by the DAs and fonts in the floppy disk's System. The Installer preserves the existing fonts and DAs from the System file you're replacing.

1st Aid Kit

1st Aid Kit is a $99 program from 1st Aid Software that you use to recover files from a hard or floppy disk whose directory is damaged. If your Mac tells you your hard disk is unreadable, you can often use 1st Aid Kit to read the files on the disk anyway. Even if the disk has a damaged directory, 1st Aid Kit can locate files by finding the markers that indicate the beginnings and ends of files. This is the first program you should try to use if you have valuable files on your hard disk that aren't backed up onto floppy disks. There are other disk repair programs, but many of them may repair a disk by writing a completely new file directory, which will make it even *more* difficult to access the files on that disk.

Disk First Aid

Disk First Aid is a disk testing and repair program that has been supplied free with every Apple system since the spring of 1987. It works with both 800K floppy disks and hard disks, but only those formatted with the HFS System. Even if you bought your Mac before 1987, you can get a copy of Disk First Aid free from an Apple dealer or user group along with an updated System file.

Disk First Aid verifies the files on a disk and looks for damaged file structures—the markers that the Mac inserts at the beginning and end of each file, and the directory on the disk that tells your Mac where every file and folder is. If your disk becomes unreadable, you can run Disk First Aid, and it will attempt to repair any problems it finds. Disk First Aid may write a new, blank directory to the disk during the repair process, though.

MacTools

MacTools is a collection of disk utility programs from Central Point Software. It is included on the disk when you buy Copy II Mac. MacTools does a lot of things, including verifying disks, copying disks, locking or unlocking files, and renaming files or disks, but for troubleshooting, it has an option called Mount.

Like Disk First Aid, Mount verifies a disk to determine if it has problems and then tries to remedy them. Mount's remedy for a disk is to replace its directory with a completely new, empty directory. If you use Mount and it is successful, your hard disk will appear to be empty of files. The files are still there, however, and you can then use the Undelete feature in MacTools to recover the files so they appear again. The problem with MacTools is that it won't recover files from a disk with a new directory unless you have installed two special Init programs, CPS SaveDeletes and CPS TagFix, in your System Folder. Any files written to the disk before these two Inits were installed can't be recovered by MacTools.

Setting Up Software Tools

One of the problems with using a program to repair a hard disk is that the System and/or Finder won't recognize the hard disk. A software tool can't examine or repair a disk it doesn't recognize. But if the Finder doesn't recognize your disk, your software tool might. Here's the best way to prepare for disk troubleshooting:

1. Copy each troubleshooting program to its own floppy disk.
2. Place a copy of the current System Folder on each disk.
3. Boot the floppy disk and make the troubleshooting program the Startup Application by selecting it and choosing Set Startup from the Special menu in the Finder.

When you have a problem in which your hard disk isn't being recognized or can't be read, you can't simply boot your troubleshooting program using the current System and Finder, because that System and Finder aren't recognizing your hard disk. Instead, you'll restart your Mac using the floppy for the troubleshooting tool you want to use. The Finder will be bypassed and the program itself will load, and it may recognize your hard disk.

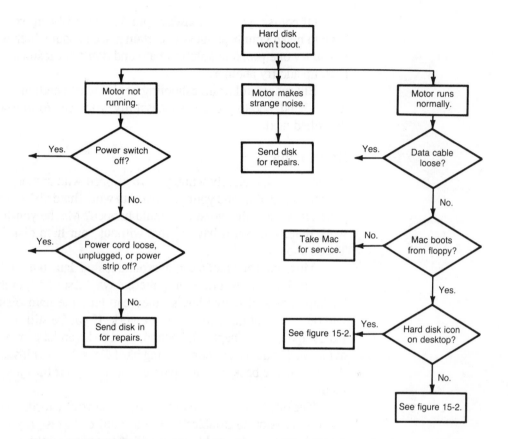

Figure 15–1. This diagram maps out the paths you might take to determine the type of problem you're having with a hard disk.

Basic Troubleshooting

The troubleshooting techniques covered here apply to any sort of breakdown, whether it's your hard disk, your car, or a household appliance.

The block diagram in Figure 15–1 shows how you might begin to isolate specific problems with a hard disk. As you can see, the process is a matter of trying one option, judging the result, and then either trying another option or moving forward toward a more precise definition of the problem.

Of course, you can't always pin down a problem exactly, and you'll have to make your best guess at certain places about which way to proceed. If you try one problem/solution path and don't get results, you can always back up and try another.

But successful troubleshooting begins with a certain attitude about the task at hand, and to proceed successfully, you need to follow certain steps, described next.

Don't Panic

It's hard to think clearly while you're gripped with anxiety about what will happen to your data and your productivity with a hard disk out of action. Calm yourself. What's the worst that could happen? Maybe you'll lose an hour's work time, and you'll have to live without your hard disk for a few days. That's about it.

Most fears and panic center around losing data, but total data loss from a hard disk failure is a rare thing these days. First of all, most people make backup copies of their files, so they can take the hard disk out of action without interrupting their ability to work. If you're still not on the backup bandwagon, read Chapter 9. Second, hard disk vendors are pretty competent at recovering data from nonworking hard disks. In most instances, your hard disk will come back to you repaired, and with your files just where you left them.

The other source of anxiety is knowing you're losing work time. If you make a decision to troubleshoot your hard disk, resign yourself to setting aside the time to do so. Maybe it will have to wait until after work, or your lunch hour, but if you set aside a specific time to do the work, you won't be worried about not being able to do something else during that time.

One Thing at a Time

During scientific experiments, researchers use a group of subjects that are each changed in only one way. Only one change is made to each group because only then is it possible to see what effect each change has. If two changes are made to one group, it's impossible to tell whether the result was due to one change, the other change, or a combination of the two.

In troubleshooting a hard disk, isolate problems and apply potential remedies one at a time, then measure the results after each attempt. If you try multiple remedies at once, you may correct the problem and then never know which remedy was responsible, which will probably mean you won't know exactly what the problem was. If you ever have the problem again, you'll have to go through the whole process again.

Many times, you have to start from the general and move to the specific, applying tests at each point to eliminate possible problems. If your hard disk won't boot, for example, the problem could be mechanical, electrical, or software-related; but if you hear the motor running, it becomes more likely that the problem is software-related.

Eliminate the Obvious

Hard disks need mechanical parts, electricity and electric components, and software to run properly. Before plunging into a major diagnostic effort, look at these three problem areas and do a quick check to eliminate obvious problems. You can take one problem area at a time.

Mechanical   Ask yourself these questions:

- Can you hear the drive motor running?
- Can you hear the read/write heads at work when you load or save a file?
- Can you hear any abnormal noises coming from the drive?

Electrical   Ask yourself these questions:

- Does the power come on when you turn on the drive?
- Does the indicator light come on when you turn on the drive?
- Is the power switch on?
- Is the power strip switch (if you're using one) on?
- Are all power cords plugged in firmly?
- Is there power to the outlet you're using?
- Is the data cable plugged in firmly to both the computer and the disk drive?
- Are the cable connector pins all straight?

Software   Ask yourself these questions:

- Are you running a compatible version of the System? (Some hard disks won't work with System 3.0 or earlier.)
- Does the problem occur with only one application program or all of them?
- Is your startup floppy readable, and does it contain the files you need to start the disk? (This is for serial port hard disks only.)

Surprisingly, many hard disk problems really are caused by something simple like a loose cable or power plug. You should be so lucky yourself. But if checking the plugs and power switches (and the files and readability of your startup floppy, if you have one) doesn't do the trick, you'll have to dig deeper.

Ask for Help

After checking the obvious, call the hard disk manufacturer's technical support line and describe the problem. You'll probably be asked specific questions about what the drive is doing, and the technical support person will suggest specific remedies, from using software tools to sending the drive back. If possible, it's best to let the people who deal with hard disk problems every day take a crack at yours before you spend your time on it.

If you still want to work on the problem after your talk with the disk's manufacturer (or if you weren't able to reach the manufacturer), you can continue the troubleshooting procedure.

Look at the Big Picture

Look at the general categories of things that could be causing a problem. As we've said, a hard disk runs on mechanical, electrical, and software components. By isolating the problem in one of these three areas, you'll know which specific path to follow, as in Figure 15–1. These are the types of components that can go wrong in each area:

- Mechanical problems (the motor, spindle, disks, heads, positioning arm)
- Electrical components (the power supply, controller circuits, and interface circuits)
- Software problems (your Mac's System software or the application software you're running)

Be Practical

Look at problems in terms of your ability to deal with them. If you can identify certain symptoms, you will have to send the disk drive out for repairs, and your troubleshooting session will be over. Don't waste time trying to pinpoint or resolve a problem that only the manufacturer can fix. If you hear a horrible screeching noise from your drive, for example, just shut if off and send it back. The following problems require a trained technician to solve.

- The drive motor doesn't run.
- The indicator light doesn't come on.
- The read/write heads won't move.
- The drive is making a horrible noise.

Most of the easily identifiable hard disk problems are mechanical or electrical in nature, and these are also the ones that you probably won't be able to fix yourself. But it may not be easy to determine whether a problem is electrical or software-related. Naturally, you can diagnose a bad motor or power supply, but if the problem is with an internal connection or a bad chip, it will be harder to pin down.

Pinpoint Problems with Specific Solutions

Once you've eliminated all the obvious problems and all the problems you can't fix yourself, the only area left is software. The problem may still be electrical, but the only way to tell is to try software solutions to see if they work. Each solution becomes a test; if the solution works, you know that was the problem, and if it doesn't, the problem is elsewhere and you have to try another solution.

Common Symptoms of Hard Disk Problems

There are two classic symptoms that signal a hard disk problem. This section will talk about these major symptoms, and their most common causes.

Hard Disk Won't Boot

The failure of the hard disk to boot up is the most common (and the most obvious) symptom. This manifests itself in one of three ways:

- The initial Mac icon (showing the disk with the blinking question mark) doesn't go away. It doesn't change into the smiling Mac face as it is supposed to.

- The smiling Mac icon appears, indicating a good startup disk, but then the screen goes crazy: Either the Welcome to Macintosh box starts jittering, or the screen turns black and the sad Mac icon appears.
- The question mark icon immediately changes to a sad Mac icon.

Often, these symptoms are caused by hardware problems you can't fix, but there are some causes that you can tackle:

- The hard disk isn't on, either because the power is off, the power cord isn't plugged in, or the data cable is loose or disconnected.
- The boot blocks on the hard disk are bad.
- You have one or more incompatible Init programs in the System Folder.
- The System files are corrupted or incompatible.
- Your Mac's Parameter RAM is corrupted.

We'll look at how to apply solutions to these specific problems later in Hard Disk Problems You Can Tackle.

Hard Disk Icon Missing from Desktop

The other major symptom of trouble is that the icon representing the hard disk doesn't appear in the Finder once you've started up or when you return to the Finder after quitting an application. When this happens, you frequently get the message, "This disk is unreadable, do you wish to Initialize it?"

Frequently, you can resolve the problems associated with this symptom. The most likely causes of trouble are:

- The desktop file is corrupted.
- The disk directory is corrupted.
- The System files are corrupted or incompatible.
- You have an incompatible Init program installed in the System Folder.
- Your Mac's parameter RAM is corrupted.

Now let's look at the user-addressable problems that might cause the hard disk to be unbootable or its icon to disappear from the desktop in the Finder.

Hard Disk Problems You Can Tackle

All the hard disk problems users can address have to do with software. Either a crucial file on the hard disk is damaged or missing, or a portion of the Mac's memory that stores important System settings has become garbled.

File Corruption Problems

A common problem on any type of storage disk is that files sometimes are written or rewritten in such a way that they are no longer usable. In this situation, it is as if the disk's read/write heads make a small error when writing information, and the information is not readable afterwards. Sometimes, a file can be corrupted simply by being read.

In hard disk operations, there are several crucial files or groups of files that can become corrupted, and once corrupted, can prevent your hard disk from working properly. Often, these corrupted files can be rebuilt or replaced to restore your disk to working order. Following are descriptions of the files that can cause problems.

Bad Boot Blocks   The boot blocks are the first area on the disk the computer looks to when it starts up. The boot blocks contain instructions that tell the Mac where to find the System files needed for startup. These instructions include the definitions of the Startup Application, the startup sound, and the system beep. If the boot blocks become corrupted, the Mac will never be able to get past them to the System files elsewhere on the disk.

Desktop File Corrupted   The desktop file is an invisible file that keeps track of the desktop icons and their positions in the Finder, and stores System comments about each file. If you've ever wondered why there are always 4K to 7K of space used on supposedly blank disks, it's the space required for the desktop file. The desktop file can store an icon for a file even after the file has been deleted from the disk. As a result, the file can grow to be rather large, especially on a hard disk. Every once in a while, this file gets screwed up and needs to be rebuilt.

Directory Corrupted   Every floppy or hard disk has a directory that lists the name and location of every file stored on that disk. If this directory is corrupted, the disk can no longer find the files it needs, and your Mac will consider the disk unreadable.

Bad System Files   An additional possibility is corrupted System files. The two vulnerable elements are the Finder and the System file. Every once in a while the particular copy of either of these files will develop a problem and need to be replaced. This is not to say that the other elements in the System Folder are invulnerable to problems, but except for incompatible Inits (described momentarily), they won't cause problems getting the hard disk to boot.

Other Software Problems

Two other problem areas for hard disk users are Init programs, which can be incompatible with other software, and Parameter RAM, which stores System file information.

Incompatible Inits   Depending on the version of the System you are running, and depending on your Startup Application, some Init files can cause conflicts with the System or desktop files. Because Inits load automatically upon startup, you can usually detect any problems with them either on startup or when you launch an application. (For more on Inits, see Chapters 2 and 12.)

Parameter RAM Problems   Most of the RAM in the computer is powered by external electricity and is wiped clean like a blackboard every time the computer is turned off. This means that strange problems that stem from something unusual in the RAM will be removed when you restart the computer. There is, however, a small area called the parameter RAM that is powered by the Mac's battery and is thus continually on. This area stores information such as the current date and time, and what serial port is being used for what purpose, as well as some information about the SCSI port. If something happens to corrupt this area of memory, the problem will continue even after you restart your computer.

Using the Troubleshooting Diagram

The troubleshooting diagram in Figure 15–2 shows the steps you take to resolve hard disk problems once you've diagnosed them as well as you can.

As you can see, the tree contains several main paths to follow, depending on what the basic symptom is, and whether or not individual remedies have any effect. We'll look at the solutions for the several problems one at a time, starting with what to do when the disk won't boot.

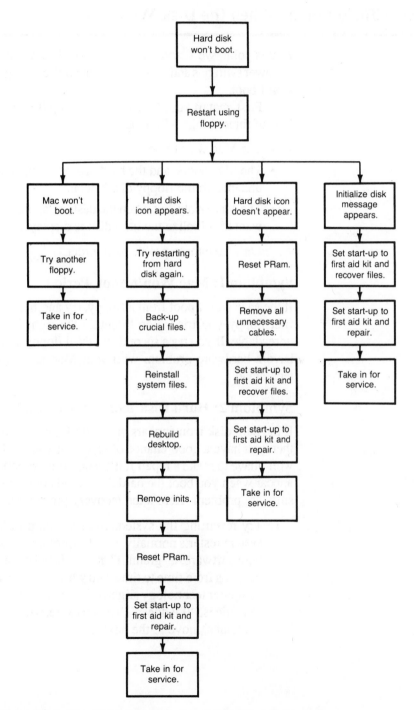

Figure 15–2. This diagram shows routes you can follow for correcting two common hard disk problems.

Specific Solutions When the Disk Won't Boot

At this point, we'll assume that you've checked the obvious problems such as power switches and cables, and that you're sitting with a Mac hard disk that won't boot.

First, restart your Mac using a startup floppy disk in the internal drive. One of three things will happen:

- The Mac won't boot.
- The Mac boots, and the hard disk icon appears on the desktop directly underneath the floppy disk's icon.
- The Mac boots, but when the desktop appears, a message asking if you want to initialize the hard disk is displayed.

Let's take these problems in order.

Symptom 1: Mac Won't Boot, Period

If the Mac won't boot from a floppy, try another floppy. It could be that the first floppy you tried didn't contain the right System files or that it was unreadable. If you try a second and third floppy and get the same result, you have a hardware problem with your Mac and should take it to a service technician.

Symptom 2: Hard Disk Icon Appears on Desktop

If the hard disk icon appears on the desktop after you boot with the floppy, then you have a good chance of repairing your disk. It's even possible you won't have to make a repair if it's a one-time situation. Failure of the icon to appear when you boot the hard disk could come from either a hardware or a software problem. Here's the recovery procedure:

1. Try restarting the system from the hard disk one more time. If the system restarts normally, then the problem was a minor incompatibility with software, a "gremlin" that surfaced once and then not again. This happens from time to time, and while it might shake your confidence in computer technology slightly, it's no cause to undertake major repairs. The rule is, "If it doesn't happen twice, it doesn't count." If the problem continues, move to the next step.

2. While you have access to the icon (and the files on the hard disk), back up any files that you might have forgotten to back up before. You may need to reinitialize the disk if all remedies fail, so be ready to rebuild from scratch.

3. Remove all Init files from the System Folder.

   a. Start up the System again from a floppy disk.

   b. Open the hard disk's icon on the desktop.

   c. Open the System Folder on the hard disk.

   d. Create a new folder inside the System Folder and name it Inits.

   e. Drag all Init programs from the System Folder to the Inits folder. Once the Inits are hidden in the Inits folder, they won't work any more (and they can't screw up your System any more, if they're the problem).

   f. Try restarting the Mac from the hard disk. If it works, the problem is an incompatible Init program.

   g. To find out exactly which Init program is causing the problem, drag the Inits back out of the Init folder and into the System folder one at a time, restarting the machine after each new Init is added. At some point, the problem will recur, and then you'll know which Init is causing it. At that point, remove that Init from your disk completely. If your Mac still won't boot from the hard disk with all the Inits removed, leave them in the Init folder for the time being.

4. Reinstall your hard disk's System files. If these files are corrupted, reinstalling them should clear up the problem. You can use the Installer program supplied by Apple, which has the advantage of replacing your System and Finder files without erasing any fonts or DAs you may have installed, or you can simply drag new System and Finder files into your hard disk's System Folder. Sometimes, the Installer won't work if you're replacing a bad System file, so you'll have to drag the new System onto the old one.

   a. In either case, though, you must use a floppy disk to start up your Mac, and the floppy disk's System file must be in control. Start up your Mac from a floppy disk.

   b. If you want to use the Installer, run the Installer program and follow the instructions in your Macintosh user's manual.

c. If you want to completely replace your System files and wipe out any fonts or DAs you have stored, simply drag the System Folder from the floppy disk to the hard disk. Alternatively, you can drag just the System and Finder files from your floppy disk to your hard disk.

d. After replacing your System files, try booting from the hard disk again. If it still doesn't boot, move to Step 5.

5. Rebuild the desktop file, beginning by restarting the Mac from a floppy disk.

   a. Hold down the Option and Command keys as soon as the icon for the floppy disk appears on the desktop. At this point, you will be shown a dialog box that asks if you want to rebuild the desktop, as shown in Figure 15–3.

   b. Click the Yes button to rebuild the desktop. Once you've rebuilt the desktop, try restarting your system from the hard disk again. If it still won't boot, move to Step 6.

6. Use Disk First Aid. Here, you'll use the floppy disk you prepared with Disk First Aid as the Startup Application.

   a. Restart your Mac with the floppy disk where you stored Disk First Aid as the Startup Application. Disk First Aid's screen will be displayed, as in Figure 15–4.

   b. Click the Drive button on the Disk First Aid screen to select your hard disk.

   c. Choose the Repair Automatically command from the Options menu.

   d. Click the Start button to try restarting your Mac from the hard disk after using Disk First Aid. If it doesn't boot, proceed to Step 7.

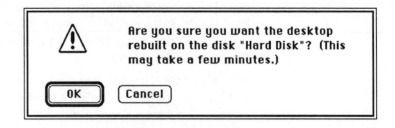

Figure 15–3. You can display the Rebuild Desktop dialog box by holding down the Command and Option keys when the startup disk's icon appears on the desktop.

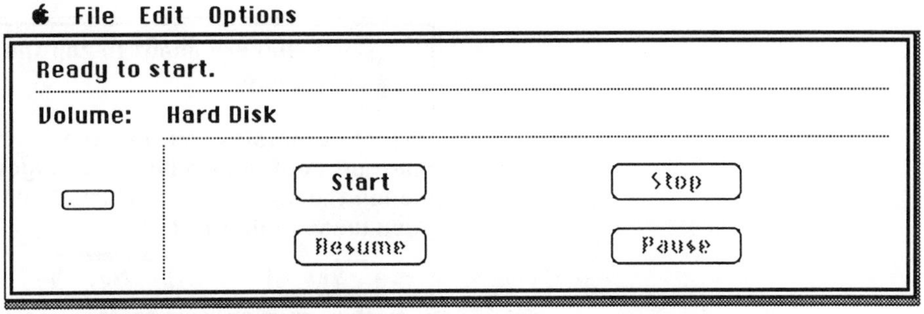

 File   Edit   Options

Ready to start.

Volume: Hard Disk

[   ]   [**Start**]   [Stop]

           [Resume]   [Pause]

Figure 15–4. Disk First Aid can help you repair your hard disk after you rebuild the desktop.

7. Flush the parameter RAM. The second to last remedy is what is affectionately known as a *lobotomy*. It may be that your Mac's internal memory is corrupted, which prevents it from accepting your hard disk as the boot disk. To remedy this, you can reset or flush out the parameter RAM that permanently stores many of your System settings. Unlike ordinary RAM, which is erased whenever you turn your Mac's power off, parameter RAM is maintained by a battery. There are three ways to flush the Parameter RAM, described next.

    a. Removing the Battery (Mac 512K and Mac Plus): The 128K, 512K, and Mac Plus models have a battery located inside a door on the back of the machine, above the power switch. Because this battery maintains the parameter RAM, all you have to do to flush the RAM is remove the power source for a few minutes. Simply remove the battery for a period of three to five minutes, and the RAM will be flushed. You can then replace the battery. (You'll also have to reset your Mac's clock/calendar.)

    b. Keyboard Commands (Mac SE and Mac II): The newer Macintosh SE and Mac II have batteries that are soldered onto their main logic boards, so you can't remove them. But these machines have keyboard commands that flush the parameter RAM. To flush the RAM on an SE or Mac II, hold down the Option, Command, and Shift keys while you select the Control Panel from the Desk Accessory menu. A dialog box will ask if you want to clear out the parameter RAM. Click the Yes button. (By the way, if you click the No button at this point, it will take 20 to 30 seconds for the dialog box to go away. This is normal.)

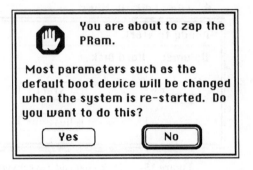

Figure 15–5. The PRAM program empties your Mac's parameter RAM or changes some of its stored settings.

    c. Software: One other option for flushing parameter RAM is to use a shareware program by Ken Winograd called PRAM. PRAM lets you change or clear out parameter RAM settings. Figure 15–5 shows the PRAM dialog box. Once you clear out the parameter RAM, try rebooting your system from the hard disk again. If it doesn't work this time, there's only one remedy left.

  8. Reinitialize the disk. If all the previous steps have failed to fix the problem, your only course at this point is to reinitialize your disk. This will erase all the files on it, wiping away any corrupted files and problem areas and letting you start with a clean slate. To erase your disk, you must restart your Mac from a floppy disk and then use one of two options:

    • Use the formatting utility (if you have one) that came with your hard disk (you can get this from the floppy where you backed up your hard disk's utility files); or

    • Select your hard disk's icon on the desktop and then use the Erase Disk command on the Special menu.

Symptom 3: Hard Disk Icon Does Not Appear on Desktop

If the hard disk icon doesn't appear on the desktop, there will be one of two symptoms—either you won't see anything at all as an indication that the Mac knows about the hard disk, or you'll get a message saying the disk is unreadable and asking if you want to reinitialize the disk. Let's look at these situations individually.

No Sign of the Disk   If your Mac doesn't appear to be "seeing" the hard disk at all, there are only two remedies to try:

1. Flush the Parameter RAM. Using the technique described above, flush out your Mac's Parameter RAM, and then try rebooting. If your hard disk still isn't recognized, go on to the next step.

2. Remove all the serial cables from the back of your Macintosh, so the only cables that remain connected are the hard disk cable (if it's an external hard disk), and the mouse and keyboard cables. Sometimes a short in a serial cable can cause the Mac to not recognize a hard disk. If the hard disk boots after removing the serial cables, you know this is the problem. Usually, removing and replacing the serial cables will clear up the problem, but if it recurs, it's time to send your Mac and its serial cables in for service.

Hard Disk Is Unreadable   If your Mac can't read the hard disk and wants to reinitialize it, that's a good sign: At least the Mac knows there's a disk there. If you reinitialize the disk at this point, you'll lose all the files on the disk. Save that option as a last resort. Instead, click the Eject button in the dialog box, because this is your only choice other than reinitializing. Once you've backed away from the reinitializing option, you can try a couple of alternatives, but be aware that this problem is more serious and therefore less likely to be solved with software repair solutions. Follow these steps:

1. If you haven't backed up all your important files to floppies, use 1st Aid Kit to try recovering the files you need. The hard disk will have been "ejected" from your Mac, which means it will no longer be recognized. Because 1st Aid Kit must recognize a disk to read its files, you can't simply reboot your Mac from a floppy and start Disk First Aid. This is the main reason why you must set 1st Aid Kit as the Startup Application on the floppy disk where you stored it. If you've had the MacTools Inits installed in your System Folder you can also try recovering files with MacTools. (See the description of MacTools at the beginning of this chapter.) If your backup floppies are up to date (or when you're finished using 1st Aid Kit), move to Step 2.

2. Use Apple's Disk First Aid program to attempt repairs on the disk. Either Disk First Aid will rescue the disk and make it bootable again, or it will write a new directory to the disk so the disk looks empty. In this latter case, you'll have to reinitialize the disk and start over again, using your backup floppies to restore the hard disk. Of course, if

reinitializing the disk fails, you'll have to send the disk in for professional help.

Enough, Already

One of the most important parts of troubleshooting is knowing when to quit. The techniques and remedies described in this chapter will resolve a lot of hard disk problems, and if you can resolve problems yourself you'll have your disk back in working order quickly. But if none of these remedies works, give it up and send the disk out for repairs. If you're even slightly tempted to open up your disk drive's case and begin poking around, think about how it will void your warranty or at least make things more difficult for the person who really ends up fixing it.

There's a sense of accomplishment in being able to repair a disk yourself, but hard disks are complex devices, and sometimes it takes a skilled technician to do the job.

APPENDIX

A

Glossary of Terms

cdev A control program (cdev stands for control device) which, when you install it in the System Folder, adjusts an aspect of the Mac's interface. When placed in the System Folder, a cdev program appears as an icon in the Control Panel (in System 4.1 or later). You can then click on the cdev in the Control Panel to gain access to settings controlling mouse movement, the desktop pattern, the keyboard responsiveness, colors of menus and window items on the Macintosh II, and so on. Some cdevs are supplied with Apple's System software, and others are offered by third parties.

Chooser Resource A controller, or driver, for an external device such as a printer, network modem, or file server. Chooser Resources are installed in the System Folder, and then appear as options in the Chooser. (*See also* Chooser.)

Client A computer that has access to remote files on another computer or server over a network.

Directory 1. A listing on a disk that contains the locations and names of that disk's files and folders. 2. A specific area of a disk containing a group of files. (*See also* Subdirectory.)

FKey   A utility program that is installed in the System file with a special installer program and that is activated by pressing a specific keyboard sequence at any time, no matter which program the Mac is running.

Folder   Under HFS, a device that contains a group of files to set them apart from others in a disk's directory. Folders can contain either files or other folders. Under MFS, a folder is a cosmetic device that temporarily hides files or other folders from view, but does not set them apart in a disk's directory. (*See also* Directory, HFS, and MFS.)

HFS   Hierarchical Filing System. The more recent Macintosh filing system that enables you to divide the files on a disk into specific groups, or directories and subdirectories. (*See also* Directory and Subdirectory.)

Init   A program that, when placed inside the System Folder of a startup disk, automatically runs when you're up the Mac. (*See also* Startup Disk.)

Installer   An application program provided by Apple that facilitates the installation of Chooser resources and updated System files on the Macintosh. Some third-party programs, such as TOPS, have their own installer programs as well.

Laser Prep File   One of the two files—the other is the LaserWriter Chooser resource—used by the Macintosh to print onto a LaserWriter or other PostScript device. The Laser Prep file translates the Mac screen's Quick-Draw image into the PostScript language for printing. (*See also* Chooser Resource, QuickDraw, and PostScript.)

MFS   Macintosh Filing System. The older filing system on the Macintosh that did not allow for the arrangement of a disk's files into various subdirectories. (*See also* Subdirectory.)

Parameter RAM (PRAM)   An area of the Mac's RAM that stores the current time and date, the current configuration of the Mac's serial ports, and the default system fonts. Parameter RAM is maintained by a battery inside the Mac.

Path   The specific route to be navigated from a disk directory and through folders or subdirectories to locate a particular file or folder. (*See also* Path Name.)

Path Name   The written expression of a path. A file called Reports inside a folder called Business on a disk called Work would have the path name Work:Business:Reports. Path names always contain colons between the directory, folder, and file names, without any extra spaces, as shown in the example.

PostScript   The page description language used by the LaserWriter and other PostScript-compatible printers to specify exactly what is printed from a file.

Printer Spooler   An application that takes over the process of printing a file, handling the processing and transmission of the printed file from a special area of a disk or memory so you regain use of the computer more quickly than if the Mac's normal resources had to handle printing.

QuickDraw   The set of built-in instructions the Mac uses to represent text and graphics on its screen.

RAM   Random Access Memory. The working memory of the Mac that stores currently active application programs and files.

ROM   Read-Only Memory. A type of memory in which instructions are permanently etched into a computer chip. The Mac's QuickDraw instructions are stored in ROM, for example.

SCSI (pronounced Scuzzy)   Small Computer Systems Interface. The communications port in a Mac through which most hard disks as well as some types of scanners and hard disk backup units are connected. Up to eight SCSI devices can be connected to a Mac in a chain, from one device to the next.

SCSI Address   The numeric identification of an SCSI device connected to a Mac. Each SCSI device must have a unique address numbered between 0 and 7.

Sector   A physical area of a disk that stores a specific amount of data. On an 800K floppy disk, one sector can store up to 512 bytes.

Server   A computer whose files are made available to other computers on a network. (*See also* Client.)

SFGet Box   The standard dialog box that allows Mac users to select files or programs to open from a list, such as the Open... box found in most programs.

SFPut Box   The standard dialog box that you use to save files to a disk, such as the Save or Save As... dialog boxes found in most programs.

Spool Folder   A folder created on a disk by a printer spooler for storing print files during processing and printing.

Standard File Box   A general name for SFGet and SFPut boxes.

Startup Disk   The disk used to start a Macintosh and whose System file is used by the Mac.

Subdirectory   A subgroup of files grouped together inside a directory of files. On the Macintosh under HFS, subdirectories are known as folders. (*See also* Directory and HFS.)

SubFinder   A finder alternative that offers fewer functions than Apple's Finder.

Suitcase File   A storage file for fonts or desk accessories.

SuperFinder   A Finder alternative that offers more functions than Apple's Finder.

Terminator   A physical device used to signify the ends of a chain of SCSI devices. The first and last SCSI devices connected to a Mac in a chain must each have a terminator.

List of Products

1st Aid Kit
1st Aid Software
42 Fadnor Road
Boston, MA 02135
617-783-7118
$99.95

AppleShare
Apple Computer
20525 Mariani Ave.
Cupertino, CA 95014
408-996-1010
$795.00

**Art Grabber & Cheap Paint
(Graphic Utilities Disk)**
MacroMind
1029 W. Wolfram
Chicago, IL 60657
312-871-0987
$49.95

AutoBlack
Itty Bitty Computers
P.O. Box 6539
San Jose, CA 95150
$5.00

Bernoulli Box
Iomega Corp.
1821 W. 4000 South St
Roy, UT 84067
801-778-1000
$1295.00 and up

CatMac
Phenix Specialties, Inc.
2981 Corvin Dr.
Santa Clara, CA 95051
408-733-9625
$16.95

Change Application Font
Loftus Becker
41 Whitney St.
Hartford, CT 06105
Free

Copy II Mac and MacTools
Central Point Software
9700 SW Capitol Highway, #101
Portland, OR 97219
503-244-5782
$39.95

DataFrame Hard Disks
SuperMac Technologies
295 N. Bernardo Ave.
Mountain View, CA 94043
415-962-2900
$995.00 and up

Disk Dup+
Roger Bates
Route 1 Box 865
Hillsboro, OR 97124
$10.00

Disk First Aid
Apple Computer
20525 Mariani Ave.
Cupertino, CA 95014
408-996-1010
Free

DiskExpress
Alsoft, Inc.
PO Box 927
Spring, TX 77383-0927
713-353-4090
$49.95

DiskFit
SuperMac Software
295 N. Bernardo Ave.
Mountain View, CA 94043
415-962-2900
$74.95

DiskInfo
Maitreya Design
P.O. Box 1480
Goleta, CA 93116
$10.00

Disktop 3.0
CE Software
P.O. Box 65580
West Des Moines, IA 50265
515-224-1995
$49.95

Fastback
Fifth Generation Systems, Inc.
2691 Richter Ave., Suite 107
Irvine, CA 92714
714-553-0111
800-225-2775
$99.00

Findswell
Working Software
321 Alvarado, Suite H
Monterey, CA 93940
408-375-2828
800-851-1986
$49.95

Font/DA Juggler
ALsoft
PO Box 927
Spring, TX 77383-0927
713-353-4090
$49.95

Font/DA Mover
Apple Computer
20525 Mariani Ave.
Cupertino, CA 95014
408-996-1010
Free

HDBackup
PBI Software
1111 Triton Dr.
Foster City, CA 94404
415-349-8765
$49.95 (Free with Apple Hard
Disks)

HFS Backup
Personal Computer Peripherals
Corporation
6204 Benjamin Rd.
Tampa, FL 33634
813-884-3092
800-622-2888
$49.95

HFS Navigator
Think Technologies
420 Bedford St.
Lexington, MA 02173
617-863-5595
$59.95

HyperCard
Apple Computer
20525 Mariani Ave.
Cupertino, CA 95014
408-996-1010
$49.95

ImageWriter II
Apple Computer
20525 Mariani Ave.
Cupertino, CA 95014
408-996-1010
$595.00

JClock
Available from BCS•Mac
48 Grave St.
Somerville, MA 02144
617-625-7080

LaserSpeed
Think Technologies
420 Bedford St.
Lexington, MA 02173
617-863-5595
$99.00

LaserWriter IINT
Apple Computer
20525 Mariani Ave.
Cupertino, CA 95014
408-996-1010
$4599.00

LaserWriter IINTX
Apple Computer
20525 Mariani Ave.
Cupertino, CA 95014
408-996-1010
$6599.00

LaserWriter IISC
Apple Computer
20525 Mariani Ave.
Cupertino, CA 95014
408-996-1010
$2799.00

MacBottom Hard Disks
Personal Computer Peripherals
Corporation
6204 Benjamin Rd.
Tampa, FL 33634
813-884-3092
800-622-2888
$895.00 and up

MacTree
Software Research Technologies
22901 Mill Creek Dr., Suite B
Laguna Hills, CA 92653
714-472-0795
$69.95

Mass Copier
CE Software
P.O. Box 65580
West Des Moines, IA 50265
515-224-1995
$15.00

MegaDrive
Jasmine Technologies
555 De Haro St.
San Francisco, CA 94107
415-621-4339
$999.00

MultiFinder
Apple Computer
20525 Mariani Ave.
Cupertino, CA 95014
408-996-1010
$49.00 (Free with new Macs)

PackIt
Harry Chesley
1850 Union St. #360
San Franscisco, CA 94123
$10.00

PhoneNet Plus
Farallon Computing, Inc.
2150 Kittredge St.
Berkeley, CA 94704
415-849-2331
$59.95

PowerStation
Fifth Generation Systems, Inc.
2691 Richter Ave., Suite 207
Irvine, CA 92714
714-553-0111
800-225-2775
$59.95

PRAM
Ken Winograd
2039 Country Club Dr.
Manchester, NH 03105
$5.00

Public Domain Disks
BMUG
1442A Walnut St., Suite 62
Berkeley, CA 94709
415-549-2684
$3.00

Public Domain Software
BCS•Mac
48 Grove Street
Somerville, MA 02144
617-625-7080
$4.00

QDial
Leo Laporte
743 Hemlock Lane
Carol Stream, IL 60188
Free

QuickKeys
CE Software
P.O. Box 65580
West Des Moines, IA 50265
515-224-1995
$99.95

SideKick
Borland International
4585 Scotts Valley Drive
Scotts Vally, CA 95066
408-438-8400
800-255-8008
$99.95

StuffIt
Raymond Lau
100-04 70 Avenue
Forest Hills, NY 11375
$15.00

Suitcase
Fifth Generation Systems, Inc.
2691 Richter Ave., Suite 207
Irvine, CA 92714
714-553-0111
800-225-2775
$59.95

Super LaserSpool
SuperMac Software
295 N. Bernardo Ave.
Mountain View, CA 94043
415-962-2900
$149.00

SuperGlue
Solutions International
29 Main St. PO Box 989
Montpelier, VT 05602
802-229-9146
$89.95

SuperSpool
SuperMac Software
295 N. Bernardo Ave.
Mountain View, CA 94043
415-962-2900
$59.95

Tempo
Affinity Microsystems
1050 Walnut St.
Boulder, CO 80302
303-442-4840
800-367-6771
$99.00

Thunder
Electronic Arts
2755 Campus Dr.
San Mateo, CA 94403
415-571-7991
$49.95

TOPS
TOPS
950 Marina Village Parkway
Alameda, CA 94501
800-445-TOPS (in California)
800-222-TOPS (elsewhere in U.S.)
$189.00

Index

=====

HyperTalk™ Programming
Dan Shafer

This exciting new book is a comprehensive tutorial covering every feature of HyperTalk including the concepts behind the language, object-oriented programming, and sample scripts for ready-made applications. It is an essential guide for all HyperCard™ users and programmers.

Whether you're an experienced programmer or merely acquainted with basic programming concepts, this workbook lets you begin programming your own HyperCard stacks right away. The book thoroughly explains the powerful programming aids used for the design and development of HyperCard applications including the use of sound, graphics, and communications. It also presents language extensions and how to use them to extend HyperTalk with C or Pascal programming.

Topics covered include:
- Building and Designing Stacks
- Object-Oriented Programming
- HyperCard Refresher
- HyperCard Building Blocks
- HyperTalk Basics and System Messages
- Mouse, Keyboard, and File I/O
- Control Structures and Logical Operators
- Card, Text, and Data Management
- Dialog Boxes
- Graphics Commands and Visual Effects
- Sound and Music Basics
- Math Operators and Functions
- Commands
- Tips, Traps, and Techniques
- Tools and Programming Aids

576 Pages, 7¾ x 9¼, Softbound
ISBN: 0-672-48426-9
No. 48426, $24.95

IBM® PC and Macintosh® Networking
Stephen L. Michel

IBM PC and Macintosh owners and users who want to combine the power of their machines will welcome this complete resource for networking the IBM PC and the Macintosh using TOPS and AppleShare.

This book details the specifics of using the Macintosh and the IBM PC on the same network, including transferring files, sharing printers, transporting data from IBM software to Mac and vice versa, and mixing word processing and spreadsheet programs.

Full of networking details, this thorough coverage of TOPS software (one of *PC Magazine's* "The Best of 1986" products) details how to create useful files and share printers and external disk drives.

Topics covered include:
- How the Macintosh and PC Really Differ
- TOPS
- AppleShare
- Coexistence
- Managing the Network
- Appendices: Glossary, ASCII Character Sets, Using PostScript Printers

328 Pages, 7¾ x 9¼, Softbound
ISBN: 0-672-48405-6
No. 48405, $21.95

Advanced Macintosh® Pascal
Paul Goodman

Beginning where most Pascal books leave off, this book introduces programmers to the advanced skills needed to produce "real" applications.

Not only does this book discuss Pascal's "power" structures, thoroughly examining sets, pointers, and records, it also covers basic and advanced QuickDraw routines, data types, programming techniques, and how to use the Macintosh Toolbox.

Topics covered include:
- Macintosh System and Memory Overview
- Advanced Pascal Structures
- Files and File Programming
- ISAM
- Event Programming
- QuickDraw Techniques
- The Inline Routines—Accessing the Toolbox
- Advanced QuickDraw
- A Complete Application—The Logger
- The Standard Apple Numerical Environment
- Appendices: Macintosh Pascal Version 2.0, Inline Routine Trap Addresses, and Decimal to Hexadecimal Table

304 Pages, 7¾ x 9¼, Softbound
ISBN: 0-672-46570-1
No. 46570, $19.95

MacAccess: Information in Motion
Dean Gengle and Steven Smith

This book examines the software and hardware required for successful data transfer and offers a step-by-step discussion of a sample telecommunications session, clearly explaining how to send and receive text files. During detailed presentation of the telecommunications session, the focus is set on solutions to common communications problems.

It includes in-depth discussions on connecting the Macintosh® to other computers, sharing and transferring data between machines, protocols, cabling, and conversion procedures.

With this book, you can easily and efficiently share data between your Macintosh and other computers and keep your vital information flowing to where it will do you the most good.

Topics covered include:
- Information in Motion
- Executives Backgrounder
- Telecommunications
- A SofTour of MicroPhone
- Communication Command Languages
- Links and Hints
- Telephone Management
- Advanced Topics by Section
- Appendices: Mac ASCII Chart, File to File Import/Export Charts, Sources Directory, Families, Bibliography for Further Reference, and Feedback and CTG Newsletter Sheet

304 Pages, 7¾ x 9¼, Softbound
ISBN: 0-672-46567-1
No. 46567, $21.95

Visit your local book retailer, use the order form provided, or call 800-428-SAMS.

Macintosh® Multiplan®
Lasselle and Ramsay

Drive your Macintosh through income statements, sales reports, and expense budgets with the powerful electronic worksheet, Multiplan.

Here is all you need to create, use, and revise Multiplan to your specifications. The step-by-step instructions simplify critical functions like how to enter text labels, numbers, and formulas, how to adjust worksheets, and how to use Multiplan templates.

Topics covered include:

- Using Your Macintosh
- Entering Information in a Worksheet
- Revising a Worksheet
- Absolute and Relative Cell References
- Inserting Rows and Columns
- Changing Columns
- Templates

224 Pages, 7¾ x 9¼, Softbound
ISBN: 0-8104-6555-8
No. 46555, $16.95

Basic Microsoft® BASIC for the Macintosh®
Coan and Coan

Develop a solid foundation in programming of Microsoft BASIC with step-by-step instructions, sample programs, and screen illustrations that guide you in writing control routines, subroutines, and complete programs quickly and easily.

Learn how to access Macintosh QuickDraw, ROM, highlight short and simple programs with additional capabilities, save memory with options base, initialize options, and much more.

Topics covered include:

- Getting Started
- Adding Features
- Writing Programs
- Loops
- Packages in BASIC: Functions, Subroutines, and Subprograms
- Picture Windows: Using Macintosh Features
- Pigeonholes Galore (Arrays)
- Miscellaneous Applications
- Graphics
- Using Macintosh QuickDraw Graphic Routines
- Files
- Random-Access Files
- Random-Access Address List
- Appendices: The Microsoft BASIC Menu Bar, Using the Disk, ASCII and Special Character Chart, Microsoft BASIC Functions, Listing of Programs, Solution Programs for Even-Numbered Problems

448 Pages, 7¾ x 9¼, Softbound
ISBN: 0-8104-6558-2
No. 46558, $19.95

HyperTalk™ Tips and Techniques
Dan Shafer

Written for programmers and developers, this book is a collection of more than 100 helpful pieces of information about HyperTalk, the programming language built into Apple® 's HyperCard™. It offers readers with some experience in HyperTalk programming a chance to learn the ins and outs of programming from one of the best-known and widely recognized HyperTalk scripting experts.

Solutions to dozens of bugs, deficiencies, and pitfalls lying in wait for the unsuspecting HyperTalk programmer are documented as are suggestions for handling some of the most often needed HyperTalk tasks. The book provides special shortcuts, speed-ups, and enhancements and a wealth of additional information that isn't available from any other source.

Topics covered include:

- Creating an Invisible Cursor
- Building an Index of Stack Contents Automatically
- Checking a Field's Content for Data Type
- Multiword and Multifield Signs
- Protecting a Stack and Script from Mis-use
- How to Construct HyperText Applications in HyperCard
- Dealing with HyperCard's Limits and Performance Issues

300 Pages, 7¾ x 9¼, Softbound
ISBN: 0-672-48427-7
No. 48427, $21.95

Understanding HyperTalk™
Dan Shafer

Understanding HyperTalk brings the power and fascination of programming in HyperTalk to those Macintosh® owners who want to customize their environment with Apple® 's HyperCard™.

Written by the author of the best-selling *HyperTalk Programming*, this book will be most useful to people who are deciding whether to buy HyperCard and to people who want to teach themselves or others HyperCard programming and stacks.

Topics covered include:

- Programming Basics
- Object-Oriented Programming Ideas
- HyperCard Refresher
- HyperTalk Building Blocks
- System Messages
- Input/Output
- Loops and Conditional Processing
- Navigational Commands
- Data Management Commands
- User Interface Commands
- Graphics and Visual Effects
- Sound and Music
- Math Functions and Operators
- Action-Taking Commands
- Property
- Interface to the Outside World
- Stack Design Considerations

300 Pages, 7 x 9, Softbound
ISBN: 0-672-27283-0
No. 27283, $17.95

Visit your local book retailer, use the order form provided, or call 800-428-SAMS.